Advance praise for *Georgia Irvin's Guide to Schools*

"Simply put, no one knows more abo[...] [...]n area than Georgia Irvin. And no one [...] [...]e school search and application maze. *Georgia Irvin's Guide to Schools* will be an invaluable resource to families . . . and a critical reference source for all educational professionals working in the national capital area."
— **Mark H. Sklarow,** Executive Director, Independent Educational Consultants Association

"Congratulations and thanks to Georgia Irvin for this much-needed, comprehensive compendium."
— **Priscilla L. Vail,** learning specialist and author

"The key to educational success is finding a school that is the right match for each child. Every parent needs this book! Georgia Irvin combines a wealth of information and years of experience with D.C. schools. What shines through most, however, is her wisdom about children, which helps families find their way through the confusion to a happy ending."
— **Susan Piggott,** Director, National Child Research Center

"Georgia Irvin is a skillful and seasoned educational consultant who knows the schools and students of metropolitan Washington, D.C. Her guide takes the mystery out of the admissions process by aiding parents and prospective students in understanding what to expect and how to choose a public or independent education."
— **Bruce Stewart,** Head of School, Sidwell Friends School

"Georgia Irvin is a most knowledgeable source for information on schools in the Washington area. Her advice to parents is right on target."
— **Dr. Regan Kenyon,** President, Secondary School Admission Test Board

Georgia Irvin's
Guide to Schools:
METROPOLITAN
WASHINGTON

INDEPENDENT AND PUBLIC/PRE-K–12

Georgia Irvin's Guide to Schools:
METROPOLITAN WASHINGTON

INDEPENDENT AND PUBLIC/PRE-K–12

Georgia K. Irvin

MADISON BOOKS
Lanham • New York • Oxford

First Madison Books edition 2002

Published by Madison Books
A Member of the Rowman & Littlefield Publishing Group
4720 Boston Way
Lanham, Maryland 20706
12 Hid's Copse Road
Cumnor Hill, Oxford OX2 9JJ, England

Distributed by National Book Network

Library of Congress Cataloging-in-Publication Data

Irvin, Georgia K., 1932–
  Georgia Irvin's guide to schools : Metropolitan Washington: independent and public/
pre-k–12 / Georgia K. Irvin.— 1st Madison Books ed.
    p. cm.
  ISBN 1-56833-251-3 (pbk. : alk. paper)
      1. Private schools—Washington Metropolitan Area—Evaluation—Directories.
  2. Public schools—Washington Metropolitan Area—Evaluation—Directories.
  3. Education—Parent participation—Washington Metropolitan Area. I. Title:
  Guide to schools. II. Irvin, Georgia, 1932– Guide to schools. III. Title.

L903+   2002003049

♾™ The paper used in this publication meets the minimum requirements of American
National Standard for Information Sciences—Permanence of Paper for Printed Library
Materials, ANSI/NISO Z39.48–1992. Manufactured in the United States of America.

For my children and grandchildren

Contents

Preface

As a parent, you want the best possible education for your child. The process of determining which school or school system best meets your family's needs can be daunting. This is particularly true in Metropolitan Washington, D.C., where more than 450 independent schools and a number of public school districts serve the nation's capital and its vicinity.

This book is designed to help alleviate the anxiety associated with the school search process and is in response to many clients who have encouraged me to develop a book. It is the culmination of nearly four decades of experience as a parent, grandparent, public school teacher, independent school admission officer, and educational consultant.

Here, you will find:

- In-depth profiles of more than 100 independent schools.
- An overview of the independent school admission process: how to apply and what to expect.
- General information on eight public school districts that serve the area.

- The names and addresses of schools with high-achieving students in those eight public school districts.
- Suggestions on what to look for as you visit the public schools.
- Answers to frequently asked questions on education and parenting.

As you use this book, please keep in mind that:

- This book is designed to serve as a neutral source. None of the schools has paid to be included, and it is not intended to be an advertisement for them.
- Consistent with my philosophy that no one school is best for every student and that the best school for a child is the one that fits his or her unique needs, I have neither rated, ranked, nor critiqued the schools.
- No two schools have identical admission procedures. The overview of the application process is just that. **It is important that you observe the specific policies of the schools to which you apply.**

A word about the independent schools chosen for inclusion: one of the hallmarks of the schools in the Washington area is variety. I included schools that represent a broad range of options and vary in size, philosophy, educational methodologies, and student composition. I sent a questionnaire to 117 schools with which I have had some engagement over the years. A total of 101 responded prior to the deadline for inclusion here. Nursery schools are not included.

Please note that a school's presence or absence from the book represents neither an endorsement nor censure.

I have focused on schools in eight public school districts that serve Metropolitan Washington; the schools are in the District of Columbia, five districts in Virginia (City of Alexandria, City of Falls Church, Arlington County, Fairfax County, and Loudoun County), and two in Maryland (Montgomery County and Prince George's County).

Within each public school system, I have provided information on specific schools with high-achieving students. The data on these schools is drawn from their publications, websites, and conversations with a representative from each of the eight districts. Individual schools were selected for inclusion on the basis of test scores and from my personal knowledge of the school. Because Maryland, Virginia, and the District of Columbia use completely different assessments and different methods for reporting scores, the test data is inconsistent. It is impossible to compare the schools on the basis of these tests.

A quick look at the defining characteristics of the four broad school types may prove useful:

- Public schools are open to all students, funded by tax dollars, governed by an elected board of education, and require teachers to be certified. Charter schools are a part of the public school system.
- Parochial schools are nonprofit, tax-exempt institutions similar to independent schools. However, they receive a significant subsidy from a specific religious institution that exercises direct governance. Some schools with a religious affiliation are considered independent because they are governed and funded independently of that religion. In the Washington area, most parochial schools are Roman Catholic. In this book, the parochial schools are considered independent schools.
- For-profit or proprietary schools are owned by individuals or corporations, are run like a business, pay taxes, and are privately financed. Each state sets standards for these schools. They are free from many of the regulations governing public and nonprofit institutions. These are also included in the section on independent schools.
- Independent schools are nonprofit, tax-exempt institutions that receive income from tuition, endowments, foundations, and gifts. They are governed by a self-perpetuating board of trustees, and can select faculty, students, and curriculum consistent with their mission.

Accreditation for independent schools varies by state. Membership in the National Association of Independent Schools (NAIS) indicates compliance with high standards of governance and academic excellence, and accreditation by an NAIS-approved organization. Membership in regional organizations, the Association of Independent School of Greater Washington (AISGW), the Association of Independent Schools of Maryland (AIMS), and the Virginia Association of Independent Schools (VAIS) indicates compliance with standards established by the respective organization. For additional information on these organizations, consult their websites: www.nais.org, www.aisgw.org, www.aimsmd.org, and www.vais.org.

The Middle States Association of Colleges and Schools provides accreditation to many public and independent elementary and secondary schools in Maryland and the District of Columbia. Schools in Virginia may be accredited by the Southern Association of Colleges and Schools. Most of the schools in this book are accredited by either the Middle States or the Southern Association of Colleges and Schools. Accreditation, however, was not a condition for inclusion in this book.

In this book all of the schools comply with state and local health and safety regulations and applicable laws regarding discrimination. All non-public schools are referred to as "independent schools" rather than "private schools," which implies exclusivity. Most independent schools offer need-based financial aid; a few also offer merit scholarships.

It is my hope that this book will help strengthen your understanding of the many fine educational opportunities in Metropolitan Washington and enable you to make important decisions with greater confidence and ease.

The information in this book was gathered in the Spring of 2002. The data from schools changes frequently, and parents should rely only on information they have received directly from a school. In particular, parents should seek specific information from schools on deadlines for applications and application criteria.

This book is sold on the terms and understanding that the publisher, author, consultants and editors are not responsible for the results of any actions taken on the basis of information in this book, nor for any error in or omission from this book.

The publisher and the author, consultants and editors, expressly disclaim all liability and responsibility to any person, whether a purchaser or reader of this book or not, in respect of anything, and of the consequences of anything, done or omitted to be done by any such person in reliance, whether wholly or partially, upon the whole or any part of the contents of this book.

GEORGIA IRVIN

Georgia K. Irvin and Associates, Inc.

Educational Consultants

Chevy Chase, Maryland

www.gkirvin.com

301-951-0131

Acknowledgments

T he enthusiastic contribution of many people to this project has been deeply gratifying. Hundreds of colleagues have provided information, and thoughtful officials in public schools have shared their time and resources.

The more I learn about schools, the greater respect and appreciation I have for teachers. This book is about them and the miracles they perform every day.

I am grateful to my clients who have trusted my judgment in important decisions regarding their children. It has been a privilege to be a part of their lives. Their expressions of appreciation and loyalty continue to inspire me, as does the thoughtfulness of many of the students who share their achievements with me.

Special credit must be given to Nicole Chardavoyne, my associate and indefatigable colleague, whose good humor, companionship, and commitment to excellence in all endeavors have touched me deeply and moved the project forward. Edith Furber Zhang, the principal researcher, provided resources, insights, and expertise in every detail. Her two-year old son, Miles, who attended many meetings, was a joyful reminder of the curiosity and creativity that are natural in children and the reason my work is important to me. Helen Colson, my beloved friend, mentor, and advisor, has supplied perspective and words when my own failed me.

Over the years, The Reverend H. Stuart Irvin, H. Stuart Irvin Jr., and Kate Kennedy Irvin have encouraged my professional activities, and their support has enabled me to realize my dreams. For this book, my son, Stuart Irvin, has contributed legal expertise and was also an insightful reader and critic. Carrie Chimerine Irvin, my daughter-in-law, gave valuable time to critique and edit early drafts. Eileen Chimerine was always the ready listener. Many friends and family members gave me confidence and were patient as I devoted countless hours to collecting information and writing.

Others to whom I am deeply grateful are my associate, Pamela Tedeschi, who has added her knowledge and skills at every stage, and Christie Woodfin, who provided invaluable support. I appreciate the advice of Nicholas Karambelas of Sfikas, Karambelas & Akaras LLP, and Virginia Carson. A heartfelt thanks to Françoise Paddack, a precious friend who worked with me for ten years and whose dedication and professionalism have been crucial to the success of the business.

Too many friends and colleagues contributed directly or indirectly to the work for me to even begin to acknowledge all of them, but Braxton McKee, Lisa Catalone, and Cathy Kreyche played special roles.

And, most importantly, to my daughter, Kate, goes endless love and gratitude for her wisdom and encouragement every day and especially throughout this project.

To each of you and many more, my profound thank you.

May 2002

About the Author

Georgia K. Irvin, a Certified Educational Planner, is considered one of the premier educational consultants in the country. She specializes in day schools in Metropolitan Washington and boarding and therapeutic schools nationwide.

Since 1984, as founder and president of Georgia K. Irvin and Associates of Chevy Chase, Maryland, she has helped thousands of students and families from all backgrounds and from all over the world select educational options that best meet each child's needs.

For fifteen years, Ms. Irvin was Director of Admission and Financial Aid at Sidwell Friends School in Washington, DC. She has served on numerous boards, including the Black Student Fund, the School and Student Services for Financial Aid (SSS), the Independent Educational Consultants Association (IECA), the advisory board of a public school, and as a trustee of an independent school. She is a frequent lecturer at schools and conferences. The Secondary School Admission Test Board (SSATB) honored her with the prestigious William B. Bretnall Award for "exemplary contribution to the field of independent school admissions."

Independent Schools

Applying to an independent school is a process that can involve a considerable commitment of time. However, it is time well spent when, in the end, you make an informed decision on behalf of your child. This chapter provides the following: a timetable and detailed explanation of the steps in the process and what to expect; a directory of more than 100 independent schools; maps that show the schools' locations; a chart that indicates the grade range and gender of the students enrolled in the independent schools; and a worksheet to organize your information as you submit applications.

HOW TO APPLY TO AN INDEPENDENT DAY SCHOOL IN METROPOLITAN WASHINGTON

This section is designed to demystify the admission process and enable you and your child to pursue your school options with less stress and greater confidence.

1

A MESSAGE FOR PARENTS

Keep in mind that applying to an independent school is not about getting into the "right" or most prestigious school. It is about matching your child's abilities with a school that will maximize his or her potential and in which he or she will feel happy and rewarded. An independent school will have a major influence on the future of your child; it is also a significant financial investment. As parents, you should consider your options and conduct research as carefully as you would when making any other major decision.

Schools with widespread name recognition have track records that reflect their reputations, but they are not the only excellent schools in the area. In fact, often the less well-known schools meet the needs of some students better than the well-known ones. The "best" school is the one in which your child will succeed.

In recent years, the number of applications for many of the area's independent schools has far exceeded the available places. It is important to realize that if your child is not accepted into your first choice school, it does not necessarily reflect any inadequacies on his or her part, but more likely is a consequence of the intense demand for a relatively limited number of places in some schools. There are enough schools in the area that a fine and appropriate one is nearly always an option.

Begin the process of researching, visiting, and applying to independent schools after Labor Day and continue throughout the fall and early winter of the year before your child will enter. The chronological receipt of an application (prior to the deadline) is rarely a determining factor in admission. It is wise to submit applications early to allow ample time to complete each step in the process and reschedule visits or tests that may be delayed by snow days or illness.

Following you will find an ideal timetable and checklist to use as you apply to independent day schools as well as a detailed discussion of the application process. Some families move to the area after deadlines have passed and others become interested in options later in the year. For those families, it is possible to adapt this schedule to the extent that school deadlines and space constraints allow. Older students applying to boarding schools also may use the schedule following.

APPLICATION PROCESS CHECKLIST

Begin one year or more prior to enrollment

I. **September or Earlier: Do Your Homework**
   - ✔ Consider your child's strengths and needs.
   - ✔ Gather information on schools through websites and brochures.
   - ✔ Identify schools you wish to visit.
   - ✔ Consider working with an educational consultant; schedule an appointment if you decide to work with one.
   - ✔ If you are eligible, contact the Black Student Fund or the Latino Fund.

II. **October–January: Prepare to Apply**
   - ✔ Arrange to attend open houses and school tours.
   - ✔ Narrow your list of schools to those to which you will apply.
   - ✔ Determine deadlines for the receipt of applications.
   - ✔ Determine due dates for all materials pertinent to each application.

III. **Before the Deadlines**
   - ✔ Submit the applications.
   - ✔ Arrange test dates, interviews, or play dates.
   - ✔ Distribute recommendation forms to current teachers.
   - ✔ Request that a transcript be sent directly to each school by the applicant's current school.
   - ✔ Submit financial aid forms.

IV. **February: Follow-Up**
   - ✔ Contact each school to confirm the receipt of all application materials.
   - ✔ Continue to schedule or follow through with the appointments for tests, interviews, or play dates.

V. **If You Miss the Deadlines**
   ✔ Evaluate your options.

VI. **March: Admission Decisions**
   ✔ Schools notify parents of acceptance, denial, or a place
   on the waiting list.

VII. **April: Respond to Schools**
   ✔ If your child is accepted at the school of your first
   choice, read the contract carefully, sign and return it
   immediately to the school.
   ✔ If your child is accepted at more than one school and
   you are unsure which is the best choice, revisit the
   school or let an older student revisit. If admitted to only
   one school and you are unsure, also revisit. Attend
   meetings and programs designed for accepted students
   and families. Consult with current parents and other
   professionals, if necessary.
   ✔ After accepting a place in a school, notify the other
   schools to which your child was accepted.
   ✔ If you wish to have your child's name remain on waiting
   lists, contact each school immediately. In April, after
   those who were accepted have responded, admission
   officers can inform parents of the likelihood of places
   becoming available.

VIII. **May–August: Show Continued Interest**
   ✔ Keep schools advised of your continued interest in
   remaining on the waiting list; send them your child's final
   report card and notify them of any recent achievements.
   ✔ If your child was denied, call the school to discuss
   the reasons.

DO YOUR HOMEWORK

Start "doing your homework" by evaluating your child. Research and select schools about which you want to learn more. You may decide to work with an educational consultant.

Consider Your Child's Strengths and Needs

Begin your school search by honestly assessing your child's development. In comparison with contemporaries, consider the following:

- Language development: receptive and expressive skills, articulation, vocabulary, intonation, understanding the nuances of language, ability to expand on a topic, gestures and facial expressions appropriate to the topic.
- Organization of known information or ability to recount a story or event in sequence.
- Short- and long-term memory for facts and events.
- Attitudes toward school, specific subjects, and homework.
- Attention span, tenacity, and frustration level.
- Motor skills: fine and gross.
- Problem-solving skills.
- Curiosity (which involves not only asking questions, but a genuine interest in finding answers).
- Physical stamina.
- Social skills.
- For young children, the ability to separate from parents.
- Relationships with peers, teachers, and other adults.
- Use of leisure: reading, playing team sports, music, playing with technological toys, drawing, writing.
- A passion, interest, or commitment to a subject or activity.
- Sources of self-esteem.
- Maturity: physical, intellectual, social, emotional.
- Medical conditions that may affect the selection of a school (wheelchair accessibility, presence of a nurse to administer medications, etc.).

Gather Information about Schools

Contact the admission office of schools in which you are interested and request current information and application materials. A few schools ask parents to visit before providing an application. Check available websites. As you review materials, remember that there is no perfect child or perfect school!

Ask yourself:

- What is important to me?
- What is important to my child?
- Are my interests consistent with my child's needs and style?
- Which schools are a reasonable commute?
- What transportation options are available?
- Which schools would enhance my child's strengths?
- Which schools would uphold and reinforce my family's values?
- Which schools would have the appropriate level of challenge, pressure, or competition?
- Which schools would maximize my child's potential?
- While my child's needs are paramount, can I see myself as a parent in this school?

Understand Schools' Academic Demands and Characteristics

I group schools into four broad categories based on the general characteristics of their students. Each group includes schools that may be traditional, or "structured," as well as those considered innovative, flexible, and informal. Although students from each group may be enrolled in any school, this characterization provides a general guideline for the likelihood of admission.

- Some schools are highly selective and look for students who already have a record of achievement, or who evidence enthusiasm for learning and a disciplined approach to new ideas and activities. Instruction moves quickly and is geared to students who are inquisitive and receptive to consistently high expectations. Older applicants have good grades and a commitment to extracurricular interests.

- Some schools look for "potential," even if the child has not fully demonstrated it yet. These schools see their primary task as nurturing and assisting students as they acquire skills and identify talents that will allow them to advance in ways consistent with their ability. Students who want to learn and are willing to work and become active and engaged in the life of the school are selected for admission.

- A third group of schools recognizes that for many children, school is not easy and that happiness for these students depends upon relationships with teachers who can inspire and engage them. The pace of instruction may be slower. In these schools, teachers' comments do not communicate, "Your child could do better if he or she tried harder" because teachers know success usually begets motivation. These students may have experienced disappointments, be immature and unsure of themselves, or need to be nurtured and appreciated for who they are.

- Some schools are designed to meet the needs of children with specific learning difficulties. Typically, teachers in these schools have advanced degrees in special education and expertise in using nontraditional teaching methods and materials. Class sizes are small and emphasis is on remediation and learning compensatory skills. In addition to a patient and skilled faculty, these schools offer other support services, such as occupational and speech therapy.

No school wants to enroll a student who will be more frustrated than rewarded; parents should share that perspective. Parents sometimes like to think a child will rise to the occasion and stretch and reach in order to master a challenging program. However, the child who has not shown a propensity for stretching and reaching is rarely prepared for vigorous academic work and typically will not be successful in more rigorous programs. Look for schools in which you have reasonable confidence that your child will be challenged and enjoy success.

Schools begin and end at various grade levels. Schools that end at second and third grades are usually called primary schools. Those that continue through sixth grade are called elementary schools, and those that end at eighth are often called junior schools. (See the chart at the end of this chapter.)

The Washington area differs from some other metropolitan areas in that there are relatively few "feeder" schools whose graduates are expected to continue their education at specific schools. Although some religious schools, especially Episcopal and Catholic schools, give preference in admission to children enrolled in other schools of the same denomination, there are only a few formal "feeder" school relationships. Do not presume that enrolling in a specific nursery, elementary, or junior school will guarantee future enrollment in any other school.

Understand Costs

Many parents sacrifice to send their children to independent schools; however, tuition does not cover the entire cost of educating a child in most schools. Nonprofit schools need philanthropy. Parents are encouraged to participate in fund-raising activities and, whenever possible, donate money to the school's causes.

Usually, the cost of your child's education will increase as he or she advances through the grades. Tuition increases are typically announced each spring. Parents should inquire about the following, even if they are not recipients of financial aid:

- What are the options for paying tuition?
- When and in what amount are tuition payments due?
- How much is the average annual increase in tuition?

Financial Aid

A few schools offer merit scholarships that are based on academic achievement and personal qualities instead of financial need. Most schools assume the position that, to the extent that a family is able, they are responsible for paying the tuition. Schools are committed to having a socio-economically diverse student body and want to provide as much assistance as their resources allow. Sources of funds for financial aid (the term used more frequently than scholarships) are a school's endowment, gifts, fund-raising events, and a portion of the annual operating budget. Some families in special needs schools are reimbursed by the public school system if it is proven that the public school cannot meet the child's needs. Most independent schools offer a variety of grants which do not require repayment, and some offer low-interest loans based upon financial need. A number of schools offer no-interest payments over a ten-month period.

Determining Eligibility

The service most widely used to determine financial need is the School and Student Service for Financial Aid (SSS) in Princeton, New Jersey. The SSS application form is available from schools and should be submitted in January. Small schools often have their own ways of determining need and most Catholic high schools use their own financial assistance forms, which are available from the schools. Forms for tuition assistance from the Archdiocese of Washington are available from the schools and must be submitted by mid-December. Visit the website, www.adw.org, for detailed information. Schools may request a current tax return; it is important to prepare and file your tax return as soon as possible if you plan to apply for aid.

In recent years, the SSS has adjusted its methods of computing financial need to make independent schools more affordable to middle-income families. In addition, a geographic index represents the higher cost of living in metropolitan areas. Because schools have limited funds, some families may qualify for more aid than schools can afford to provide. The financial aid officers work closely with families to explain financial assistance and to offer aid to as many students as possible.

The following chart is based on SSS formula and shows how much a family would be expected to pay.

How Much Might I Have to Pay?

Number of children attending a day school	Parental contribution* with income of $100,000	
	Net worth: $100,000	Net worth: $200,000
One child	$13,339	$18,320
Two children	$6,670 per child	$9,160 per child
Three children	$4,446 per child	$6,107 per child

*Based on methodology used by the School and Student Service for Financial Aid (SSS) for 2002–2003 academic year.

Assumptions used in calculations: parents' age 43; three children in the family; net worth includes income, home equity, investments, bank accounts, other resources, and liabilities; average state and other taxes for District of Columbia; standard federal income tax (no itemization); no student contribution.

Source: Mark J. Mitchell, Director of Information and Research Team, National Association of Independent Schools.

The Black Student Fund and the Latino Student Fund

The Black Student Fund (BSF) and the Latino Student Fund (LSF) provide a wide range of services to students attending pre-kindergarten through twelfth grades in selected independent schools. Each organization has an annual school fair at which representatives from many schools are available to discuss their programs and enrollment options. Independent schools and families are grateful for the work of the BSF and LSF as they assist in preparing all children for life in a multicultural world.

The Black Student Fund, founded in 1964, provides grants and essential support services to black students in Maryland, Virginia, and the District of Columbia. The BSF works toward creating an equitable learning experience for all students. During the 2001–2002 school year, 269 students received $290,000 in financial aid. For further details visit the BSF website, www.blackstudentfund.org or call 202-387-1414.

The Latino Student Fund, founded in 1994, provided $76,500 in financial assistance to about 70 students in 2001–2002. The LSF also provides a bilingual school directory, bilingual assistance, tutoring, and mentoring. For more information call 202-452-1500.

Identify Schools to Visit

After reviewing the materials, create a list of the schools you want to visit and make appointments. You may wish to include a variety of schools—single sex and coeducational, religious and secular, large and small. As you visit each school, look for evidence that it lives up to its stated mission and goals.

Not all schools accept new students at every grade level. Determine at which grades each school accepts applications and how difficult it may be to gain admission at each grade. If possible, find out how many places are usually available to families new to the school. Each school's admission process is different. Make note of the differences. (See the worksheet at the end of this chapter.)

Consider an Educational Consultant

Certified Educational Planners or educational consultants are full-time, experienced professionals who have gained extensive knowledge of educational options through personal visits and frequent contact with many schools. They may specialize in day schools, boarding schools, therapeutic programs, or colleges. Most consultants meet personally with the student and family to help clarify a child's educational needs and to identify his or her strengths and talents, as well as to assist parents in understanding what to look for in a school. The consultant will provide a customized list of options and information about each school's admission criteria, academic rigor, extracurricular opportunities, and student population that can aid parents in making decisions. For a list of Certified Educational Planners, contact the Independent Educational Consultants Association at 703-591-4850 or visit its website at www.IECAonline.com.

Parents interested in long-term planning may begin working with a consultant several years before admission; others start during the spring or summer before the application process begins—or later.

PREPARE TO APPLY

Do not expect to learn everything you may wish to know in your initial research. The purpose of the initial research is to identify schools to which you want to apply. The final decision about enrollment will follow. Do not apply to a school with a philosophy or culture that is not compatible with your family's values or whose program is not right for your child's learning needs. However, be open to learning about schools with which you are unfamiliar.

Visit the Schools

Each school has a different system for introducing parents to the school and getting to know applicants, but in general the application process includes one or more of the following on-campus visits:

- Open house or tour—Designed to provide a group of prospective parents and older students an opportunity to tour the campus and meet faculty, enrolled students, and their parents. Some are by appointment. No application or fee is required.
- Pre-application visit—Required by a few schools. Parents make an appointment to meet with a school official and tour the campus before receiving an application form.
- Play date—The visit of an applicant or group of applicants to pre-kindergarten through, usually, fourth grade. An application and fee must have been submitted.
- Student visit or interview—Typically involves taking a campus tour followed by meeting individually with a teacher or admission officer, or participating in activities with a small group of other applicants, or spending a portion of the day in the classroom. An application and fee must have been submitted.
- Visit following acceptance—Parents and students who have been accepted are invited to return to the campus to learn more about the school.

Open Houses and Tours

Open houses and tours are scheduled throughout the year, but most occur in the autumn. These visits take about two hours and are usually optional. They provide an opportunity to meet faculty and students, see the facilities, and learn about the school's programs. Ideally, classes are in session, and you can observe methods of instruction and teacher/student interaction during a normal school day; however, many schools hold open houses and tours only on weekends.

If you know you want to apply to a school, you may submit an application before an optional tour. Unless attendance by the student is required, students younger than ten years old should not attend tours. Interviews or play dates, which are scheduled after you submit the application, provide an opportunity for all applicants and parents to visit the school.

Don't forget: get directions to the school and find out where to park beforehand. Be on time. Make every effort to keep scheduled appointments.

What to Look for and Ask During Your Visit

You will want to observe and inquire about the grades in which your child will be enrolled in the next few years; however, if you are applying for a young child to a school that continues, observe the upper grades as well. Often the differences in schools are more visible in the middle and upper schools.

The qualities or characteristics listed below are meant to be as comprehensive as possible. Not all will apply or be available in each school. You must determine which features are most important to you. Some of the answers are available in published materials and websites. Remember: schools are human institutions and none is perfect.

As you visit, be sensitive about the tone of your inquiry. You want to establish a relationship with the school based on mutual understanding and trust.

School Community

- Size of school; grade levels included.
- Religious affiliation; mandatory courses, prayers, chapel; religious holidays that are celebrated; spiritual climate; moral values.
- Governance: role of the board of trustees, head of school, principals, other administrators; if for-profit, who makes final decisions.
- School accreditation and memberships.
- Urban or suburban location.
- Length of school day.
- Availability of before- and after-school care.
- Availability of school transportation, car pools, access to Metro.
- Culture, climate, personality, atmosphere, formal or informal style, general ambiance of the institution.
- Demeanor of the students.
- School traditions, school "spirit."
- Supervision of playgrounds and free time.
- Additional personnel (nurse, community service coordinator, resource teachers, media specialist, etc.).
- Counselors: academic, college or next school placement, psychologist.
- Colleges or schools attended upon graduation.
- Opportunities for and evidence of parent involvement.
- Rate of attrition (annual number of students who do not return; local average is about 9%). Source: Mark Mitchell, Director of Information and Research Team Leader, National Association of Independent Schools
- Future plans for programs or facilities.
- Financial stability of the institution; endowment, if any.

Student Body

- Age at which a student is eligible for admission (schools have different birthday cut-off dates).

- Single-sex or coeducational; if coed, boy/girl ratio.
- Range of academic abilities.
- Racial diversity or multiculturalism.
- Percent of families who receive financial aid.
- Level of mutual respect of students to one another within the community.
- Evidence that your child will be comfortable in the social setting.
- Evidence of the values that you want in your child's friends.

Faculty

- Academic background.
- Age range, experience, average years of service.
- Male/female ratio.
- Racial diversity or multicultural composition.
- Average class size and total teaching load.
- Responsibilities: classroom and extracurricular.
- Professional mentoring and development opportunities.
- Evidence of excitement and commitment.
- Camaraderie among teachers.
- Rapport with students.

Facilities

- A safe and hospitable climate in the halls and classrooms.
- Equipment and supplies that are appropriate to the grade/age.
- Classrooms: arrangement of desks, maps, and other furniture; content and format of bulletin boards; organization and quality of science labs; availability of space for the arts; cleanliness; cheerfulness.
- Use of other space: faculty room and supplies, conference room, tutoring space, nurse's office, library or media center, gymnasium, playground and playing fields that are well maintained, safe, and age-appropriate.

• Food service: optional, required, additional expense; nutritional value; ability to accommodate special diets; atmosphere of dining room or eating area.

Curricular Offerings and Teaching Methods

• Curriculum: required and elective subjects.
• Advanced courses: Advanced Placement (AP), International Baccalaureate (IB), honors and gifted programs, consortium courses, independent study.
• Accommodation of special learning needs: tutoring, study skills, extra help, extended time on tests, use of laptop computers or calculators, waiver of a foreign language requirement, reduced course load, optional math courses, etc.
• Remediation of learning differences through specialized instruction.
• Teaching styles:
    * Teacher-directed, classical courses in a traditional setting.
    * Innovative, student-initiated activities with experiential learning.
    * A combination of styles.
• Fine and performing arts programs, requirements, opportunities to participate.
• Athletic options, requirements, level of competition, opportunities to participate.
• Clubs, publications (e.g., look for a student newspaper and year-book), other activities.
• Homework expectations at each grade level.
• Methods of teaching, especially math, reading, and writing.
• Current text books, maps, and other teaching tools.
• Character/religious education.
• Unique courses or programs such as Asian or classical languages, orchestra, film-making, outside-of-school internships, travel or study abroad, distinguished speakers' forum, other enrichment opportunities.
• Opportunities to try new activities or pursue an individual interest.

- Foreign languages: grades introduced, courses offered, requirements.
- Technology: how computers are integrated into the curriculum, availability, location, sophistication of equipment; faculty training.
- Availability of elective courses listed in the program of studies (offered annually; limited number of students can enroll; pre-requisites).
- College or next-school placement counseling procedures.

School Policies

- Costs, availability of financial aid.
- Hidden costs: books, activity fees, field trips, athletic equipment.
- Safety issues: measures in place to handle emergencies.
- Requirements for graduation.
- Community service opportunities or requirements.
- Advisor/advisee or mentoring system.
- Dress code or uniform.
- Disciplinary measures.
- Policy on drugs, smoking, sex education, if age-appropriate.
- "Open campus" or freedom to leave campus during school hours.
- Students' cars: allowed on campus, use during the school day, parking.
- In single-sex schools, opportunities to meet the opposite sex.
- Method and frequency of communicating grades and progress.
- Use of standardized tests and other forms of assessment.

You may understand more about the culture of a school if you attend a middle or upper school athletic or arts event. Listen to students and talk to parents. This can be especially helpful if your child has an interest in a specific sport, artistic endeavor, or other activity.

Birthday Cut-Off Dates

It is not unusual for schools to require that applicants be three, four or five years old by a specific date before enrolling. This date varies from school to school but can be as early as July before a fall enrollment; many are between August 31 and October 1. Schools that are firm about their birthday cut-off dates for admission to the early grades also realize that they must not put "an intellectual lid" on a child's head. They try to keep each child appropriately challenged in every subject area. The goal is to maximize the child's academic potential while remaining with a chronological age group that is appropriate socially and healthy emotionally.

The birthday cut-off dates are usually less rigid at seventh grade and above because the maturation pace has leveled off. The late bloomer's skills have caught up with those of the early bloomer, and indications of maturity other than age are given more consideration in admission decisions.

It can be difficult to discern the best grade placement for children with summer birthdays. There are many advantages to being among the oldest, but each child's readiness for the program in a specific school must be considered.

SUBMIT APPLICATIONS

A completed application may include a student and/or parent essay and a photograph. Separately, test scores, recommendations, and a transcript must be submitted. In addition, a visit or interview must be scheduled and attended.

Elements in Submitting the Applications

Finalize the list of schools to which you will apply and comply with each school's requirements in submitting each application. The number of applications you submit depends upon your comfort level with alternatives. In general, six should be a maximum. If attendance at an independent school is important to you, apply to more than just the most highly selective schools.

Time Table

Learn the deadlines for each school, some of which are as early as November. Try to submit your applications no later than January 1, even if the deadlines are later. Applications must be submitted before the student's interview or play date is scheduled.

Format

If a typewriter is not available, write legibly, in ink. Schools that are equipped for on-line applications prefer that you use the Internet.

Student's Essay or Writing Sample

Older students may be asked to submit a paper that has been graded by a teacher. Most schools ask that the applicant to write an essay. This should be the student's work, and unless the school indicates that using the computer is acceptable, it should be in his or her own handwriting, in ink. Parents may discuss the topic with the student, but editing is not appropriate. An essay is required on some of the admission tests. If there is a discrepancy between the essay written at home and at school, it may raise questions. There never seems to be a good time to write those essays, but it is probably best to do it during the Thanksgiving holiday because it does not get easier to find time later.

Parents' Comments

Some schools provide a questionnaire for parents to complete. If the space on the page is insufficient or you prefer to use a computer, it is appropriate to attach a page, but be mindful of length. The fact that the space provided is limited indicates that schools do not want an exhaustive family history or curriculum vitae. Stick to the questions. Too much information is not as helpful as a few relevant, insightful comments. If the school does not provide a questionnaire and you want to convey information that is pertinent to your child's application, include your comments in a brief letter.

Photograph

If requested, a school picture or a snapshot is fine. Do not have a professional photograph taken for the application.

Recommendations

Schools usually mail forms and instructions after receipt of the completed application. Follow the instructions from each school. Some want recommendations to be completed after January 1 by current teachers, usually English, math, and one other person. Other schools wish to have former teachers' recommendations as well. Write the student's name in the appropriate blank before giving it to the teachers and supply stamped envelopes addressed to the schools. Be sure the teacher knows the due date. Giving teachers ample time to complete the forms is not only a courtesy, it may enhance the quality of the recommendation. Parents are not privy to these comments and should not request a copy.

Recommendations from personal friends are useful when they tell the admission officers something they may not otherwise know. The most useful letter is from someone who knows both the applicant and the school well. Letters on fancy letterheads from celebrities or others who do not know the school or the student are not helpful to an admission committee. Members of the board of trustees are usually asked to write on behalf of numerous students, and schools are unable to accept every student recommended by a board member. A general rule to follow on "when to ask" is that if you do not know someone well enough to know where his or her children go to school or if he or she serves as a trustee, it is reasonably safe to assume that a recommendation from that person may not be effective.

Be selective; too many letters are inappropriate. There is an old adage among admission officers, "The thicker the file, the thicker the child!"

Transcript

For students applying to third grade and above, parents should request, in writing, that a transcript be sent directly to each school to which an application has or will be submitted. The transcript should include standardized test results and grades. Some schools' application materials include a card for parents to sign requesting a transcript from the current school. It is acceptable to ask the current school for an unofficial copy for review. On occasion, mistakes have been detected and corrected. Schools will not release a transcript until outstanding bills have been settled.

Tests

Parents must make arrangements for the appropriate test or tests to be administered. General comments about testing are difficult because schools in this area use many different kinds of tests, and some schools accept existing test results. Read each school's information to determine what is required at each grade level, the dates on which the test will be administered, and how to register or make an appointment to take the test.

Some schools do not require formal tests for any of their applicants. Instead, they conduct an informal assessment on the day of the interview. Applicants to nursery programs are not tested. Usually they accompany their parents for a brief visit to the school.

The following tests are administered to groups of students on specified Saturdays at designated schools. They contain sections on mathematics, reading, vocabulary, and writing and last about two-and-a-half hours.

- **The TerraNova Survey Battery** admission test is used by Roman Catholic schools in the Catholic Archdiocese of Washington for applicants to ninth and tenth grades and Roman Catholic schools in the Catholic Diocese of Arlington for applicants to ninth grade. For applicants to other grades, existing test data is used. For additional information and application forms, visit the website, www.adw.org, or call 301-853-4516.
- **The Secondary School Admission Test** (SSAT) is accepted by most independent schools for applicants to sixth through twelfth grades. It is administered one Saturday each month from November through April at local schools or by appointment at various locations. The test can be taken more than once in an academic year. Tutoring for the SSAT should familiarize students with test-taking skills and increase self-confidence. While using the practice booklet published by SSAT can be beneficial, many educators question the

effectiveness of prolonged tutoring for the purpose of prepping for specific questions that might be on the test. For registration information, consult the *Student Registration Guide*, available at the schools that require the test or at www.ssat.org.

• **Independent School Entrance Exam** (ISEE) is used exclusively by some independent schools and accepted by most for applicants to fifth through eleventh grades. Three levels of the test address the age and grade of the applicants. It can be taken only when making a formal application to a school requiring the ISEE and only once in a six-month period. The test is administered from November through March at several schools, on various Saturdays. Consult the *ISEE Student Guide*, available at schools that require the test, or visit www.iseetest.org for registration and the practice book, *What to Expect on the ISEE,* which includes a practice test. Tutoring for the test is not recommended.

Special arrangements can be made for individual and extended time testing for the SSAT and ISEE. For more information, contact individual schools, SSAT at 609-683-4440, or ISEE at 800-446-0320.

The following tests are administered by a qualified diagnostician to an individual student. In general, these tests provide an objective assessment of development, comparing children of the same age range. Students acquire the skills measured on these individually administered tests through communication with adults, games, reading, and other age-appropriate activities.

According to the protocols for these tests, students should not take the test more than once in a twelve-month period. For that reason and to avoid over-testing, many of the schools have an understanding with various testers to send the test results to more than one school. You need to arrange to have the test administered only once and instruct the administrator to send a copy, which is done at no additional expense, to each school to which you apply that requires it. Schools that do not require this type of testing often appreciate receiving a copy, which you can mail.

All tests are subject to up-date or change. In this category, the following are the most commonly used tests:

- **The Detroit Tests of Learning Aptitude-Primary: Second Edition (DTLA-P:2)** is used primarily for applicants to pre-kindergarten. It provides information on verbal and nonverbal processing abilities, fine motor, attention, concentration, and memory skills. The test is administered orally and takes about thirty minutes.
- **The Wechsler Preschool and Primary Scale of Intelligence-Revised** (WPPSI-R) is used primarily for applicants to kindergarten and first grade. The test is composed of two scales, each of which has subtests. The Verbal Scale measures language development, verbal reasoning, comprehension, factual knowledge, memory, concentration, and listening, among other things. The Performance Scale measures nonverbal problem-solving, fine motor coordination, organization, spatial perception, logic, alertness to visual detail, and speed, among other things. The test is administered orally and takes about an hour and fifteen minutes.
- **The Wechsler Intelligence Scale for Children-Third Edition (WISC-III)** is used primarily for applicants to second through fifth grades. The test is administered the same way as the WPPSI-R, measures the same abilities, and takes about the same amount of time.

Another type of individually administered test measures achievement in reading, math, written language, and general knowledge and is used to determine the level of mastery a student has achieved in specific subject areas.

- **The Woodcock-Johnson Tests of Achievement-Third Edition (WJ-III)** or the **Wechsler Individual Achievement Test-Second Edition (WIAT-II)** can be used for applicants to first grade and above. This type of assessment is requested infrequently. Both tests serve the same purpose and only one is needed, but some schools prefer the WJ-III and others prefer the WIAT-II. These tests take several hours to administer.

The results of other tests the student has taken may also be considered. (See also the section on Admission Decisions.)

Some schools place a greater emphasis on test scores than others, but all schools look beyond the performance on one test in determining acceptance. Admission tests can be a "gate keeper," with good reason. Schools want their students to be happy and successful. They know the scores of their students who have been successful and the scores of those who have been more frustrated than rewarded. Therefore, when scores appear to be below those that predict success in their program, schools are cautious about offering a place. However, it should be noted that schools admit students with a range of test scores and do not always admit those with the highest scores.

Applicants from Out-of-Town

Most schools require parents who are moving to the area to bring their children for a play date or interview, even if it requires a long trip. If possible, try to arrange to be in the area at the time of a regularly scheduled play date or group visit. Sometimes several schools will have a scheduled visit during the same week; more frequently special arrangements will be needed to accommodate you while you are in the area. Plan in advance. Try to make these arrangements before winter weather, when snow days can disrupt schedules. Do not schedule more than two schools in one day. Even the most resilient child will have a meltdown when overscheduled. Plan to arrive early so that your child can have a weekend to recover from travel fatigue or jet lag. If you also are scheduling a test, schedule the visits to schools before the test. Not only is the child apt to be less tired for the test, it can motivate him or her to do well if more is known about the schools for which the test is taken.

Working with the Office of Admission

Admission office personnel are gracious and grateful for your interest in their school; however, sometimes the pressure of numbers limits their ability to respond immediately to questions and requests. There are times when your patience is necessary. Keep your calls to a minimum and your communication focused and organized. Not all faculty and staff can answer all questions. Most schools allow time for parents to speak in private with an admission officer at the time of the visit or interview. If this is not scheduled, use your judgment about requesting this meeting. In many schools, you will have an opportunity to meet the head of school or principal.

Preparing Students for a Test or Interview

The best preparation for a test or interview is a good night's sleep, breakfast, and an on-time, unhurried arrival. In an age-appropriate way, explain the process to your child. Familiarize the older child with the schools you intend to visit by reviewing catalogues (sometimes called viewbooks), CD-ROMs, videos, and websites. It is best to tell young children only a few days in advance about the visit. If the campus or test site is unfamiliar, ride by the school or test location and speculate about the visit. Explain that there are lots of wonderful schools and some will not have enough space for everyone who visits, but they are still worth investigating. Make sure your attitude and conversation do not convey anxiety or pressure. Do not become invested in any one school to the exclusion of others. If admission to that school is denied, your child might feel personal failure or that he or she has disappointed you. This is not only unhealthy, it could preclude his or her ability to be happy in another equally fine institution.

Play Dates and Interviews

School personnel like to meet both parents. Since scheduling can be difficult, plan well in advance. If it becomes impossible for both parents to attend, it is often better to keep the appointment because rescheduling can be an even greater challenge. Parents with a pre-determined first-choice school often ask if that school should be scheduled first or last. Although you know your child's response to new situations better than anyone else, I do not believe that the sequence of the visits makes a difference. Try to arrange the visits over a period of time rather than in rapid succession. Most schools provide information on what to expect at a play date or interview.

If your child is ill, reschedule. If your child gets sick following an interview or play date (fever or other disabling symptoms), advise the admission office of the condition.

Dress

Look at pictures of students in the school materials and encourage your child to dress similarly. In general, boys should wear shirts with collars and girls should wear a comfortable, simple dress, skirt, or pants. Young children should wear comfortable play or school clothes. Shoes should be comfortable, and hair should be kept out of the child's face. Do not overdress. Parents should dress in casual, but professional attire.

Advice to Give Students Entering Fourth Grade and Above

Some schools will invite you to spend part of the day at school and have lunch. A student guide often gives a tour, and you can participate in or observe a class. Other schools invite you for a visit/interview that lasts about two hours. You will tour the school and talk to a teacher or admission officer. The interview serves two purposes. One is to give you an opportunity to get to know more about the school, and the other is for the school to learn more about you. Your goal is to be thoughtful and confident during your conversations. Most students have a wonderful time. Remember to do the following:

- Review the catalog or view book, CD-ROM, or website before your visit.
- Relax and be yourself.
- Present a firm handshake, if it seems appropriate to shake hands.
- Maintain eye contact.
- Take an active role in the conversation; give more than "yes" or "no" answers.

- Talk freely about yourself and your interests but keep focused on the topic.
- Ask questions: a good interview will be a mutual exchange of ideas and information.

Examples of Questions an Applicant Might Ask the Interviewer

- How much homework is there on a typical night?
- What is the average size of an English class (or other favorite subject)?
- What is the time commitment involved in playing sports, or participating in drama, orchestra, or other activities?
- On what days are athletic games played? What schools do you play?
- Can I play sports and also be in a school play?
- Does the school plan weekend activities? What are some examples?
- How good do I have to be to play on a team, act or be involved in a play, play in the band, or participate in other activities?
- When is extra help or extra credit work available?
- Is there a "buddy system," or are there other arrangements to help a new student feel comfortable?
- Ask about anything that is important to you.

Examples of Questions an Applicant Might Ask the Student Guide

- What do you like the best about this school? What do you like the least?
- Which courses are the most interesting? The hardest?
- How much time do you spend on homework on an average night?
- What are your extracurricular activities? How much time do you spend on them?
- As a new student, how long did it take you to feel comfortable?

Examples of Questions the School Interviewer Might Ask an Applicant

- How would your teachers describe you?
- Can you name a book or magazine that you would recommend to a friend? Why?
- If you were in charge of your present school, what would you change?
- What do you like to do in your free time?
- What were your impressions of the tour? Were there any surprises?

Advice Regarding Children Entering Third Grade and Below

Many schools invite small groups of children to visit on a weekday or Saturday morning. Age-appropriate activities are used to evaluate skills a student needs in order to succeed in the school's program and to assess reading, writing, and math skills. Children have a good time. Do not try to "prep" your child. Let him or her know that other children and parents will be there too. Assure him or her that nice teachers will have interesting things to do. Say something reassuring such as, "I'll be here when you finish." It may be helpful to say, "Remember to follow directions!" Resist saying there will be games because the younger children may interpret that as meaning they can make up their own rules.

FOLLOW UP

Once the application has been submitted and steps completed, continue to be active in the process. Consider what you have learned about the school and ways to enhance the application.

Questions to Ask Yourself after the Visit or Student Interview

Your answers to the following questions may be useful when you make final decisions. Following your visit to each school ask yourself:

- Can I envision my child in this setting?
- Can I see myself as a parent in this school?
- Whose needs am I considering? Mine? My child's?
- Will my child be sufficiently challenged?
- Will my child be more frustrated than rewarded?

Children do not like to be asked a lot of questions after a visit. Let them tell you their impressions. Do not try to impose your ideas. For an older student, suggest that he or she make a few notes on what seemed interesting or different or any questions that remain.

Many schools will inform you when your child's file is complete or tell you what is missing. If in doubt, call the school when you think the application should be complete.

Enhancing the Application

While you do not want the application file to be overly thick, sending copies of awards, artwork, published articles, or any applicable information is appropriate. Be your child's advocate, but be honest. If you provide an aggrandized description of your child, the school may question whether you are realistic. It is unwise for a family to become deeply committed to only one school. However, you may advise one school of the seriousness of your application by indicating that it is your first choice and if your child is admitted, you will accept. This does not guarantee acceptance and should be done only when you will honor your commitment. Students sometimes write a letter expressing a keen desire to attend. Be cautious about this because, if the student is not admitted, it may add to his or her disappointment.

IF YOU MISS THE DEADLINES

Some families move to the area after all the schools' deadlines have passed, or may need to enroll after school has started. Many schools will already be at capacity. Fire marshals, zoning regulations, and health officials set firm limits on the number of students who can be enrolled; therefore, schools cannot simply "make a place." By calling different schools, parents may be fortunate enough to find a place, or one parent may commute until appropriate schools can be found for the children. Parents may decide to consult with an educational consultant. (See page 11 for information on finding an educational consultant.) After meeting the student, consultants can advise families of possible options, may call appropriate schools to determine if there is a place for a student with the skills and interests of this child (or children), assist with short- and long-term plans, and provide useful information about the transition.

ADMISSION DECISIONS AND PARENTS' RESPONSES

Usually, an Admission Committee will review the files and make the final decisions. The head of school, principal, admission officers, and selected faculty often serve on the committee. These committees meet over the course of several weeks to consider carefully all of the information on each child. The decision to accept or deny is not based on a single item in the file. Each school uses different criteria for making final decisions. The school's mission and the committee's judgment about who "complements the class" contribute to the selection from among those who are qualified.

Most schools seek racial, economic, and cultural diversity. "Complements the class" means enrolling a diverse group of students who can contribute to the academic and non-academic programs and, in coeducational schools, having an equal number of boys and girls. Schools weigh various factors differently, but dependent upon the age of the applicant, among the factors considered are the student's character, evidence of self-discipline, problem-solving skills, and extracurricular interests or activities. In addition to test results, consideration is given to the interview or play date, recommendations, grades, parent comments, student essay, and any other pertinent information in the file.

Schools often state in their admission materials that qualified siblings of current or former students, children of alumni and faculty, and members of the religious denomination (if the school has a religious affiliation) are given preference. Cousins, stepchildren, and half- or step-siblings may be given preference. While schools want to keep families together, sometimes there are not enough available spaces to accommodate all priority applicants. Thus, guarantees of enrollment are rare.

No school wants to admit a child who is likely to fail. However, when possible, schools may accept a student with some questionable qualifications in the hope that with extra attention, he or she will succeed. Adding to the complexity of the decision-making process is the fact that teachers can manage only a limited number of time-intensive students in a class. The needs of each child in the class must be considered. Making admission decisions can be a complicated and often emotionally difficult process.

School Notification and Parents' Responses

Some schools mail letters advising parents of the decision as early as February, but most are mailed in mid-March. Letters indicate to parents that their child's application is accepted (usually a thicker envelope containing a contract), denied, or placed on a waiting list.

Accept

Your family may receive one or more thick envelopes! Parents and older students often are invited to revisit the schools to which they have been admitted. It is especially important for older students to take advantage of this opportunity. It helps determine the compatibility of the student and the school, and it enhances the student's confidence about entering in the fall. Because friends are particularly important to older students, having an opportunity to meet future classmates and teachers allows newly admitted students to begin to feel comfortable. Previously unanswered questions can be asked. Admission officers are pleased to provide assistance to facilitate the decision for those who have been accepted. Current parents are often available to answer questions.

For families applying for financial aid, information about the award is usually provided at the time of acceptance. Generally, you do not have to accept a place that has been offered until the school advises you of the size of the grant.

The role that older students play in the final decision is important. If you have established some parameters for the selection within a narrow range of schools, your child can usually be trusted to make the final decision.

Read your school enrollment contract carefully. When you decide upon a school, submit the contract and enrollment fee promptly. Notify other schools of your decision not to accept their offer of admittance and withdraw from other waiting lists. A prompt response may allow another student on the waiting list to be admitted.

Deny

Denial is often the result of the large number of well-qualified applicants relative to the total number of places. Some schools may have more than 200 applications for 25 places. Neither you nor your child should feel any sense of failure. Some children may be advised to reapply at a later date. Although often no single factor can be identified as the reason for not being accepted, on occasion, the committee feels that the school cannot meet the student's specific needs. Admission officers will discuss decisions with parents, and may refer them to an educational consultant who can direct them to schools with more spaces or a more appropriate program.

Waiting List or Waiting Pool

The waiting list or pool indicates that your child is qualified and, if space permits, will be admitted. If you want to remain on the list, notify the school immediately and convey your enthusiasm. Schools rarely rank students on the waiting list; selection from the list depends upon many factors, including the number of students who accept the places already offered, and the withdrawal of currently enrolled students. With the expectation that not all families will accept the places offered, schools may admit more students than the exact number of places available; therefore, when an accepted student refuses a place, it may not immediately create a place for someone on the waiting list. After the deadline for parents to respond to an acceptance, admission officers can better "guesstimate" the odds of acceptance from the waiting list. Continue to keep the school informed of your interest, and forward recent grades or evidence of a recent achievement. First semester tuition is usually due in July, and, on occasion, spaces become available at that time. However, a place can become available as late as the beginning of the school year.

When you no longer wish to remain on the waiting list, immediately inform the school of your decision to withdraw. Waiting lists usually cease to exist after school opens and one has to reapply for future consideration. Some schools modify the process for a re-application.

Enrolling in a New School

Rejoice over your child's new school and continue to be vigilant and actively involved in his or her education. No school is perfect, nor does any one school meet the needs of every child equally well every year. Even the best teachers may have a bad year, and the chemistry of a class may or may not be ideal. Parents have a right to high expectations—but must be realistic. Monitor your child's academic progress, know the teachers, know your child's friends and their parents, be available to support school programs, and attend parent meetings and as many of your child's activities as you possibly can. Remember you and the school are co-educators or partners in education, and by working together, the common goal of your child's success and happiness can best be achieved.

Independent
School Directory

AIDAN MONTESSORI SCHOOL (THE)

Year founded: 1961
2700 27th Street, NW
Washington, DC 20008
Head of School:
Kathy Minardi

GENERAL
Grade range: PN-6th   Coed
Religious affiliation: Nonsectarian
Average class size: 12 (age 18 months-age 3), 25 (age 3-6th)
School day: 9:00-12:00 (Toddler-PK), 9:00-3:00 (K-6th)
Morning or after-school care: 8:00-6:00

CAMPUS/CAMPUS LIFE
Facilities:
Montessori-designed environment with library, playground

Lunch provided: No
Boarding option: No
Bus service: No
School uniform or dress code: None
Handicapped access available: Yes
Community service requirement: None

Director of Admission:
Christine Kranz Smith
Phone: 202-387-2700
Fax: 202-387-0346
E-mail:
c.smith@aidanschool.org
Website:
www.aidanschool.org

ADMISSIONS
Application deadline: March 1
Application fee: $50
Application process:
Application, school visit, academic records (K-6th), teacher recommendations (K-6th), informal assessment, transcript
Number of students applied/enrolled: 91 / 25

COSTS
Tuition: $8,280 (toddler), $7,690 (primary half day), $11,470 (primary full day), $11,940 (1st-6th)
Average additional fees: $300 (enrollment fee), $1,800 (development fee, one time only, one per family)
Financial aid budget: $30,000
Average grant size: $3,250
% of Students receiving financial aid: 6.2%

NOTE: This data applies to the 2002–2003 school year.

ACADEMIC PROFILE
Number of faculty: 11 Full Time
1 Part Time (plus assistants)
Languages and grades offered:
Spanish (age 3-6th grade)
Number of AP classes offered:
Not applicable
Tutors/learning specialists:
Yes: at an additional fee
Schools three or more graduates have attended over the past five years:

SPECIAL FEATURES
Montessori curriculum, after-school
enrichment program includes
Mandarin Chinese, French, outdoor
games, creative arts

ENROLLMENT
Total number of students attending and graduating class size: 148 /
Birthday cut-off:
% Diversity: 33%
Grades with openings: toddler (6-8)
in Sept & Feb, 3-5 years old (28),
plus attrition

SUMMER PROGRAMS
Yes: various programs (18 months
to 6 years)

ART PROGRAMS
Art, music

SPORTS
None

LONG-RANGE PLANS

HISTORY AND MISSION STATEMENT
Aidan Montessori was founded by a group of parents who based the school's curriculum on the philosophy of Dr. Maria Montessori. At Aidan, we respect the individual child's needs and strive to meet those needs by providing a child-centered learning environment. We offer an education for the development of the whole child. Our student body, faculty and staff provide a rich cultural diversity, which contributes to an enriching educational experience.

NOTE: This data applies to the 2002–2003 school year.

ALEXANDRIA COUNTRY DAY SCHOOL

Year founded: 1983
2400 Russell Road
Alexandria, VA 22301
Head of School:
Alexander "Exie" Harvey, IV

GENERAL
Grade range: K-8th   Coed
Religious affiliation: Nonsectarian
Average class size: 11 (K), 15
(1st-8th)
School day: 8:30-2:45 (K-2nd),
8:15-3:00 (3rd-8th)
Morning or after-school care:
7:00-6:00

CAMPUS/CAMPUS LIFE
Facilities:
Art studio, computer lab, gym,
library, playing field, science lab
Lunch provided: Yes: additional fee
Boarding option: No
Bus service: Yes
School uniform or dress code:
Dress code: white or green
collared shirt, khaki pants/
shorts/skirt
Handicapped access available: No
Community service requirement: Yes

Director of Admission:
Julia Love
Phone: 703-548-4804 x303
Fax: 703-549-9022
E-mail:
admissions@acdsnet.org
Website:
www.acdsnet.org

ADMISSIONS
Application deadline: January 31
Application fee: $75
Application process:
In-house assessment (K-4th),
ISEE (5th-8th), teacher
recommendations, student visit,
parent tour
**Number of students
applied/enrolled:** 165 / 45

COSTS
Tuition: $12,025 (K-3rd),
$13,370 (4th-8th)
Average additional fees: $300
Financial aid budget: $140,000
Average grant size: $3,000
**% of Students receiving
financial aid:** 15%

NOTE: This data applies to the 2002–2003 school year.

ACADEMIC PROFILE

Number of faculty: 35

Languages and grades offered:
Spanish (K-8th), German and
Swedish (language clubs)

Number of AP classes offered:
Not applicable

Tutors/learning specialists:
Yes: counselor, resource teachers
in language arts, math, science

**Schools three or more graduates have
attended over the past five years:**
Bishop Ireton, Bishop O'Connell,
Bullis, Edmund Burke, Episcopal,
Flint Hill, Georgetown Day,
Georgetown Visitation, Madeira,
National Cathedral, Potomac,
St. Albans, St. Stephen's & St. Agnes,
St. Andrew's, Sidwell Friends,
Thornton Friends

SPECIAL FEATURES

Small classes, individualized
attention, nurturing environment,
technologically advanced,
academically oriented,
close community

ENROLLMENT

**Total number of students
attending and graduating
class size:** 250 / 25

Birthday cut-off: September 30

% Diversity: 9%

Grades with openings: K (24),
1st (8), 2nd (2), 3rd-8th (3-6)

SUMMER PROGRAMS

K-2nd: week-long content-based
programs, 6th-8th: Potomac
Exploration science/outdoor camp

ART PROGRAMS

Intensive six-week middle
school course; weekly class for
1st-6th, K has in-class art spaces

SPORTS

Basketball, cross-country, softball,
track, (5th-8th); soccer (6th-8th)

LONG-RANGE PLANS

Build an addition with space for
science labs, art & music
studios, cafeteria and kitchen,
expand to 275 students, add
handicapped accessibility,
and lacrosse program

HISTORY AND MISSION STATEMENT

The Alexandria Country Day School engenders and nurtures enthusiasm, compassion, and self-confidence in its students by means of developmentally appropriate academic and other programs, high behavioral expectations, and an emphasis on citizenship.

NOTE: This data applies to the 2002–2003 school year.

BARNESVILLE SCHOOL

Year founded: 1969
21830 Peach Tree Road, P.O. Box 404
Barnesville, MD 20838
Head of School:
Jaralyn Hough

GENERAL
Grade range: PK-8th   Coed
Religious affiliation: Nonsectarian
Average class size: 15
School day: 8:30-3:00 (PK-5th),
8:15-3:00 (6th-8th)
Morning or after-school care:
7:00-6:00

CAMPUS/CAMPUS LIFE
Facilities:
40 acre rural campus, 2 buildings,
art room, basketball court, gym/
performing arts center, music tech lab,
science lab, soccer field
Lunch provided: No
Boarding option: No
Bus service: Yes
School uniform or dress code:
Dress code: respectful, safe and
appropriate for a learning environment
Handicapped access available: Yes
Community service requirement:
Yes: every grade participates

Director of Admission:
Sally Mullen
Phone: 301-972-0341
Fax: 301-972-4076
E-mail:
smullen@barnesville-school.com
Website:
www.barnesville-school.com

ADMISSIONS
Application deadline: January 15
Application fee: $50
Application process:
In-house testing (PK-4th),
ISEE (5th-8th)
**Number of students
applied/enrolled:** 137 / 45

COSTS
Tuition:
$5,085 (PK), $8,475 (K-5th),
$9,070 (6th-8th)
Average additional fees: $300
Financial aid budget: $66,000
Average grant size: $2,000
**% of Students receiving
financial aid:** 5%

NOTE: This data applies to the 2002–2003 school year.

ACADEMIC PROFILE
Number of faculty: 21 Full Time
7 Part Time
Languages and grades offered:
Spanish (5th-8th)
Number of AP classes offered:
Not applicable
Tutors/learning specialists:
Yes: school provides space,
parents employ tutor
Schools three or more graduates have attended over the past five years:
Bullis, Connelly School of the Holy Child, Holton-Arms, Landon, Potomac, St. Andrew's, Sandy Spring Friends

SPECIAL FEATURES
Mountain biking program in Middle School

ENROLLMENT
Total number of students attending and graduating class size: 250 / 25
Birthday cut-off: December 31
% Diversity: 12%
Grades with openings: PK (20), K (8-10), plus attrition

SUMMER PROGRAMS
Yes: computers, drama, music, sports camps

ART PROGRAMS
Art, drama, music

SPORTS
Basketball, lacrosse, mountain biking, soccer, softball

LONG-RANGE PLANS
Continue to invest in the 'whole child' educational experience and maximize the options for the post-Barnesville years.

HISTORY AND MISSION STATEMENT
Founded as a primary school, Barnesville expanded to 8th grade in the 1990's with two classes of each grade and a student body of 250. Barnesville students are part of a nurturing community which cares for its greater community through service and learning as an integral part of the curriculum.

NOTE: This data applies to the 2002–2003 school year.

BARRIE SCHOOL

Year founded: 1932
13500 Layhill Road
Silver Spring, MD 20906
Head of School:
Julia A. Wall, Interim Head

GENERAL
Grade range: PN-12th   Coed
Religious affiliation: Nonsectarian
Average class size: 18-20 (2-3 year olds),
25 (PK-5th), 16 (6th-12th)
School day: 9:00-12:30 (2-3 year olds),
9:00-3:20 (PK-5th), 8:10-3:20 (6th-12th)
Morning or after-school care:
7:00-6:00

CAMPUS/CAMPUS LIFE
Facilities:
44 acre wooded campus with outdoor
swimming pools, amphitheater, 200 seat
theater Center for Athletics & Performing
Arts with full gymnasium (1999),
fitness center, 3 libraries, photography
darkroom, science rooms, stables
Lunch provided: No
Boarding option: No
Bus service: Yes
School uniform or dress code:
Dress code: neat, clean, appropriate
and non-revealing
Handicapped access available: Limited
Community service requirement:
Yes: 60 hours for graduation

Director of Admission:
Julie C. Lewis
Phone: 301-871-6200
Fax: 301-871-6706
E-mail:
jlewis@barrie.org
Website:
www.barrie.org

ADMISSIONS
Application deadline: February 1
Application fee: $50
Application process: Applicant visit,
records, teacher recommendations,
WPPSI-R or WISC III (1st-5th),
SSAT (6th-12th)
**Number of students
applied/enrolled:** 250 LS; 135 MS;
130 US /

COSTS
Tuition: $8,850 (half day N),
$11,900 (full day N-K), $13,350
(1st-5th), $14,960 (6th-8th),
$16,980 (9th-12th)
Average additional fees: $600
Financial aid budget: Need based
starting at kindergarten
Average grant size: Maximum of
50% of tuition
**% of Students receiving
financial aid:** 12-15%

NOTE: This data applies to the 2002–2003 school year.

ACADEMIC PROFILE

Number of faculty: 56 Full Time
6 Part Time
Languages and grades offered:
French (6th-12th),
Spanish (2 year olds-12th)
Number of AP classes offered: 12-15
Tutors/learning specialists:
Yes: learning specialists, counselors
on staff
**Schools three or more graduates have
attended over the past five years:**
American, Bryn Mawr, Georgetown,
Howard, Harvard, Northwestern,
Princeton, University of Chicago,
University of Michigan, Vanderbilt,
Vassar, Wake Forest

SPECIAL FEATURES

The Extension Days Program supports
science/cultural/environmental studies
with field trips and on-campus activities.
Extended Study Week offers Middle and
Upper Schools students opportunities
such as visiting China and Senegal or
working on a Navajo reservation.
Interships for Juniors and Seniors have
included placements at the U.S. Naval
Academy, Johns Hopkins Hospital, and
WJLA television.

ENROLLMENT

**Total number of students
attending and graduating
class size:** 510 / 28
Birthday cut-off: September 1
(2 year olds), December 31 (K)
% Diversity: 29%
Grades with openings:
2 year olds (18-20), plus attrition

SUMMER PROGRAMS

Yes: arts & crafts, camping, canoe-
ing, computer, counselor training,
drama, horseback riding, nature
study, sports, studio art, swimming

ART PROGRAMS

Art history and studio art, chorus,
drama and technical theater, music

SPORTS

Baseball, basketball, cross-country,
golf, horseback riding, lacrosse,
racquetball, soccer, tennis,
track & field

LONG-RANGE PLANS

Facilities: Master Site Plan in process
Program: expand technology
curriculum

HISTORY AND MISSION STATEMENT

Barrie is committed to educating students to be independent thinkers, resource-
ful problem solvers, good citizens, and life-long learners. Barrie is committed to
its Montessori philosophy and college preparatory rigor, which embrace interac-
tive and self-directed learnning, academic excellence, respect and appreciation for
the environment, and the celebration of all people and cultures.

NOTE: This data applies to the 2002–2003 school year.

BEAUVOIR, THE NATIONAL CATHEDRAL ELEMENTARY SCHOOL

Year founded: 1933
3500 Woodley Road, NW
Washington, DC 20016
Head of School:
Paula J. Carreiro

GENERAL
Grade range: PK-3rd   Coed
Religious affiliation: Episcopal
Average class size: 20 with 2 teachers
School day: 8:00-3:00
Morning or after-school care:
3:00-6:00

CAMPUS/CAMPUS LIFE
Facilities:
Newly renovated classrooms, gym,
library, performing arts room,
technology
Lunch provided: Yes
Boarding option: No
Bus service: Yes
School uniform or dress code:
None
Handicapped access available: Yes
Community service requirement:
No requirement, but active participation

Director of Admission:
Margaret Hartigan
Phone: 202-537-6493
Fax: 202-537-5778
E-mail:
mhartigan@cathedral.org
Website:
www.beauvoirschool.org

ADMISSIONS
Application deadline: January 10
Application fee: $65
Application process: School visit,
teacher recommendations, Detroit
(PK*), WPPSI-R (K), WISC III
(1st-3rd)
(*Subject co change)
**Number of students
applied/enrolled:** 333 / 90

COSTS
Tuition: $17,200
Average additional fees:
Financial aid budget:
Average grant size: $10,280
**% of Students receiving
financial aid:** 16%

NOTE: This data applies to the 2002–2003 school year.

ACADEMIC PROFILE

Number of faculty: 51 Full Time
4 Part Time
Languages and grades offered:
Spanish (PK-3rd)
Number of AP classes offered:
Not applicable
Tutors/learning specialists:
Yes: math, reading resource specialists
Schools three or more graduates have attended over the past five years:
Bullis, Georgetown Day, Holton-Arms, Landon, Maret, National Cathedral, National Presbyterian, Potomac, St. Albans

SPECIAL FEATURES

ENROLLMENT

Total number of students attending and graduating class size: 389 / 75
Birthday cut-off:
August 31
% Diversity: 28%
Grades with openings: PK (63), K (20), 1st-3rd (attrition only)

SUMMER PROGRAMS
Yes

ART PROGRAMS
Art, music, performing arts

SPORTS
Physical education

LONG-RANGE PLANS

HISTORY AND MISSION STATEMENT

Beauvoir, The National Cathedral Elementary School founded in 1933, is a primary school dedicated to educating a diverse student body within a caring and creative environment. Our program is designed to nurture the spiritual, ethical, intellectual, emotional, physical, and social development of our children. We seek to foster a spirit of inquiry and a joy in learning.

NOTE: This data applies to the 2002–2003 school year.

BISHOP IRETON HIGH SCHOOL

Year founded: 1964
201 Cambridge Road
Alexandria, VA 22314
Head of School:
Rev. Kevin Nadolski, OSFS

GENERAL
Grade range: 9th-12th   Coed
Religious affiliation: Catholic
Average class size: 25
School day: 8:00-3:00
Morning or after-school care:
No

CAMPUS/CAMPUS LIFE
Facilities:
Auditorium, gymnasium, labs, library
Lunch provided: Yes
Boarding option: No
Bus service: No
School uniform or dress code:
Uniform
Handicapped access available: Yes
Community service requirement:
Yes: 30 hours

Director of Admission:
Peter Hamer
Phone: 703-751-7606
Fax: 703-212-8173
E-mail:
phamer@bishopireton.org
Website:
www.bishopireton.org

ADMISSIONS
Application deadline: February 2
Application fee: $35
Application process: Terra Nova

Number of students
applied/enrolled: 600+ / 235

COSTS
Tuition: $7,300-$11,100
Average additional fees: $600
Financial aid budget: $250,000
Average grant size:
% of Students receiving
financial aid: 10%

NOTE: This data applies to the 2002–2003 school year.

ACADEMIC PROFILE
Number of faculty:
Languages and grades offered:
French, German, Latin, Spanish,
Russian (9th-12th)
Number of AP classes offered:
All subjects except PE and religion
Tutors/learning specialists:
Yes
Schools three or more graduates have
attended over the past five years:
Air Force Academy, Georgetown,
Notre Dame, University of Virginia,
Virginia Technology, West Point

SPECIAL FEATURES
New building, performance hall,
technology curriculum, writing center

ENROLLMENT
Total number of students
attending and graduating
class size: 800 / 172
Birthday cut-off:
Not applicable
% Diversity: 20%
Grades with openings: 9th (200)

SUMMER PROGRAMS
Yes: limited

ART PROGRAMS
Art, drama, music

SPORTS
Baseball, basketball, cross-country,
football, golf, ice hockey, lacrosse,
soccer, softball, swimming &
diving, tennis, track & field,
volleyball, wrestling

LONG-RANGE PLANS

HISTORY AND MISSION STATEMENT

NOTE: This data applies to the 2002–2003 school year.

BLESSED SACRAMENT SCHOOL

Year founded: 1923
5841 Chevy Chase Parkway, NW
Washington, DC 20015
Head of School:
Frances Scango

GENERAL
Grade range: K-8th   Coed
Religious affiliation: Catholic
Average class size: 26
School day: 8:10-3:10
After-school care:
3:10-6:00

CAMPUS/CAMPUS LIFE
Facilities:
Urban campus with auditorium/cafeteria,
computer lab, gym, library
Lunch provided: Yes: additional fee
Boarding option: No
Bus service: No
School uniform or dress code:
Uniform
Handicapped access available: Yes
Community service requirement:
Yes: 20 hours in 8th

Director of Admission:
Eleanor Clark
Phone: 202-966-6682 x336
Fax: 202-966-4938
E-mail:
eclark@blessedsacramentdc.org
Website:
www.blessedsacramentdc.org

ADMISSIONS
Application deadline: Rolling
Application fee: None
Application process: Application,
informal assessment, transcript,
birth certificate, baptismal
certificate, teacher recommendation
**Number of students
applied/enrolled:** 94 / 50

COSTS
Tuition: $7,780 (non-parishioners),
$4,560 (parishioners)
Average additional fees: $400
Financial aid budget:
Average grant size: Case by case basis
**% of Students receiving
financial aid:**

NOTE: This data applies to the 2002–2003 school year.

ACADEMIC PROFILE
Number of faculty: 36 Full Time
21 Part Time
Languages and grades offered:
French, Spanish (3rd-8th)
Number of AP classes offered:
Not applicable
Tutors/learning specialists:
Yes: educational psychologist,
guidance counselor, 2 resource teachers
Schools three or more graduates have attended over the past five years:
Connelly School of the Holy Child,
Georgetown Prep, Georgetown
Visitation, Gonzaga, Good Counsel,
Holy Cross, St. Albans, St. Anselm's,
St. John's College High, Stone Ridge

SPECIAL FEATURES

ENROLLMENT
Total number of students attending and graduating class size: 490 /
Birthday cut-off:
% Diversity: 5%
Grades with openings: K (50),
plus attrition

SUMMER PROGRAMS
None

ART PROGRAMS
Art, band, choir, drama, music

SPORTS
Parish sponsors CYO basketball

LONG-RANGE PLANS
Significant renovation to be
completed Fall of 2003, new media
center, art studio and 40% more
classroom space will reduce
class sizes

HISTORY AND MISSION STATEMENT
Blessed Sacrament is a parish, neighborhood school dedicated to excellence within an atmosphere of Christian love and concern. The curriculum incorporates a balance of basic educational needs and advanced materials. The school setting provides children with opportunities for the practice of Christian virtues and values as they deal with their own personal growth and development and their relationships with others.

NOTE: This data applies to the 2002–2003 school year.

BRITISH SCHOOL OF WASHINGTON

Year founded: 1998
4715 16th Street, NW
Washington, DC 20011
Head of School:
Lesley P. Stagg

GENERAL
Grade range: N-11th   Coed
Religious affiliation: Nonsectarian
Average class size: 17
School day: 8:45-3:30
Morning or after-school care:
8:00-6:00

CAMPUS/CAMPUS LIFE
Facilities:
3 campuses, urban setting
Lunch provided: No
Boarding option: No
Bus service: Yes
School uniform or dress code:
Uniform: red, white and blue
Handicapped access available: No
Community service requirement:
None

Director of Admission:
Deborah Blott
Phone: 202-829-3700
Fax: 202-829-6522
E-mail:
admission@britishschool.org
Website:
www.britishschool.org

ADMISSIONS
Application deadline: Rolling
Application fee: $150
Application process: Informal
assessment, report from current
school
**Number of students
applied/enrolled:**

COSTS
Tuition: $6,400 (Nursery,
mornings only)
$12,000 (N-5th)
$13,500 (6th and up)
Average additional fees: $1,000
Financial aid budget:
Average grant size:
**% of Students receiving
financial aid:**

NOTE: This data applies to the 2002–2003 school year.

ACADEMIC PROFILE
Number of faculty: 36 Full Time
7 Part Time
Languages and grades offered:
French (N-11th), Latin (5th-11th),
Spanish (5th-11th)
Number of AP classes offered:
Not applicable
Tutors/learning specialists:
None: no ESL provision
Schools three or more graduates have attended over the past five years:
No graduates yet

SPECIAL FEATURES
United Kingdom National Curriculum
and school calendar, year round
enrollement, many extra-curricular
activities.

ENROLLMENT
Total number of students attending and graduating class size: 300 /
Birthday cut-off:
August 31
% Diversity: 40% American,
40% British, 20% other nationalities
Grades with openings: All grades

SUMMER PROGRAMS
Yes: summer camp for BSW
pupils only

ART PROGRAMS
Art, dance, drama, music

SPORTS
Basketball, cricket, gymnastics,
rounders, rugby, soccer, softball,
tennis

LONG-RANGE PLANS
IB Diploma will commence
September 2003

HISTORY AND MISSION STATEMENT
The British School of Washington currently accepts children from age three to sixteen years old. The curriculum is modelled on the National Curriculum (England). Pupils are taught by UK trained, experienced teachers who are dedicated to realising the potential of each child within a structured learning environment.

BROOKSFIELD SCHOOL

Year founded: 1987

1830 Kirby Road

McLean, VA 22101

Head of School:

Anita Labetti

GENERAL

Grade range: PK-3rd   Coed

Religious affiliation: Nonsectarian

Average class size:

School day: 9:00-12:00 *or* 9:00-3:00

Morning or after-school care:

7:30-5:30

CAMPUS/CAMPUS LIFE

Facilities:

5 wooded acres

Lunch provided: Yes

Boarding option: No

Bus service: No

School uniform or dress code:

None

Handicapped access available:

Community service requirement:

Director of Admission:

Sandi Metro

Phone: 703-356-2187

Fax: 703-356-6620

E-mail:

brksfield@aol.com

Website:

www.brooksfieldschool.org

ADMISSIONS

Application deadline: February 1

Application fee: $50

Application process: Informal assessment

Number of students applied/enrolled:

COSTS

Tuition:

Average additional fees:

Financial aid budget:

Average grant size:

% of Students receiving financial aid:

NOTE: This data applies to the 2002–2003 school year.

ACADEMIC PROFILE

Number of faculty:

Languages and grades offered:
Spanish (PK-3rd)

Number of AP classes offered:
Not applicable

Tutors/learning specialists:

Schools three or more graduates have attended over the past five years:
Flint Hill, Langley, Nysmith, Potomac, Sidwell Friends

SPECIAL FEATURES
Montessori based curriculum

ENROLLMENT

Total number of students attending and graduating class size:

Birthday cut-off:

% Diversity:

Grades with openings:

SUMMER PROGRAMS
Yes: half and full day summer camp

ART PROGRAMS
Arts focus with 2 experienced art teachers, dance, music, theater

SPORTS
Outdoor adventure program, physical education program

LONG-RANGE PLANS
Expand

HISTORY AND MISSION STATEMENT

Brooksfield School was founded upon the belief that learning happens through the joys of friendship, shared experiences and self discovery. Mission statement: To nurture the creative spirit while facilitating academic excellence.

NOTE: This data applies to the 2002–2003 school year.

BROWNE ACADEMY

Year founded: 1941
5917 Telegraph Road
Alexandria, VA 22310
Head of School:
Mort Dukehart

GENERAL
Grade range: N-8th   Coed
Religious affiliation: Nonsectarian
Average class size: 18
School day: 8:30-3:30
Morning or after-school care:
7:00-6:00

CAMPUS/CAMPUS LIFE
Facilities:
Three classroom buildings including
library, computer lab, science labs,
music and art departments set on
11 acres with stream, playing fields,
swimming pool, basketball court,
and outdoor amphitheater.
Lunch provided: Yes
Boarding option: No
Bus service: No
School uniform or dress code:
Dress code
Handicapped access available: Yes
Community service requirement:
No: Community service is inherent
in the school's mission

Director of Admission:
Kerri Bennett
Phone: 703-960-3000
Fax: 703-960-7325
E-mail:
kbennett@browneacademy.org
Website:
www.browneacademy.org

ADMISSIONS
Application deadline: February 9
Application fee: $50
Application process: Detroit (PK*),
WPPSI-R (K), WISC III (1st-8th),
application, teacher recommendation,
transcript, classroom visit, parent
interview (*Subject to change)
**Number of students
applied/enrolled:**

COSTS
Tuition: $6,118-$12,193 (N),
$14,715 (K-8th)
Average additional fees:
$900-$1,500
Financial aid budget: 7% of budget
Average grant size: Not available
**% of Students receiving
financial aid:** 20%

NOTE: This data applies to the 2002–2003 school year.

ACADEMIC PROFILE
Number of faculty: 67 Full Time
15 Part Time
Languages and grades offered:
French (N-8th), Spanish (5th-8th)
Number of AP classes offered:
Not applicable
Tutors/learning specialists:
Yes
Schools three or more graduates have attended over the past five years:
Bishop Ireton, Bishop O'Connell, Episcopal High, Flint Hill, Georgetown Day, Madeira, Maret, Potomac, St. Stephen's & St. Agnes, Sidwell Friends, Thomas Jefferson

SPECIAL FEATURES

ENROLLMENT
Total number of students attending and graduating class size: 330 / 27
Birthday cut-off:
September 30
% Diversity: 30%
Grades with openings: N (18), PK (15), K (5), 1st-4th (6), 5th-8th (8)

SUMMER PROGRAMS
Yes

ART PROGRAMS
Art, ballet, band, choir, drawing, flute, handbells, jazz, painting, percussion, piano

SPORTS
Basketball, soccer, softball, tae kwon do

LONG-RANGE PLANS
Build new gym, multipurpose building

HISTORY AND MISSION STATEMENT

Browne Academy is a coeducational, independent day school for children in Preschool through 8th Grade. We are committed to developing independent, passionate, lifelong learners who will actively participate as responsible, caring citizens in a global community. We are passionate about Excellence, Diversity, Character, and Community. Browne offers a challenging academic environment with an interdisciplinary curriculum fostering critical thinking skills as well as leadership and social responsibility.

NOTE: This data applies to the 2002–2003 school year.

BULLIS SCHOOL (THE)

Year founded: 1930
10601 Falls Road
Potomac, MD 20854
Head of School:
Thomas B. Farquhar

GENERAL
Grade range: 3rd-12th   Coed
Religious affiliation: Nonsectarian
Average class size: 15
School day: 8:00-3:30
Morning or after-school care:
3:30-5:30

CAMPUS/CAMPUS LIFE
Facilities: Art center, 2 computer labs,
football stadium, gymnasium, library,
4 science labs, indoor tennis courts, track
Lunch provided: Yes
Boarding option: No
Bus service: Yes
School uniform or dress code:
Dress code: boys - ties/khakis; girls -
plaid skirt or khakis, polo shirt in
warmer weather
Handicapped access available: Yes
Community service requirement: Yes

Director of Admission:
Nancy Spencer
Phone: 301-983-5724
Fax: 301-299-9050
E-mail:
nancy_spencer@bullis.org
Website:
www.bullis.org

ADMISSIONS
Application deadline: February 1
Application fee: $50
Application process: WISC III (3rd),
ERB (4th-5th), interviews and
SSAT or ISEE (6th-12th),
teacher recommendations,
essays, and interview/group visit
(3rd-12th)
**Number of students
applied/enrolled:** 600 / 125

COSTS
Tuition: $16,150 (3rd-5th),
$18,340 (6th-8th), $19,150
(9th-12th)
Average additional fees: $1,000
Financial aid budget: $960,000
Average grant size: $10,000
**% of Students receiving
financial aid:** 14%

NOTE: This data applies to the 2002–2003 school year.

ACADEMIC PROFILE

Number of faculty: 90 Full Time
5 Part Time
Languages and grades offered:
French (4th-12th), Latin (6th-12th),
Spanish (3rd-12th)
Number of AP classes offered:
15
Learning specialist:
1 in Upper School, part time in lower/
middle school
Schools three or more graduates have attended over the past five years:
American, Amherst, Colby, Columbia,
Kenyon, Princeton, Rice, Skidmore,
Stanford, University of Maryland,
University of Pennsylvania

SPECIAL FEATURES

ENROLLMENT

Total number of students attending and graduating class size: 600 / 92
Birthday cut-off:
September 1 (guideline)
% Diversity: 19%
Grades with openings: 3rd (28),
6th (20), 7th (15), 9th (30),
plus attrition

SUMMER PROGRAMS

Yes: academic courses, sports camps

ART PROGRAMS

Acting, art, ceramics, chorus,
dance, drawing, field trips, mixed
media, music, music theory,
painting, sculpture, theater

SPORTS

Baseball, basketball, cross-country,
field hockey, football, golf, ice
hockey, lacrosse, soccer, swimming,
tennis, track & field, wrestling

LONG-RANGE PLANS

HISTORY AND MISSION STATEMENT

The Bullis School is an independent, college preparatory day school offering boys and girls in grades 3 through 12 an educational program of excellence in a community that values integrity, respect, responsibility, diversity, and service. A caring and supportive faculty fosters a positive attitude about learning and challenges our students to achieve their highest potential in academics, the arts, and athletics.

NOTE: This data applies to the 2002–2003 school year.

BURGUNDY FARM COUNTRY DAY SCHOOL

Year founded: 1946
3700 Burgundy Road
Alexandria, VA 22303
Head of School:
Gerald L. Marchildon

GENERAL
Grade range: PK-8th   Coed
Religious affiliation: Nonsectarian
Average class size: 16-28 with 2 teachers
School day: 8:30-3:00
Morning or after-school care:
3:00-6:00

CAMPUS/CAMPUS LIFE
Facilities:
Amphitheater, art studios, auditorium, farm, new gymnasium and middle school building, media center/library, photography and science labs, pond, pool, woods; in West Virginia, 300 acre campus
Lunch provided: No
Boarding option: No
Bus service: Yes
School uniform or dress code:
None
Handicapped access available: Yes
Community service requirement:
Yes: many opportunities in PK-5th including partnership with DC public school; 8 hours (6th), 10 hours (7th), 12 hours (8th)

Director of Admission:
Patricia Harden
Phone: 703-960-3431
Fax: 703-960-5056
E-mail:
info@burgundyfarm.org
Website:
www.burgundyfarm.org

ADMISSIONS
Application deadline: February 1
Application fee: $50
Application process: Detroit (PK),*
WPPSI-R (K), WISC III (1st-8th), teacher recommendations, classroom visit, school transcripts (2nd-8th) (*Subject to change)
**Number of students
applied/enrolled:** 242 / 49

COSTS
Tuition: $14,400 (PK-5th),
$15,115 (6th-8th)
Average additional fees: $500
Financial aid budget: $420,000
Average grant size: $8,500
**% of Students receiving
financial aid:** 16%

NOTE: This data applies to the 2002–2003 school year.

ACADEMIC PROFILE
Number of faculty: 33 Full Time
10 Part Time
Languages and grades offered:
French, Spanish (begins at
6 years old)
Number of AP classes offered:
Not applicable
Tutors/learning specialists:
Yes
Schools three or more graduates have attended over the past five years:
Bishop Ireton, DeMatha, Edmund Burke, Field, Flint Hill, Georgetown Day, Gonzaga, Madeira, Maret, National Cathedral, Potomac, St. Albans, St. Stephen's & St. Agnes, Sidwell Friends, Thomas Jefferson

SPECIAL FEATURES

ENROLLMENT
Total number of students attending and graduating class size: 280 / 32
Birthday cut-off:
September 30
% Diversity: 33%
Grades with openings: PK (16), K (10-12), 6th (4), plus attrition

SUMMER PROGRAMS
West Virginia: residential natural science camp
Alexandria campus: day camp featuring arts, crafts, computers, performing and visual arts, science, sports, swimming

ART PROGRAMS
Art, drama, music

SPORTS
Basketball, soccer

LONG-RANGE PLANS
Complete 10 year campus renovation program

HISTORY AND MISSION STATEMENT

Founded as a parent cooperative. Racially integrated in 1950, first school in Virginia to integrate. Philisophically, the school is in the Progressive tradition. The school's stated vision is, "Preparing the Whole Child for the Whole World" in a school community that has as its core values: citizenship, collaboration, cooperation, human diversity, learning by doing, responsibility for oneself and others.

NOTE: This data applies to the 2002–2003 school year.

BUTLER SCHOOL

Year founded: 1971
15951 Germantown Road
Darnestown, MD 20874
Head of School:
Cheryl B. Rowe

GENERAL
Grade range: N-8th   Coed
Religious affiliation: Nonsectarian
Average class size: 25
School day: 8:45-3:15
Morning or after-school care:
8:00-5:15

CAMPUS/CAMPUS LIFE
Facilities:
22 acre rural campus with library, pool,
stables, tennis courts
Lunch provided: No
Boarding option: No
Bus service: Yes: limited
School uniform or dress code:
Uniform: Elementary - plain polo shirt
(red, navy yellow, white), khaki or
navy pants
Handicapped access available: Yes
Community service requirement:
Yes

Director of Admission:
Cheryl B. Rowe
Phone: 301-977-6600
Fax: 301-977-2419
E-mail:

Website:
www.butlerschool.org

ADMISSIONS
Application deadline: March 1
Application fee: $25
Application process:
Informal assessment
Number of students
applied/enrolled:

COSTS
Tuition: $5,300 (half day N),
$8,350 (K-6th), $8,725 (7th-8th)
Average additional fees:
$1,000 (7th-8th)
Financial aid budget:
Average grant size:
% of Students receiving
financial aid: 10%

NOTE: This data applies to the 2002–2003 school year.

ACADEMIC PROFILE
Number of faculty:
Languages and grades offered:
French, Spanish (K-8th)
Number of AP classes offered:
Not applicable
Tutors/learning specialists:
Yes
Schools three or more graduates have attended over the past five years:
Various independent and public schools

SPECIAL FEATURES
AMI Montessori program

ENROLLMENT
Total number of students attending and graduating class size: 175 /
Birthday cut-off:
December 31
% Diversity:
Grades with openings:

SUMMER PROGRAMS
Yes: day camp, outdoor adventures

ART PROGRAMS
Fine arts, music, piano lessons (optional)

SPORTS
Equestrian, ropes challenge course

LONG-RANGE PLANS

HISTORY AND MISSION STATEMENT
Butler School directs all of the efforts and talents of its staff to the development of a total education program. This direction sees education in all forms as a "help to life." The principles of Dr. Maria Montessori provide the framework for program development in all areas.

CAPITOL HILL DAY SCHOOL

Year founded: 1968
210 South Carolina Avenue, SE
Washington, DC 20003
Head of School:
Catherine M. Peterson

GENERAL
Grade range: PK-8th   Coed
Religious affiliation: Nonsectarian
Average class size: 24
School day: 8:10-3:10, 8:10-2:10 W
Morning or after-school care:
3:10-6:00

CAMPUS/CAMPUS LIFE
Facilities: 4 story building &
neighboring townhouse
Lunch provided: No
Boarding option: No
Bus service: Yes
School uniform or dress code:
Dress code: appropriate

Handicapped access available: No
Community service requirement:
Yes: 7th serves within the school and
8th serves with the Church of Brethren
Soup Kitchen and Friendship House
Daycare

Director of Admission:
Mary Beth Moore
Phone: 202-547-2244 x120
Fax: 202-547-0510
E-mail:
mbmoore@chds.org
Website:
www.chds.org

ADMISSIONS
Application deadline: January 18
for application, February 1 for
all materials
Application fee: $50
Application process: Tour,
application, assessment, teacher
recommendation, transcript
(2nd-8th), child visit, Detroit (PK*),
WPPSI-R (K-1st), WISC III
(2nd-8th) (*Subject to change)
**Number of students
applied/enrolled:** 152 / 33

COSTS
Tuition: $14,650 (PK-5th),
$15,250 (6th-8th)
Average additional fees:
$900 (one time fee)
Financial aid budget: $262,000
Average grant size: $6,800
**% of Students receiving
financial aid:** 16%

NOTE: This data applies to the 2002–2003 school year.

ACADEMIC PROFILE

Number of faculty: 23 Full Time
17 Part Time
Languages and grades offered:
French, Spanish (PK-8th)
Number of AP classes offered:
Not applicable
Tutors/learning specialists:
Yes: reading, child development
Schools three or more graduates have attended over the past five years:
Edmund Burke, Field, Georgetown Day, Georgetown Visitation, Gonzaga, Maret, National Cathedral, St. Andrew's, Sidwell Friends, Stone Ridge, Washington International

SPECIAL FEATURES

Educational field trip program augments entire curriculum, neighborhood public schools collaboration

ENROLLMENT

Total number of students attending and graduating class size: 230 / 24
Birthday cut-off:
October 1
% Diversity: 29%
Grades with openings: PK (24), plus attrition

SUMMER PROGRAMS

Yes: history camp, summer camp

ART PROGRAMS

Art, drama, music, poetry emphasized throughout the curriculum

SPORTS

Baseball, basketball, soccer, squash, track & field

LONG-RANGE PLANS

New long-range plan now being developed

HISTORY AND MISSION STATEMENT

Located in a historic District of Columbia school building, Capitol Hill Day School offers a strong academic program in a creative environment. Children focus on patterns and relationships in studies of science, mathematics, literature, language, history, and culture. Self-expression is stressed through art and writing, and children are taught to respect each other's ideas and differences. To help children understand that learning occurs beyond the classroom walls, extensive use is made of resources of the Washington area, as children regularly visit sites related to their studies. Community participation is stressed through cooperative activities. Parents participate actively in school life.

NOTE: This data applies to the 2002–2003 school year.

CHARLES E. SMITH JEWISH DAY SCHOOL

Year founded: 1965
K-6th: 1901 East Jefferson Street,
Rockville, MD 20852
7th-12th: 11710 Hunters Lane,
Rockville, MD 20852
Head of School:
Jonathan Cannon

GENERAL
Grade range: K-12th   Coed
Religious affiliation: Jewish
Average class size: 20 (Lower School),
16-18 (Upper School)
School day: 8:15-3:30 (Lower School),
8:00-3:45 (Upper School)
Morning or after-school care:
No

CAMPUS/CAMPUS LIFE
Facilities:
2 renovated campuses
Lunch provided: Yes: additional fee
Boarding option: No
Bus service: Yes
School uniform or dress code:
Dress code
Handicapped access available: Yes
Community service requirement:
Yes

Director of Admission:
Susan Cohen (K-6th),
Robin Shapiro (7th-12th)
Phone: 301-881-1400
Fax: 301-984-7834
E-mail:
cesjds@cesjds.org
Website:
www.cesjds.org

ADMISSIONS
Application deadline: January 18
Application fee: $75
Application process: Application,
teacher recommendations,
transcript, in-house testing
**Number of students
applied/enrolled:** 400 / 270

COSTS
Tuition: $11,550 (K-6th),
$14,600 (7th-11th), $7,300 (12th)
Average additional fees: $300
Financial aid budget: $1,200,000
Average grant size:
**% of Students receiving
financial aid:** 25%

NOTE: This data applies to the 2002–2003 school year.

ACADEMIC PROFILE
Number of faculty:
Languages and grades offered:
French (7th-12th), Hebrew (K-12th),
Spanish (7th-12th)
Number of AP classes offered:
Tutors/learning specialists:
None
Schools three or more graduates have
attended over the past five years:
Columbia, Northwestern, Princeton,
University of Maryland, University of
Michigan, University of Pennsylvania

SPECIAL FEATURES
Dual language program

ENROLLMENT
Total number of students
attending and graduating
class size: 1,485 / 79
Birthday cut-off:
December 31
% Diversity:
Grades with openings:

SUMMER PROGRAMS

ART PROGRAMS
Art, drama, music

SPORTS
Baseball, basketball, cross-country,
soccer, softball, tennis, track,
volleyball

LONG-RANGE PLANS

HISTORY AND MISSION STATEMENT
The Charles E. Smith Jewish Day School of Greater Washington is an independent, community day school, serving students from kindergarten through twelfth
grade. The School is dedicated to creating an environment in which students can
grow to their fullest potential as responsible and dedicated members of the Jewish
people, and of American society. The Mission of our school is based on six basic
Jewish precepts.

NOTE: This data applies to the 2002–2003 school year.

CHELSEA SCHOOL (THE)

Year founded: 1976
711 Pershing Drive
Silver Spring, MD 20910
Head of School:
J. Timothy O'Connor

GENERAL
Grade range: 5th-12th   Coed
Religious affiliation: Nonsectarian
Average class size: 6-8
School day: 8:30-3:09
Morning or after-school care:
Not at this time

CAMPUS/CAMPUS LIFE
Facilities: 4.87 acres, gymnasium, library
Lunch provided: No
Boarding option: No
Bus service: Yes: county transportation
School uniform or dress code:
None
Handicapped access available: Yes
Community service requirement:
Yes: 60 hours for graduation, school-wide community service events offered twice a year

Director of Admission:
Ms. Dale Frengel
Phone: 301-585-9320
Fax: 301-585-5865
E-mail:
dfrengel@chelseaschool.edu
Website:
www.chelseaschool.edu

ADMISSIONS
Application deadline: Rolling
Application fee: $50
Application process: Complete psychoeducational evaluation and any other relevant reports, interview, applicant attends classes for two full days
Number of students applied/enrolled:

COSTS
Tuition: $29,006 (2001-02) 2002-03 not yet set
Average additional fees: Dependent upon number of related services
Financial aid budget: Most students funded through public school system or private grants
Average grant size: $16,000
% of Students receiving financial aid: 85%

NOTE: This data applies to the 2002–2003 school year.

ACADEMIC PROFILE
Number of faculty: 28 Full Time
2 Part Time
Languages and grades offered:
Spanish
Number of AP classes offered:

Tutors/learning specialists:
Yes: related services program provides
access and treatment to students who
need additional support, occupational
therapy, speech/language therapy,
psychological services
**Schools three or more graduates have
attended over the past five years:**
American, Bowdoin, Corcoran College
of Art, Curry, David and Elkins, Goucher,
Marymount, University of Maryland,
Western Maryland College

SPECIAL FEATURES
Specialized reading and written language
methodologies and techniques, multi-
sensory teaching includes visual,
kinesthetic and auditory modalities,
extra curricular activities, community
service

ENROLLMENT
**Total number of students
attending and graduating
class size:** 121 / 16
Birthday cut-off:
Not applicable
% Diversity: 60%
Grades with openings:
All applications considered

SUMMER PROGRAMS
Yes: academic courses, field trips
(5th-12th)

ART PROGRAMS
Ceramics, color theory, design,
drawing, hand building, painting,
pottery, sculpting, three dimensional
constructing

SPORTS
Basketball, bowling, floor hockey,
golf, soccer, softball, table tennis
and regular tennis

LONG-RANGE PLANS
New facility with auditorium,
classrooms, library, lunchroom,
medical center; increase student
population

HISTORY AND MISSION STATEMENT
Betty Nehemias and Eleanor Blewitt Worthy, parents of dyslexic children, founded
Chelsea. Their dream was to establish a school that could teach and improve the
lives of students with learning based disabilities. The mission of Chelsea is to offer
a highly structured, individualized, supportive program for students with learning
disabilities. Chelsea School is accredited for students with learning disabilities.

NOTE: This data applies to the 2002–2003 school year.

CHRIST EPISCOPAL SCHOOL

Year founded: 1966
109 S. Washington Street
Rockville, MD 20850
Head of School:
Jane M. Pontius

GENERAL
Grade range: N-8th   Coed
Religious affiliation: Episcopal
Average class size: 18
School day: 8:00-3:00
Morning or after-school care:
7:30-6:00

CAMPUS/CAMPUS LIFE
Facilities: Centrally located in
historic Rockville, preschool in
an adjacent home setting, main
building has a chapel and a renovated
computer lab
Lunch provided: No
Boarding option: No
Bus service: No
School uniform or dress code:
Uniform
Handicapped access available: No
Community service requirement:
Yes

Director of Admission:
Carol Lechner
Phone: 301-424-6650
Fax: 301-424-0494
E-mail:
clechner@cesstaff.org
Website:
www.ces-rockville.org

ADMISSIONS
Application deadline: Rolling,
November 1 (for K)
Application fee: $50 (K-1st),
$125 (2nd-8th)
Application process: Informal
assessment and WPSSI (K-1st),
informal assessment and class visit
(2nd-8th), interview applicant
and parents
**Number of students
applied/enrolled:** 100 / 60

COSTS
Tuition: $4,480 (N-PK),
$8,175 (K-8th)
Average additional fees: $500
Financial aid budget: $35,000
Average grant size: $2,940
**% of Students receiving
financial aid:** 6%

NOTE: This data applies to the 2002–2003 school year.

ACADEMIC PROFILE

Number of faculty: 33

Languages and grades offered:

Spanish (K-8th)

Number of AP classes offered:

Not applicable

Tutors/learning specialists:

Yes: learning resource teacher

Schools three or more graduates have attended over the past five years:

Bullis, Connelly School of the Holy Child, Georgetown Prep, Gonzaga, Good Counsel, Landon, Stone Ridge

SPECIAL FEATURES

ENROLLMENT

Total number of students attending and graduating class size: 200 / 18

Birthday cut-off:

September 1

% Diversity: 13%

Grades with openings: N (20), PK (6-8), K (19), 1st (1), 2nd (1), 3rd (1), 4th (2), 5th (2), 6th (2-3), 7th (3), 8th (1-2)

SUMMER PROGRAMS

None

ART PROGRAMS

Variety of art media once per week

SPORTS

Physical education daily

LONG-RANGE PLANS

Increase student body, acquire additional space

HISTORY AND MISSION STATEMENT

Christ Episcopal School prepares talented boys and girls for the rigors of secondary education. Our students are members of a Christian community of learners, one that teaches them to use their minds well. A CES education instills a work ethic, a commitment to service, and an appreciation for the differences in others. We build confidence, integrity, and create an enduring sense of belonging.

NOTE: This data applies to the 2002–2003 school year.

COMMONWEALTH ACADEMY

Year founded: 1997
1321 Leslie Avenue
Alexandria, VA 22301
Head of School:
Susan Johnson

GENERAL
Grade range: 6th-12th   Coed
Religious affiliation: Nonsectarian
Average class size: 10
School day: 7:45-3:00
Morning or after-school care:
7:00-4:00

CAMPUS/CAMPUS LIFE
Facilities:
Classrooms, computer and
science labs
Lunch provided: No
Boarding option: No
Bus service: No
School uniform or dress code:
None
Handicapped access available: Yes
Community service requirement:
One project per quarter

Director of Admission:
Susan Johnson
Phone: 703-931-8018
Fax: 703-931-8093
E-mail:

Website:
www.commonwealthacad.org

ADMISSIONS
Application deadline: End of first
semester
Application fee: $100
Application process: Interview,
applicant visit
**Number of students
applied/enrolled:**

COSTS
Tuition: $16,500 (6th-12th)
Average additional fees: $1,500
Financial aid budget:
Average grant size:
**% of Students receiving
financial aid:**

NOTE: This data applies to the 2002–2003 school year.

ACADEMIC PROFILE
Number of faculty: 10 Full Time
3 Part Time
Languages and grades offered:
French, Spanish, (9th-12th)
Number of AP classes offered:
Tutors/learning specialists:
Yes: learning specialists, full time
counselor, speech and language
therapist
**Schools three or more graduates have
attended over the past five years:**
No graduates yet

SPECIAL FEATURES
Individual attention, Innerquest
activities, on-line homework,
emphasis on writing

ENROLLMENT
**Total number of students
attending and graduating
class size:** 36 / 1
Birthday cut-off:
Not applicable
% Diversity:
Grades with openings: 6th-12th

SUMMER PROGRAMS

ART PROGRAMS
Art, drama, music

SPORTS
None

LONG-RANGE PLANS
Expand student population

HISTORY AND MISSION STATEMENT

Our commitment is to offer a college prep curriculum with accomodations and alternative teaching methods for bright middle and high school-aged students with learning differences. The objective is to assist students to learn strategies to compensate for their weaknesses and master their learning style.

NOTE: This data applies to the 2002–2003 school year.

CONCORD HILL SCHOOL

Year founded: 1965
6050 Wisconsin Avenue
Chevy Chase, MD 20815
Head of School:
Denise Gershowitz

GENERAL
Grade range: N-3rd   Coed
Religious affiliation: Nonsectarian
Average class size: 17 with two teachers
School day: 8:45-12:15 (N-PK; K, MWF;
1st-3rd, F only); 8:45-3:00 (K, T/Th;
1st-3rd, M-Th)
Morning or after-school care:
8:00-8:45

CAMPUS/CAMPUS LIFE
Facilities:
Renovated building and playground,
media lab with technology, music
and art rooms, science lab
Lunch provided: No
Boarding option: No
Bus service: No
School uniform or dress code:
None
Handicapped access available: Yes
Community service requirement:
Yes: parent sponsored

Director of Admission:
Debra Duff
Phone: 301-654-2626
Fax: 301-654-1374
E-mail:
dduff@concordhill.org
Website:
www.concordhill.org

ADMISSIONS
Application deadline: January 15
Application fee: $55
Application process:
Informal assessment
**Number of students
applied/enrolled:** 133 / 26

COSTS
Tuition: $8,850 (N), $11,600 (K),
$13,180 (1st-3rd)
Average additional fees:
Financial aid budget: $40,000
Average grant size: $7,000
**% of Students receiving
financial aid:**

NOTE: This data applies to the 2002–2003 school year.

ACADEMIC PROFILE
Number of faculty: 9 Full Time
9 Part Time
Languages and grades offered:
None
Number of AP classes offered:
Not applicable
Tutors/learning specialists:
None: school works closely with
therapists providing services outside
of school
**Schools three or more graduates have
attended over the past five years:**
Bullis, Holton-Arms, Landon, Maret,
Mater Dei, National Cathedral,
National Presbyterian, Norwood,
Potomac, St. Albans, Stone Ridge

SPECIAL FEATURES

ENROLLMENT
**Total number of students
attending and graduating
class size:** 102 / 16
Birthday cut-off:
September 1 (N-PK)
December 1 (K-3rd)
% Diversity: 7%
Grades with openings: N (12),
PK (3-4), K (4-5), plus attrition

SUMMER PROGRAMS
Yes: day camp for 3-5 year olds

ART PROGRAMS
Art, music

SPORTS
None

LONG-RANGE PLANS

HISTORY AND MISSION STATEMENT
Concord Hill School is a coeducational primary school that emphasizes the developmental, as well as the academic, needs of the young child. The school's mission is to give children a firm grasp of fundamental skills; to develop the ideas, compassion and responsibility necessary to function successfully in their communities; and to nurture in each child a lifelong love of learning.

NOTE: This data applies to the 2002–2003 school year.

CONGRESSIONAL SCHOOLS OF VIRGINIA (THE)

Year founded: 1939
3229 Sleepy Hollow Road
Falls Church, VA 22042
Head of School:
Shirley K. Fegan

GENERAL

Grade range: PN-8th   Coed
Religious affiliation: Nonsectarian
Average class size: 4 (infants),
8 (1-2 year olds),
12 (2-3 year olds), 18 (PK-8th)
School day: 8:15-3:10
Morning or after-school care:
7:00-6:00

CAMPUS/CAMPUS LIFE

Facilities: 40 acres, amphitheater, art
and music studios, athletic fields,
auditorium, 2 libraries, 3 playgrounds,
2 pools, ropes course, 3 science labs,
technology center

Lunch provided: Yes
Boarding option: No
Bus service: Yes
School uniform or dress code:
Uniform: 1st-8th boys - white shirt,
navy pants, ties for 5th-8th; girls -
white blouse, jumper, kilt or navy pants
Handicapped access available: Yes
Community service requirement:
Optional

Director of Admission:
Karen H. Weinberger
Phone: 703-533-9711
Fax: 703-532-5467
E-mail: admissions@
congressionalschools.org
Website:
www.congressionalschools.org

ADMISSIONS

Application deadline: Rolling
Application fee: $75
Application process: Informal
assessment and visit (PN-PK),
WPPSI-R (K-1st), WISC III
(2nd-8th) or ISEE (5th-8th),
teacher recommendations,
transcript, school visit (PN-8th)
Number of students
applied/enrolled:

COSTS

Tuition: $240/week (6 months-age
three), $11,092 (PN-K), $11,206
(1st-2nd), $11,853 (3rd-4th),
$12,933 (5th-6th), $13,790
(7th-8th)
Average additional fees: $850 plus
books (1st-8th)
Financial aid budget:
Average grant size:
% of Students receiving
financial aid:

NOTE: This data applies to the 2002–2003 school year.

ACADEMIC PROFILE

Number of faculty:

Languages and grades offered:
French (K-8th), Spanish (5th-8th)

Number of AP classes offered:
Not applicable

Tutors/learning specialists:
Yes: guidance counselor, science
resource teacher, reading and study
skills specialist

**Schools three or more graduates have
attended over the past five years:**
Bishop Ireton, Bishop O'Connell,
Edmund Burke, Foxcroft, Georgetown
Day, Georgetown Prep, Gonzaga,
Madeira, National Cathedral, Paul VI,
Potomac, St. Albans, St. Andrew's,
St. Stephen's & St. Agnes, Sidwell
Friends, Thomas Jefferson

SPECIAL FEATURES

ENROLLMENT

**Total number of students
attending and graduating
class size:** 450 / 36

Birthday cut-off:
October 31

% Diversity: 45%

Grades with openings:

SUMMER PROGRAMS
Yes: basketball, recreation,
specialty camps

ART PROGRAMS
Art, drama, music, spring musical

SPORTS
Basketball, cross-country, soccer,
softball, track

LONG-RANGE PLANS

HISTORY AND MISSION STATEMENT

Congressional School offers a traditional, comprehensive education stressing ethics and positive moral values within a diverse community. An accelerated academic program is designed to stimulate a love of learning and prepare students for college preparatory high schools.

NOTE: This data applies to the 2002–2003 school year.

CONNELLY SCHOOL OF THE HOLY CHILD

Year founded: 1961
9029 Bradley Boulevard
Potomac, MD 20854
Head of School:
Maureen K. Appel

GENERAL
Grade range: 6th-12th   Girls
Religious affiliation: Catholic
Average class size: 16
School day: 8:10-3:20

Morning or after-school care:
No

CAMPUS/CAMPUS LIFE
Facilities:
9 acre suburban campus, 2 art studios,
gymnasium, library, playing fields,
science labs
Lunch provided: Yes: additional fee
Boarding option: No
Bus service: No
School uniform or dress code:
Uniform
Handicapped access available: No,
but renovations are underway
Community service requirement:
Yes: 30 hours for Juniors

Director of Admission:
Sheri M. Mural
Phone: 301-365-0955
Fax: 301-365-0981
E-mail:
admissions@holychild.org
Website:
www.holychild.org

ADMISSIONS
Application deadline: December 15
(9th), February 1 (6th-8th) Upper
school transfer admission (rolling)
Application fee: $50
Application process:
SSAT (6th-8th)
Terra Nova (9th)
**Number of students
applied/enrolled:**

COSTS
Tuition: $13,200 (6th-8th),
$14,275 (9th-12th)
Average additional fees:
Financial aid budget:
Average grant size:
**% of Students receiving
financial aid:**

NOTE: This data applies to the 2002–2003 school year.

ACADEMIC PROFILE
Number of faculty: 51 Full Time
8 Part Time
Languages and grades offered:
French (7th-12th), Latin (6th),
Spanish (7th-12th)
Number of AP classes offered:
9
Tutors/learning specialists:
Yes: learning specialist, math lab,
writing center
Schools three or more graduates have attended over the past five years:
Catholic, College of the Holy Cross,
Elon, Fordham, Loyola (MD),
Providence, University of Maryland,
University of Scranton, University of
Virginia, Villanova

SPECIAL FEATURES
Seminar classes offered in conjunction
with consortium schools: Holton-Arms,
Landon, St. Andrew's, and Stone Ridge

ENROLLMENT
Total number of students attending and graduating class size: 449 / 63
Birthday cut-off:
Not applicable

% Diversity:
Grades with openings: 6th, 9th,
plus attrition

SUMMER PROGRAMS
None

ART PROGRAMS
Chamber music, dance, drama,
photography

SPORTS
Basketball, cross-country, dance
team, equestrian, field hockey,
lacrosse, soccer, softball, swimming
& diving, tennis, track & field,
volleyball

LONG-RANGE PLANS

HISTORY AND MISSION STATEMENT
Connelly School of the Holy Child was opened in 1961 by the Society of the Holy Child Jesus as a college preparatory school for girls. The school is part of a network of 33 Holy Child schools in the United States, Europe and Africa, which are guided by the educational philosophy of Cornelia Connelly. A caring environment and attention to each student as a whole human being have been hallmarks of a Holy Child education for a century and a half.

NOTE: This data applies to the 2002–2003 school year.

EDLIN SCHOOL

Year founded: 1989
10742 Sunset Hills Road
Reston, VA 20190
Head of School:
Elaine Mellman & Linda Schreibstein

GENERAL
Grade range: PK-8th   Coed
Religious affiliation: Nonsectarian
Average class size: 15
School day: 9:00-3:15
Morning or after-school care:
7:30-6:00

CAMPUS/CAMPUS LIFE
Facilities:
2 acre Sylvan setting, computer lab,
playground, science lab
Lunch provided: No
Boarding option: No
Bus service: Yes
School uniform or dress code:
Dress code: dress pants, collared shirt
Handicapped access available: Yes
Community service requirement:
None

Director of Admission:
Elaine Mellman & Linda Schreibstein
Phone: 703-438-3990
Fax: 703-438-3958
E-mail:

Website:
www.edlinschool.com
Application deadline: Rolling
Application fee: $50
Application process: WISC III
(1st-8th), applicant visit, transcript,
teacher recommendation
**Number of students
applied/enrolled:**

COSTS
Tuition: $11,460
Average additional fees: None
Financial aid budget:
Average grant size: Case by case basis
**% of Students receiving
financial aid:**

NOTE: This data applies to the 2002–2003 school year.

ACADEMIC PROFILE

Number of faculty: 30 Full Time
Part Time
Languages and grades offered: 4
French (PK-8th), Latin (PK-8th),
Spanish (5th-8th)
Number of AP classes offered:
Not applicable
Tutors/learning specialists:
Yes
Schools three or more graduates have attended over the past five years:
Bishop O'Connell, Forest Valley, Flint Hill, Georgetown Prep, Gonzaga, Madeira, Notre Dame, Paul VI, Randolph Macon, St. Albans, Thomas Jefferson

SPECIAL FEATURES

Collaboration with NASA to develop aerospace technology

ENROLLMENT

Total number of students attending and graduating class size: 250 /
Birthday cut-off:
Case by case basis
% Diversity: 30%
Grades with openings: PK (25), K (20), plus attrition

SUMMER PROGRAMS

Yes: academics, sports (4 year old-8th)

ART PROGRAMS

Art, chorus, drama, instrumental music

SPORTS

Basketball, field hockey, lacrosse, soccer, wrestling

LONG-RANGE PLANS

Add an Upper School

HISTORY AND MISSION STATEMENT

Edlin is a school that defies the traditional expected idea of student-teacher relationships. It engenders laughter and excitement for learning. Bright students can explore new ideas and challenge old ideas.

NOTE: This data applies to the 2002–2003 school year.

EDMUND BURKE SCHOOL

Year founded: 1968
2955 Upton Street, NW
Washington, DC 20008
Head of School:
David Shapiro

GENERAL
Grade range: 6th-12th   Coed
Religious affiliation: Nonsectarian
Average class size: 15
School day: 8:10-3:15
Morning or after-school care:
No

CAMPUS/CAMPUS LIFE
Facilities:
Urban campus, art studios, classrooms,
community space, gymnasium, access
to playing fields, science labs
Lunch provided: No
Boarding option: No
Bus service: No
School uniform or dress code:
None
Handicapped access available: Yes
Community service requirement:
Yes: 6th-8th part of curriculum;
15 hours per year, total 60 hours for
9th-12th

Director of Admission:
Jean Marchildon
Phone: 202-362-8882
Fax: 202-362-1914
E-mail:
jean_marchildon@eburke.org
Website:
www.eburke.org

ADMISSIONS
Application deadline: January 16
Application fee: $50
Application process: Open house,
application, student interview,
transcript, teacher recommendations,
SSAT or ISEE (6th-12th)
**Number of students
applied/enrolled:** 280 / 62

COSTS
Tuition: $18,400
Average additional fees: $115
Financial aid budget: $692,070
Average grant size: $11,438
**% of Students receiving
financial aid:** 21%

NOTE: This data applies to the 2002–2003 school year.

ACADEMIC PROFILE
Number of faculty: 43 Full Time
8 Part Time
Languages and grades offered:
French, Latin, Spanish (6th-12th)
Number of AP classes offered:
10
Tutors/learning specialists:
Yes
Schools three or more graduates have attended over the past five years:
Boston University, Brown, Clark, Earlham, Emerson, Kenyon, New York University, Oberlin, Parsons School of Design, Rochester Institute of Technology, Sarah Lawrence, University of Maryland

SPECIAL FEATURES

ENROLLMENT
Total number of students attending and graduating class size: 299 / 55
Birthday cut-off: Not applicable
% Diversity: 21.7%
Grades with openings: 6th (14), 7th (18), 9th (22), plus attrition

SUMMER PROGRAMS
Yes

ART PROGRAMS
Ceramics, computer graphics, drama, drawing, instrumental and vocal music, mixed media, painting, photography, playwriting, sculpture, theater production

SPORTS
Basketball, cross-country, soccer, softball, track & field, volleyball, wrestling

LONG-RANGE PLANS
Building expansion

HISTORY AND MISSION STATEMENT
Edmund Burke consciously brings together students who are different from each other in many ways; affords them unreserved respect for who they are and actively engages them in their own education; has high expectations for them and gives them power and responsibility; sustains an environment of civil discourse. All of this is for one reason: to serve children's growth as skilled and independent thinkers who step forward to make positive contributions to the worlds they live in.

NOTE: This data applies to the 2002–2003 school year.

EMERSON PREPARATORY SCHOOL

Year founded: 1852
1324 18th Street, NW
Washington, DC 20036
Head of School:
Margot Ann Walsh

GENERAL
Grade range: 9th-12th   Coed
Religious affiliation: Nonsectarian
Average class size: 10
School day: 8:15-3:05
Morning or after-school care:
No

CAMPUS/CAMPUS LIFE
Facilities:
10 classrooms, computer lab/library,
courtyard, science lab
Lunch provided: No
Boarding option: No
Bus service: No
School uniform or dress code:
Handicapped access available: No
Community service requirement:
Yes: 100 hours of service for 1 unit
of credit

Director of Admission:
Carol Ann Humphrey
Phone: 202-785-2877
Fax: 202-785-2228
E-mail:
info@emersonprep.net
Website:
www.emersonprep.net

ADMISSIONS
Application deadline: September for
Fall Term, February for Spring Term
Application fee: $50
Application process: Interview,
teacher recommendations,
placement exams
**Number of students
applied/enrolled:**

COSTS
Tuition: $14,000
Average additional fees: $500
Financial aid budget: $20,000
Average grant size:
**% of Students receiving
financial aid:** 5%

NOTE: This data applies to the 2002–2003 school year.

ACADEMIC PROFILE

Number of faculty: 8 Full Time
10 Part Time
Languages and grades offered:
French, German, Italian, Japanese,
Russian, Spanish (9th-12th)
Number of AP classes offered: 4
Tutors/learning specialists:
Yes: tutorial services can be arranged
for extra help and to earn credit in
advanced languages, mathematics,
and science courses not offered as
regular classes
**Schools three or more graduates have
attended over the past five years:**
American University (Paris, France),
American University (Washington, D.C.),
Franklin College (Switzerland),
Georgetown, George Washington,
University of Colorado-Boulder,
University of Maryland

SPECIAL FEATURES

Concentrated academic program,
maximum of four classes for 90 minutes
per day. Opportunity to complete high
school in fewer than four years.
Enrollment options for September,
February and June.

ENROLLMENT

**Total number of students
attending and graduating
class size:** 85 / 39
Birthday cut-off: Not applicable
% Diversity: 20%
Grades with openings: Several
openings available in each grade

SUMMER PROGRAMS

Yes: 6 week academic program

ART PROGRAMS

None

SPORTS

None

LONG-RANGE PLANS

To continue the Emerson tradition
for another 150 years

HISTORY AND MISSION STATEMENT

Emerson Preparatory School provides a challenging academic curriculum and
educational community that encourages the development of the attitudes, habits
and thought processes requisite to a meaningful life.

NOTE: This data applies to the 2002–2003 school year.

EPISCOPAL HIGH SCHOOL

Year founded: 1839
1200 North Quaker Lane
Alexandria, VA 22302
Head of School:
F. Robertson Hershey

GENERAL
Grade range: 9th-12th   Coed
Religious affiliation: Episcopal
Average class size: 10-12
School day:
Morning or after-school care:

CAMPUS/CAMPUS LIFE
Facilities:
130 acres, 30 buildings, 45 classrooms,
8 dormitories, athletic fields, chapel,
2 gymnasiums, indoor track & field,
library, outdoor pool, 5 squash courts,
12 tennis courts, new arts center
Lunch provided: Yes
Boarding option: Yes /100%
Bus service:
School uniform or dress code:
Dress code: boys - shirt with tie, no
blue jeans or sneakers; comparable
for girls
Handicapped access available:
Community service requirement:
No requirement, but active participation

Director of Admission:
Douglas C. Price
Phone: 703-933-4062
Fax: 703-933-3016
E-mail:
admissions@
episcopalhighschool.org
Website:
www.episcopalhighschool.org

ADMISSIONS
Application deadline: January 31
Application fee: $50 /$100 for
international applicants
Application process: Application,
transcript, applicant interview,
teacher recommendations, SSAT
(9th-10th), SSAT or PSAT (11th)
**Number of students
applied/enrolled:** 600 / 110

COSTS
Tuition: $27,600
Average additional fees: $600
Financial aid budget: $2,100,000
Average grant size: $16,000
**% of Students receiving
financial aid:** 30%

NOTE: This data applies to the 2002–2003 school year.

ACADEMIC PROFILE
Number of faculty: 84
Languages and grades offered:
French, German, Latin, Spanish
(9th-12th), Greek (1 year)
Number of AP classes offered: 25
Tutors/learning specialists:
Yes: learning specialist
Schools three or more graduates have attended over the past five years:
Boston College, Brown, Davidson, Duke, Georgetown, Harvard, Princeton, University of North Carolina, University of the South, University of Virginia, William and Mary, Yale

SPECIAL FEATURES
Senior seminar, School Year Abroad (SYA), Washington Program, boarding only

ENROLLMENT
Total number of students attending and graduating class size: 410 /
Birthday cut-off: Not applicable
% Diversity: 20%
Grades with openings: 9th-11th

SUMMER PROGRAMS
None

ART PROGRAMS
Ceramics, choir, drama, music theory, orchestra, photography, visual arts

SPORTS
Aerobics, baseball, basketball, crew, cross-country, field hockey, football, golf, lacrosse, soccer, softball, squash, tennis, track, volleyball, wrestling

LONG-RANGE PLANS
Just completed a $95 million capital campaign, proceeds will be used for facility improvements including new arts center and endowment

HISTORY AND MISSION STATEMENT
Episcopal is dedicated to the student's pursuit of excellence and to the joy of learning and self-discovery in a caring and supportive community. Enriched by the educational and cultural resources of the nation's capital, Episcopal's dynamic academic program encourages students to develop individual talents and prepares them to attend selective colleges and universities. Students from diverse backgrounds live and learn together in a residential community based on a foundation of honor, spiritual growth, responsibility, and mutual respect.

NOTE: This data applies to the 2002–2003 school year.

EVERGREEN SCHOOL

Year founded: 1964

10700 Georgia Avenue

Wheaton, MD 20902

Head of School:

Lydia Mosher

GENERAL

Grade range: PN-6th   Coed

Religious affiliation: Nonsectarian

Average class size: 22

School day: 8:30-3:00

Morning or after-school care:

7:30-6:00

CAMPUS/CAMPUS LIFE

Facilities:

Computer lab, library, playground

Lunch provided: No

Boarding option: No

Bus service: No

School uniform or dress code:

No

Handicapped access available: Yes

Community service requirement:

None

Director of Admission:

Lorie Allion

Phone: 301-942-5979

Fax: 301-946-0311

E-mail:

admissions@evergreenschool.com

Website:

www.evergreenschool.com

ADMISSIONS

Application deadline: Rolling

Application fee: $75

Application process: Informal

assessment

Number of students

applied/enrolled: 128 / 37

COSTS

Tuition: $6,225 (half day),

$9,250 (full day), $9,650 (1st-6th)

Average additional fees:

Financial aid budget: $50,000

Average grant size:

% of Students receiving

financial aid: 9%

NOTE: This data applies to the 2002–2003 school year.

ACADEMIC PROFILE

Number of faculty:

Languages and grades offered:
Spanish (N-8th)

Number of AP classes offered:
Not applicable

Tutors/learning specialists:
None

Schools three or more graduates have attended over the past five years:

SPECIAL FEATURES

Small group and individual instruction, Montessori program

ENROLLMENT

Total number of students attending and graduating class size: 84 / 3

Birthday cut-off:

% Diversity: 40%

Grades with openings: PK (10-15), plus attrition

SUMMER PROGRAMS

Yes: 10 week summer camp

ART PROGRAMS

Performing and visual arts within classroom

SPORTS

Basketball, field games, floor hockey, soccer

LONG-RANGE PLANS

HISTORY AND MISSION STATEMENT

NOTE: This data applies to the 2002–2003 school year.

FAIRFAX COLLEGIATE SCHOOL

Year founded: 1993
4300 Evergreen Lane
Annandale, VA 22003
Head of School:
Paul Petzrick

GENERAL
Grade range: 4th-9th   Coed
Religious affiliation: Nonsectarian
Average class size: 15
School day: 8:00-3:30
Morning or after-school care:
7:30-6:00

CAMPUS/CAMPUS LIFE
Facilities:
7,500-8,000 square feet in
professional office building, PE
conducted at nearby park or
rented gym space
Lunch provided: No
Boarding option: No
Bus service: No
School uniform or dress code:
None
Handicapped access available: Yes
Community service requirement:
Yes: 2 hours per quarter

Director of Admission:
Paul Petzrick
Phone: 703-256-9380
Fax: 703-256-9384
E-mail:
inquiries@fairfaxcollegiate.org
Website:
www.fairfaxcollegiate.org

ADMISSIONS
Application deadline: Rolling
Application fee: $40
Application process: Informal
assessment, applicant and
parent interview
**Number of students
applied/enrolled:** 18 / 12

COSTS
Tuition: $7,700 (4th-5th),
$8,800 (6th-8th)
Average additional fees: $700
Financial aid budget: $8,000
Average grant size: $2,000
**% of Students receiving
financial aid:** 2%

NOTE: This data applies to the 2002–2003 school year.

ACADEMIC PROFILE
Number of faculty: 6 Full Time
1 Part Time
Languages and grades offered:
French (9th), Spanish (4th-9th)
Number of AP classes offered:
Not applicable
Tutors/learning specialists:
Yes: private tutoring, SAT/PSAT test prep
Schools three or more graduates have
attended over the past five years:
Biship Ireton, Bishop O'Connell,
Gonzaga, Madeira

SPECIAL FEATURES

ENROLLMENT
Total number of students
class size: 60 / 14
Birthday cut-off: Not applicable
% Diversity: 15%
Grades with openings: 4th (6),
5th (6), 6th (6), 7th (6), 8th (6)

SUMMER PROGRAMS
Yes: computers, math, test-taking,
video, writing enrichment (4th-9th)

ART PROGRAMS
Art, art history, computer graphics

SPORTS
Basketball, cross-country, soccer,
softball, volleyball

LONG-RANGE PLANS
Add a high school, one class at a
time beginning school year 2002,
high school classes will focus on
college placement and advanced
placement classes

HISTORY AND MISSION STATEMENT

FCS has continued growing since our founding in 1993 by continually focusing on our mission: academic excellence in a supportive and nurturing environment for students in fourth through ninth grades.

NOTE: This data applies to the 2002–2003 school year.

FIELD SCHOOL (THE)

Year founded: 1972
2301 Foxhall Road, NW
Washington, DC 20007
Head of School:
Elizabeth Ely

GENERAL
Grade range: 7th-12th   Coed
Religious affiliation: Nonsectarian
Average class size: 11
School day: 8:20-2:25
Morning or after-school care:
No

CAMPUS/CAMPUS LIFE
Facilities:
New campus
Lunch provided:
Boarding option: No
Shuttle service: Yes
School uniform or dress code:
Handicapped access available: Yes
Community service requirement:
Yes

Director of Admission:
Clay Kaufman
Phone: 202-232-0733
Fax: 202-387-1338
E-mail:
admissions@fieldschool.com
Website:
www.fieldschool.com

ADMISSIONS
Application deadline: January 16
Application fee: $60
Application process:
SSAT (7th-12th)
Number of students
applied/enrolled: 354 / 56

COSTS
Tuition: $20,580
Average additional fees: $500
Financial aid budget:
Average grant size:
% of Students receiving
financial aid:

NOTE: This data applies to the 2002–2003 school year.

ACADEMIC PROFILE
Number of faculty:
Languages and grades offered:
French, Latin, Spanish (7th-12th)
Number of AP classes offered: 5
Tutors/learning specialists:
None
Schools three or more graduates have attended over the past five years:
Bates, Colgate, New York University, Northwestern, Syracuse, University of Hartford, University of Vermont, University of Wisconsin, Wesleyan

SPECIAL FEATURES
College prep program, work internship, January term

ENROLLMENT
Total number of students attending and graduating class size: 220 / 36
Birthday cut-off: Not applicable
% Diversity: 21%
Grades with openings: 7th (32), 9th (20), plus attrition

SUMMER PROGRAMS
Yes: academic enrichment, remediation

ART PROGRAMS
Ceramics, computer arts, drama, music, photography, pottery, studio arts, theater

SPORTS
Baseball, basketball, cross-country, lacrosse, soccer, tennis, track & field

LONG-RANGE PLANS

HISTORY AND MISSION STATEMENT
The Field School values the individual and inspires creativity, compassion for others, and passion for learning. We select students with a variety of challenges, abilities, and backgrounds. Through dialogue among students and teachers, we encourage students to seek knowledge and join in community. Field connects the various realms of knowledge to help students understand their world and lead full lives.

NOTE: This data applies to the 2002–2003 school year.

FLINT HILL SCHOOL

Year founded: 1956
10409 Academic Drive
Oakton, VA 22124
Head of School:
Thomas C. Whitworth, III

GENERAL
Grade range: K-12th   Coed
Religious affiliation: Nonsectarian
Average class size: 16
School day: 8:00-3:00
Morning or after-school care:
3:15-6:00

CAMPUS/CAMPUS LIFE
Facilities: 2 campuses on 45 acres,
art, dance and music studios,
athletic fields, fully networked
classrooms, computer and language
labs, 2 gyms, learning centers,
libraries/media centers, science labs,
8 tennis courts, 300-seat theater,
400-meter track; West campus
(9th-12th) 3323 Germantown Road,
half mile from East campus.
Lunch provided: Yes: Upper School
Boarding option: No
Bus service: Limited
School uniform or dress code:
Uniform: Lower School; Dress code:
Middle and Upper Schools
Handicapped access available: Limited
Community service requirement:
Yes: 60 hours required in Upper School;
10 hours-8th grade; school sponsored
community service trips 5th-7th

Director of Admission:
Ruth Little
Phone: 703-584-2300
Fax: 703-584-2369
E-mail:
admissions@flinthill.org
Website:
www.flinthill.org

ADMISSIONS
Application deadline: February 15
Application fee: $50
Application process: Informal
assessment (PK), WPPSI-R (K),
WISC III (1st-5th), SSAT
(6th-12th), parent interview,
applicant visit
**Number of students
applied/enrolled:** 525 / 160

COSTS
Tuition: $12,000 (PK), $14,200
(K-4th), $16,000 (5th-8th),
$16,335 (9th-12th)
Average additional fees: $500
Financial aid budget: $750,000
Average grant size: $8,000
**% of Students receiving
financial aid:** 10%

NOTE: This data applies to the 2002–2003 school year.

ACADEMIC PROFILE

Number of faculty: 90 Full Time
21 Part Time
Languages and grades offered:
French (8th-12th), Latin (6th-12th),
Spanish (PK-12th)
Number of AP classes offered:
20
Tutors/learning specialists:
Yes: learning disabilities support
(15% of student body)
Schools three or more graduates have attended over the past five years:
Boston University, Cornell, Georgetown, James Madison, Johns Hopkins, Kenyon, New York University, Tulane, William & Mary, University of Virginia

SPECIAL FEATURES

Senior project and presentation, experiential education

ENROLLMENT

Total number of students attending and graduating class size: 840 / 63
Birthday cut-off: September 1
% Diversity: 26-30%
Grades with openings: PK (18), K (30), 5th (18), 6th (10), 7th (20), 9th (22), plus attrition

SUMMER PROGRAMS

Yes: arts, enrichment, field studies, remediation, sports

ART PROGRAMS

Art, drama, music

SPORTS

Baseball, basketball, cross-country, golf, lacrosse, soccer, softball, swimming, tennis, track & field

LONG-RANGE PLANS

Continue expansion of facilities, curriculum, and other programs to accomodate increased enrollment to 1,100; program additions include football, band, and electives

HISTORY AND MISSION STATEMENT

Reorganized in 1989, the School was created by a blend of constituencies. Faculty and students are encouraged to experience the joy of learning and growing in a diverse community which seeks excellence and embraces the "Driving Spirit." Honor, integrity, personal responsibility, and how we treat one another are emphasized. Students are encouraged to cherish time-tested democratic ideals of a free society, to understand diverse cultures, to think globally and analytically.

NOTE: This data applies to the 2002–2003 school year.

FOURTH PRESBYTERIAN SCHOOL

Year founded: 1999
10701 South Glen Road
Potomac, MD 20854
Head of School:
William Zimmerman

GENERAL
Grade range: PK-5th   Coed
Religious affiliation: Presbyterian
Average class size: 10
School day: 8:40-3:10 (1st-4th),
8:40-11:30 or 12:20-3:10 (PK-K)
Morning or after-school care:
No

CAMPUS/CAMPUS LIFE
Facilities:
30 acre wooded campus, 2 buildings,
art center
Lunch provided: No
Boarding option: No
Bus service: No
School uniform or dress code:
Yes: girls - plaid jumper or skirt,
white shirt with school logo;
boys - khaki or blue pants or shorts,
white shirt with logo
Handicapped access available: No
Community service requirement:
No requirement, but active participation

Director of Admission:
William Zimmerman
Phone: 301-765-8133
Fax: 301-765-8138
E-mail:
alaw@fourthschool.org
Website:
www.fourthschool.org

ADMISSIONS
Application deadline:
February 8
Application fee: $75
Application process: Application,
teacher and parent assessments,
Pastor recommendation,
Woodcock-Johnson test
administered by school, interview
with Headmaster
**Number of students
applied/enrolled:** 61 / 44

COSTS
Tuition: $3,375 (PK), $4,125 (K),
$7,875 (1st-4th)
Average additional fees: None
Financial aid budget: $45,000
Average grant size:
**% of Students receiving
financial aid:** 34%

NOTE: This data applies to the 2002–2003 school year.

ACADEMIC PROFILE

Number of faculty: 7 Full Time
5 Part Time
Languages and grades offered:
Spanish (K and continuing),
Latin (3rd and continuing)
Number of AP classes offered:
Not applicable
Tutors/learning specialists:
Yes: learning specialist
Schools three or more graduates have attended over the past five years:
No graduates yet

SPECIAL FEATURES

ENROLLMENT

Total number of students attending and graduating class size: 79 /
Birthday cut-off: October 31
% Diversity: 13%
Grades with openings: All

SUMMER PROGRAMS

Yes: "Discover the Creator" hands-on science program, sports camp

ART PROGRAMS

Art, music, visits to the National Gallery

SPORTS

LONG-RANGE PLANS

Add a grade annually through 8th grade

HISTORY AND MISSION STATEMENT

The Fourth Presbyterian, governed by an independent board of directors elected by the session of the Fourth Presbyterian Church, has as its mission to pass on the best of our cultural inheritance to our covenant children in the light of a Reformed Christian worldview so that all students may know and pursue what is good, true and beautiful. Through this pursuit, our graduates will be able to understand, evaluate and transform their world under the Lordship of Christ by contributing thoughtfully and responsibly to family life, to the church's life and mission, and to the political and cultural life of the general society, all to the glory of God.

NOTE: This data applies to the 2002–2003 school year.

FRENCH INTERNATIONAL SCHOOL (LYCEE ROCHAMBEAU)

Year founded: 1967
9600 Forest Road
Bethesda, MD 20814
Head of School:
Monique Letocart

GENERAL

Grade range: N-12th   Coed
Religious affiliation: Nonsectarian
Average class size: 25
School day: 8:30-3:30 (Lower School),
8:30-5:30 (Middle and Upper School)
Morning or after-school care:
3:30-5:30

CAMPUS/CAMPUS LIFE

Facilities:
3 campuses: Lower School campus
located at 3200 Woodbine St.,
Chevy Chase, MD 20815;
Maternelle (Nursery) 7108 Bradley
Blvd., Bethesda, MD 20817
Lunch provided: No
Boarding option: No
Bus service: Yes
School uniform or dress code:
None
Handicapped access available: No
Community service requirement:
No

Director of Admission:
Agnes Finucan
Phone: 301-530-8260 x246
Fax: 301-564-5779
E-mail:
finucan@rochambeau.org
Website:
www.rochambeau.org

ADMISSIONS

Application deadline: Rolling
Application fee: $200
Application process:
Informal assessment
**Number of students
applied/enrolled:**

COSTS

Tuition: $8,385 (N-K), $7,470
(1st-5th), $8,460 (6th-9th),
$9,685 (10th-12th)
Average additional fees: $150
Financial aid budget:
Average grant size:
**% of Students receiving
financial aid:**

NOTE: This data applies to the 2002–2003 school year.

ACADEMIC PROFILE
Number of faculty:
Languages and grades offered:
French (N-12th), German (8th-12th),
Latin (7th-12th), Spanish (8th-12th)
Number of AP classes offered:
International Baccalaureate (IB)
Tutors/learning specialists:
Yes
Schools three or more graduates have attended over the past five years:
Canadian and European universities

SPECIAL FEATURES
Students educated in the French system are admitted as space permits, all classes are taught in French except English and US History.

ENROLLMENT
Total number of students attending and graduating class size: 1163 / 50
Birthday cut-off: December 31
% Diversity: 50 nationalities
Grades with openings: All

SUMMER PROGRAMS
Yes

ART PROGRAMS

SPORTS
Basketball, soccer, volleyball

LONG-RANGE PLANS

HISTORY AND MISSION STATEMENT

NOTE: This data applies to the 2002–2003 school year.

FRIENDS COMMUNITY SCHOOL

Year founded: 1986
4601 Calvert Road
College Park, MD 20740
Head of School:
Tom Goss

GENERAL
Grade range: K-6th   Coed
Religious affiliation: Society of Friends
(Quaker)
Average class size: 15
School day: 9:00-3:00, 9:00-2:00 W
Morning or after-school care:
8:00-6:00

CAMPUS/CAMPUS LIFE
Facilities:
Main building includes 11 classrooms,
multi-purpose room, art area, new
and improved blacktop, playground,
soccer field
Lunch provided: No
Boarding option: No
Bus service: No
School uniform or dress code:
None
Handicapped access available: Yes
Community service requirement:
Yes

Director of Admission:
Tom Goss
Phone: 301-699-6086
Fax: 301-779-4595
E-mail:
gwen@friendscommunityschool.org
Website:
www.friendscommunityschool.org

ADMISSIONS
Application deadline: February 1
Application fee: $50
Application process: Application,
parent meeting, informal
assessment
**Number of students
applied/enrolled:** 77 / 34

COSTS
Tuition: $7,674
Average additional fees: $100
Financial aid budget: $129,500
Average grant size: $3,600
**% of Students receiving
financial aid:** 33%

NOTE: This data applies to the 2002–2003 school year.

ACADEMIC PROFILE
Number of faculty: 17
Languages and grades offered:
Spanish (K-6th)
Number of AP classes offered:
Not applicable
Tutors/learning specialists: 1
Schools three or more graduates have attended over the past five years:
Edmund Burke, Field, Queen Anne, St. Andrew's, Sandy Spring Friends, Sidwell Friends, Thornton Friends

SPECIAL FEATURES

ENROLLMENT
Total number of students attending and graduating class size: 142 / 20
Birthday cut-off: November 1
% Diversity: 25%
Grades with openings: K (18), 1st (6-8), 2nd (3-4), 3rd (4-5), 4th (2-3), 5th (0), 6th (0)

SUMMER PROGRAMS
Yes: arts & crafts from around the world, Spanish cultural activities, sports (ages 5-12), music and swimming/water games

ART PROGRAMS
Children are introduced to color and design theory and selected Art History

SPORTS
None

LONG-RANGE PLANS

HISTORY AND MISSION STATEMENT
Friends Community School, a Quaker Elementary School serving students from Kindergarten through 6th Grade, is under the care of Adelphi Friends Meeting Inc. As parents, educators, and Quakers, the founders felt a strong need for a school which provides a joyful and caring environment balancing the basic academic subjects with nurture of the spirit based upon Quaker values. The Mission is to teach young people to be life-long learners, courageous risk-takers, joyous peacemakers, to find that of God within themselves and others.

NOTE: This data applies to the 2002–2003 school year.

GEORGETOWN DAY SCHOOL

Year founded: 1945
PK-8th: 4530 MacArthur Boulevard, NW
Washington, DC 20007
9th-12th: 4200 Davenport Street, NW
Washington, DC 20016
Head of School:
Peter M. Branch

GENERAL
Grade range: PK-12th   Coed
Religious affiliation: Nonsectarian
Average class size: 18 (PK-8th),
15 (9th-12th)
School day: 8:15-3:15
Morning or after-school care:
3:00-6:00

CAMPUS/CAMPUS LIFE
Facilities:
Separate campuses for Upper &
Lower/Middle Schools, each with
art studios, computer labs, gym,
libraries, music studios, science labs,
theater for Upper School, media center
for Lower School
Lunch provided: No
Boarding option: No
Bus service: No
School uniform or dress code:
None
Handicapped access available: Yes
Community service requirement:
Yes: 60 hours in Upper School

Director of Admission:
Wes Gibson
Phone: PK-8th: 202-295-6210,
9-12th: 202-274-3210
Fax: PK-8th: 202-295-6211,
9th-12th: 202-274-3211
E-mail:
info@gds.org
Website:
www.gds.org

ADMISSIONS
Application deadline: January 15
Application fee: $60
Application process: Detroit (PK*),
WPPSI-R (K), WISC III (1st-5th),
SSAT or ISEE (6th-12th), transcript,
teacher recommendations, interview
(*Subject to change)
**Number of students
applied/enrolled:**

COSTS
Tuition: $17,425 (PK-K),
$18,635 (1st-5th), $19,384
(6th-8th), $19,630 (9th-11th),
$20,095 (12th)
Average additional fees: $400
Financial aid budget: $1,800,000
Average grant size: $11,000
**% of Students receiving
financial aid:** 18%

NOTE: This data applies to the 2002–2003 school year.

ACADEMIC PROFILE
Number of faculty: 160 Full Time
10 Part Time
Languages and grades offered:
French (3rd-12th), Latin (7th-12th),
Spanish (3rd-12th)
Number of AP classes offered:
19
Tutors/learning specialists:
Yes: learning specialists in Lower &
Middle Schools
**Schools three or more graduates have
attended over the past five years:**
Brown, Duke, Emory, Harvard,
Stanford, Tufts, University of Michigan,
University of Pennsylvania, University
of Virginia, Yale

SPECIAL FEATURES

ENROLLMENT
**Total number of students
attending and graduating
class size:** 1025 / 115
Birthday cut-off: June 1 (guideline)
% Diversity: 34%
Grades with openings: PK (20),
K (20), 1st (8), 3rd (6), 4th (10),
6th (12), 7th (4), 9th (35),
plus attrition

SUMMER PROGRAMS
None

ART PROGRAMS
Extensive

SPORTS
Baseball, basketball, crew, cross-
country, golf, lacrosse, soccer,
softball, tennis, track & field,
volleyball, wrestling

LONG-RANGE PLANS

HISTORY AND MISSION STATEMENT
Georgetown Day School honors the integrity and worth of each individual within a diverse school community. GDS is dedicated to providing a supportive educational atmosphere in which teachers challenge the intellectual, creative, and physical abilities of our students and foster strength of character and concern for others. From the earliest grades, we encourage our students to wonder, to inquire, and to be self-reliant, laying the foundation for a lifelong love of learning.

NOTE: This data applies to the 2002–2003 school year.

GEORGETOWN PREPARATORY SCHOOL

Year founded: 1789
10900 Rockville Pike
North Bethesda, MD 20852
Head of School:
Reverend William L. George, S.J.

GENERAL
Grade range: 9th-12th   Boys
Religious affiliation: Catholic, Jesuit
Average class size: 17
School day: 8:15-3:00
Morning or after-school care:
No

CAMPUS/CAMPUS LIFE
Facilities:
90 acre campus, 2 dormitories,
2 classroom buildings, auditorium,
field house, golf course, indoor
tennis courts, theater, 400m
synthetic track
Lunch provided: Yes
Boarding option: Yes / 98
Bus service: Yes: free shuttle from Metro
School uniform or dress code:
Dress code: solid color dress shirt,
blue blazer, tie, khaki pants, dress shoes
Handicapped access available: Yes
Community service requirement:
Yes: various activities

Director of Admission:
Michael J. Horsey
Phone: 301-214-1215
Fax: 301-493-6128
E-mail:
admission@gprep.org
Website:
www.gprep.org

ADMISSIONS
Application deadline: February 1
Application fee: $50 /$100
for international applicants
Application process: SSAT
(9th-11th), 2 teacher and
1 personal recommendations,
interview, transcript for 2
previous years
Number of students
applied/enrolled: 400 / 100 (9th)

COSTS
Tuition: $16,850 day,
$29,850 boarding
Average additional fees: $500
Financial aid budget: $1,100,000
Average grant size: $12,000
% of Students receiving
financial aid: 23%

NOTE: This data applies to the 2002–2003 school year.

ACADEMIC PROFILE
Number of faculty:
Languages and grades offered:
French, German, Ancient Greek,
Latin, Spanish (9th-12th)
Number of AP classes offered: 24
Tutors/learning specialists:
Yes: school psychologist
Schools three or more graduates have
attended over the past five years:
Columbia, Cornell, Georgetown, Notre
Dame, Princeton, Stanford, University
of Maryland, University of Virginia,
other Jesuit colleges

SPECIAL FEATURES
Low (2%) attrition rate, acclaimed
drama program, Metro accessible,
(Grosvenor station on Red Line),
4.1 AP courses per graduate, 80% AP
scores above 3

ENROLLMENT
Total number of students
attending and graduating
class size: 430 / 110
Birthday cut-off: Not applicable
% Diversity: 28%
Grades with openings: 9th (75 day,
25 boarding), 10th-11th
(10 boarding)

SUMMER PROGRAMS
Yes: foreign language trips,
mathematics for advancement

ART PROGRAMS
Art, drama, music

SPORTS
Baseball, basketball, cross-country,
fencing, football, golf, ice hockey,
indoor soccer, indoor track,
lacrosse, rugby, soccer, swimming
& diving, tennis, track & field,
wrestling

LONG-RANGE PLANS
Add a second field house with an
indoor track

HISTORY AND MISSION STATEMENT

To challenge young men to become "Men for Others" who are intellectually competent, religious, loving, open to growth, and committed to doing justice.

NOTE: This data applies to the 2002–2003 school year.

GEORGETOWN VISITATION PREPARATORY SCHOOL

Year founded: 1799
1524 35th Street, NW
Washington, DC 20007
Head of School:
Daniel M. Kerns

GENERAL
Grade range: 9th-12th   Girls
Religious affiliation: Catholic
Average class size: 19
School day: 8:00-3:00 or 3:30
Morning or after-school care:
No

CAMPUS/CAMPUS LIFE
Facilities:
23 acre campus in Georgetown with
newly renovated facilities, new
gymnasium and performing arts center
Lunch provided: Yes: additional fee
Boarding option: No
Bus service: No
School uniform or dress code:
Uniform: Fall/Spring - green kilt,
yellow polo; Winter - plaid kilt,
gray pants
Handicapped access available: Yes
Community service requirement:
Yes: 80 hours

Director of Admission:
Laurie Collins Quirk
Phone: 202-337-3350 x2241
Fax: 202-342-5733
E-mail:
Quirk@visi.org
Website:
www.visi.org

ADMISSIONS
Application deadline: December 6
Application fee: $50
Application process: Terra Nova
(9th-12th), application with essay,
transcript, teacher recommendations,
Archdiocesan test results
**Number of students
applied/enrolled:** 380 / 112

COSTS
Tuition: $13,100
Average additional fees: $200
Financial aid budget: $575,000
Average grant size: $5,000
**% of Students receiving
financial aid:** 20%

NOTE: This data applies to the 2002–2003 school year.

ACADEMIC PROFILE

Number of faculty: 100

Languages and grades offered:
French, Japanese, Latin, Spanish
(9th-12th)

Number of AP classes offered: 11

Tutors/learning specialists:
Yes

Schools three or more graduates have attended over the past five years:
Boston College, Boston University,
Carnegie Mellon, Colgate, Cornell,
Georgetown, Holy Cross, James
Madison, Loyola (MD), Princeton,
Syracuse, Tulane, University of
Virginia, William & Mary

SPECIAL FEATURES
30 clubs, new gym and performing
arts center

ENROLLMENT

**Total number of students
attending and graduating
class size:** 430 / 111

Birthday cut-off: Not applicable

% Diversity: 25%

Grades with openings: 9th (110)

SUMMER PROGRAMS
Yes: academics, performing arts,
sports

ART PROGRAMS
Dance, music, orchestra, studio
art, theater

SPORTS
Basketball, crew, cross-country, field
hockey, lacrosse, soccer, softball,
swimming & diving, tennis,
track & field, volleyball

LONG-RANGE PLANS

HISTORY AND MISSION STATEMENT

Georgetown Visitation is a college preparatory school dedicated to the education of young women from a variety of backgrounds. We are a faith-centered community which is focused on educational excellence and rooted in the Roman Catholic faith and Salesian tradition. Our mission is to empower our students to meet the demands and challenges of a rapidly changing and morally complex world. Enriching co-curricular and Christian Service programs complement the academic and spiritual life of the school and encourage our students to develop into intellectually mature and morally responsible women of faith, vision and purpose.

NOTE: This data applies to the 2002–2003 school year.

GONZAGA COLLEGE HIGH SCHOOL

Year founded: 1821
19 Eye Street, NW
Washington, DC 20001
Head of School:
Michael Pakenham

GENERAL
Grade range: 9th-12th   Boys
Religious affiliation: Catholic, Jesuit
Average class size: 25
School day: 8:15-2:35
Morning or after-school care:
No

CAMPUS/CAMPUS LIFE
Facilities:
Newly renovated campus close to
Union Station
Lunch provided: Yes
Boarding option: No
Bus service: No
School uniform or dress code:
Dress code: collared shirt, dress pants,
dress shoes
Handicapped access available: No
Community service requirement:
Yes: 40 hours senior year and other
volunteer opportunities

Director of Admission:
Reverend Bob Mattingly, S.J.
Phone: 202-336-7101
Fax: 202-454-1188
E-mail:
rmatting@gonzaga.org
Website:
www.gonzaga.org

ADMISSIONS
Application deadline: December 15
Application fee: $35
Application process: Terra Nova
(9th-12th)
**Number of students
applied/enrolled:** 700 / 225

COSTS
Tuition: $9,550
Average additional fees: $300
Financial aid budget: $1,200,000
Average grant size:
**% of Students receiving
financial aid:** 33%

NOTE: This data applies to the 2002–2003 school year.

ACADEMIC PROFILE

Number of faculty: 65

Languages and grades offered:
French, German, Latin, Spanish
(9th-12th)

Number of AP classes offered: 22

Tutors/learning specialists:
Yes

Schools three or more graduates have attended over the past five years:
Boston College, Catholic, Harvard,
Holy Cross, Loyola (MD), Naval
Academy, University of Maryland,
University of Virginia, Yale

SPECIAL FEATURES

ENROLLMENT

Total number of students attending and graduating class size: 875 / 200

Birthday cut-off: Not applicable

% Diversity: 31%

Grades with openings: 9th (220)

SUMMER PROGRAMS

Yes: academic, sports camps

ART PROGRAMS

Drawing, painting, photography,
T.V. communications

SPORTS

Baseball, basketball, crew, cross-country, football, golf, ice hockey,
lacrosse, tennis, track & field,
rugby, wrestling

LONG-RANGE PLANS

HISTORY AND MISSION STATEMENT

Gonzaga, founded by the Society of Jesus and chartered by Congress, strives to form graduates that are loving, religious, open to growth, intellectually competent and committed to social justice.

NOTE: This data applies to the 2002–2003 school year.

GOOD COUNSEL HIGH SCHOOL

Year founded: 1958
11601 Georgia Avenue
Wheaton, MD 20902
Head of School:
Arthur Raimo

GENERAL
Grade range: 9th-12th   Coed
Religious affiliation: Catholic
Average class size: 24
School day: 8:00-2:45
Morning or after-school care:
No

CAMPUS/CAMPUS LIFE
Facilities:
3 computer labs, 2 gyms, renovated
science labs
Lunch provided: Yes: additional fee
Boarding option: No
Bus service: Limited
School uniform or dress code:
Dress code: girls - skirt and blouse;
boys - dress pants, shirt and tie
Handicapped access available: Yes
Community service requirement:
Yes: 100 hours by graduation

Director of Admission:
Tom Campbell
Phone: 301-942-1155 x105
Fax: 301-942-4967
E-mail:
TCampbell@gchs.com
Website:
www.gchs.com

ADMISSIONS
Application deadline: January 10
Application fee: $25
Application process: Application,
teacher recommendations,
transcript, Terra Nova (9th-12th)
**Number of students
applied/enrolled:** 620 / 270

COSTS
Tuition: $9,560
Average additional fees: $500
Financial aid budget: $700,000
Average grant size: $2,500
**% of Students receiving
financial aid:**

NOTE: This data applies to the 2002–2003 school year.

ACADEMIC PROFILE
Number of faculty: 80
Languages and grades offered:
French, Latin, Spanish (9th-12th)
Number of AP classes offered: 11
Tutors/learning specialists:
Yes: Ryken Program for learning
disabilities
**Schools three or more graduates have
attended over the past five years:**
Duke, Georgetown, Harvard, Johns
Hopkins, Mt. St. Mary's, Massachusetts
Institute of Technology, Towson,
University of Maryland, Villanova,
Virginia Technology

SPECIAL FEATURES
International Baccalaureate Program

ENROLLMENT
**Total number of students
attending and graduating
class size:** 1050 / 233
Birthday cut-off: Not applicable
% Diversity: 20%
Grades with openings:
9th, plus attrition

SUMMER PROGRAMS
Yes: Camp Good Counsel,
basketball, football, and
lacrosse camps

ART PROGRAMS
Art, band, chorus, music

SPORTS
Baseball, basketball, cross-country,
field hockey, football, golf, ice
hockey, lacrosse, soccer, swimming
& diving, tennis, track & field,
wrestling

LONG-RANGE PLANS
Relocate to 50 acre campus in
Olney in 2005

HISTORY AND MISSION STATEMENT

Good Counsel is a Xavierian Brothers sponsored school that is committed to preparing a diverse student population with varying learning needs for the challenges of college and lifelong learning by providing programs and activities that teach gospel values, foster personal growth, and promote academic excellence.

NOTE: This data applies to the 2002–2003 school year.

GRACE EPISCOPAL DAY SCHOOL

Year founded: 1960
9115 Georgia Avenue
Silver Spring, MD 20910
Head of School:
Carol Franek

GENERAL
Grade range: N-6th   Coed
Religious affiliation: Episcopal
Average class size: 16
School day: 8:45-12:00 or 3:00 (N-K),
8:30-3:15 (1st-6th)
Morning or after-school care:
7:30-6:00

CAMPUS/CAMPUS LIFE
Facilities:
1st-6th located on second 11 acre
campus at 9411 Connecticut Ave.,
Kensington, MD 20895,
multipurpose rooms
Lunch provided: No
Boarding option: No
Bus service: No
School uniform or dress code:
Uniform: girls - jumper or pants;
boys - collared shirts and blue pants
Handicapped access available: Yes
Community service requirement:
Yes

Director of Admission:
Donna Harshman
Phone: 301-585-3513 x12
Fax: 301-585-5240
E-mail:

Website:
www.geds.org

ADMISSIONS
Application deadline: March 1
Application fee: $75
Application process: WPPSI-R (K),
WISC III (1st-6th), tour,
application, student visit,
parent interview
**Number of students
applied/enrolled:** 135 / 60

COSTS
Tuition: $3,868-$6,447 (N),
$6,447-$10,746 (PK), $10,746
(1st-3rd), $10,885 (4th-6th)
Average additional fees: $75
Financial aid budget:
Average grant size:
**% of Students receiving
financial aid:**

NOTE: This data applies to the 2002–2003 school year.

ACADEMIC PROFILE

Number of faculty: 25 Full Time
20 Part Time

Languages and grades offered:
Latin (5th-6th), Spanish (K-6th)

Number of AP classes offered:
Not applicable

Tutors/learning specialists:
Yes: math enrichment; reading
recovery teacher

Schools three or more graduates have attended over the past five years:
Bullis, Connelly School of Holy Child, Edmund Burke, Field, Holton-Arms, Landon, National Cathedral, St. Andrew's, St. John's College High, Sidwell Friends, Stone Ridge

SPECIAL FEATURES

Inclusive, comfortable envrionment, high diversity, solid foundation offered, 90% of 6th grade gets their 1st choice of school for 7th grade

ENROLLMENT

Total number of students attending and graduating class size: 292 / 28

Birthday cut-off: December 31

% Diversity: 35%

Grades with openings:

SUMMER PROGRAMS

Yes: academic enrichment; summer camps

ART PROGRAMS

Art, drama, music

SPORTS

Soccer and other lifeskill-based games and activities

LONG-RANGE PLANS

Continue renovating/ upgrading both campuses

HISTORY AND MISSION STATEMENT

Grace seeks to develop the academic potential of each student and to help prepare each student as an individual to live a creative, humane and compassionate life worthy of a child of God and to perform as a contributing member of our world community.

NOTE: This data applies to the 2002–2003 school year.

GRACE EPISCOPAL SCHOOL

Year founded: 1959
3601 Russell Road
Alexandria, VA 22305
Head of School:
Nancy Rowe

GENERAL
Grade range: N-5th   Coed
Religious affiliation: Episcopal
Average class size: 9-19 with 1-3 teachers
School day: 8:45-3:15
Morning or after-school care:
7:30-6:00

CAMPUS/CAMPUS LIFE
Facilities:
Semi-wooded campus with art,
auditorium and stage, computer,
library, music, indoor PE space,
science rooms, weather station,
soccer field, basketball court
Lunch provided: Yes
Boarding option: No
Bus service: No
School uniform or dress code:
Dress code: 1st-5th: tan/navy pants/
shorts/skirts with solid color polo shirts/
turtlenecks
Handicapped access available: Yes
Community service requirement:
Yes

Director of Admission:
Debra Jackson Busker
Phone: 703-549-5067
Fax: 703-549-9545
E-mail:
school.office@gracealex.org
Website:
www.gracealex.org

ADMISSIONS
Application deadline: February 1
Application fee: $50
Application process: WPPSI-R
(under 6 years old), WISC III
(1st-5th), tour, application, play
date or applicant visit, teacher
recommendations, transcript
**Number of students
applied/enrolled:**

COSTS
Tuition: $4,680 (N-PK, half day),
$9,770 (full day K),
$9,980 (1st-5th)
Average additional fees: $700
Financial aid budget: based on
United Way funding and donations
Average grant size: maximum 50%
of tuition
**% of Students receiving
financial aid:** 13%

NOTE: This data applies to the 2002–2003 school year.

ACADEMIC PROFILE

Number of faculty: 31 Full Time

Languages and grades offered:
French (4th-5th)

Number of AP classes offered:
Not applicable

Tutors/learning specialists:
None

Schools three or more graduates have attended over the past five years:
Alexandria Country Day, Burgundy Farm, Field, Holton-Arms, Holy Trinity, Maret, National Cathedral, Potomac, St. Albans, St. Andrew's, St. Anselm's, St. Patrick's, St. Paul's, St. Stephen's & St. Agnes

SPECIAL FEATURES
11 special enrichment faculty

ENROLLMENT

Total number of students attending and graduating class size: 115 / 11

Birthday cut-off: September 30

% Diversity: 12%

Grades with openings:

SUMMER PROGRAMS
None

ART PROGRAMS
Art, drama, music

SPORTS
None

LONG-RANGE PLANS

HISTORY AND MISSION STATEMENT

Grace Episcopal School serves students with the ability and readiness to participate and progress within an academically challenging curriculum and an enriching environment where learning is enjoyed and sharing is commonplace. Founded in 1959, we provide an excellent, developmentally appropriate education for children in Nursery through Fifth Grade. We offer a warm and nurturing environment beginning at age 3 and continuing with a progressive academic program for the elementary grades. Low student-teacher ratios give the staff the freedom to cultivate students, especially gifted and talented youngsters, to reach their maximum potential. Spiritual and moral values plus service to others are emphasized, both within the school community and beyond.

NOTE: This data applies to the 2002–2003 school year.

GREEN ACRES SCHOOL

Year founded: 1934
11701 Danville Drive
Rockville, MD 20852
Head of School:
Louis Silvano

GENERAL
Grade range: PK-8th   Coed
Religious affiliation: Nonsectarian
Average class size: 12
School day: 8:30-3:00
Morning or after-school care:
3:00-6:00

CAMPUS/CAMPUS LIFE
Facilities:
15 acre wooded campus with multiple
buildings
Lunch provided: No
Boarding option: No
Bus service: Yes
School uniform or dress code:
None
Handicapped access available: Yes
Community service requirement:
Yes: 40 hours for 7th-8th

Director of Admission:
Marge Dimond
Phone: 301-881-4100
Fax: 301-881-3319
E-mail:
annae@greenacres.org
Website:
www.greenacres.org

ADMISSIONS
Application deadline: January 15
Application fee: $75
Application process: Parent
interview, applicant visit, transcript
**Number of students
applied/enrolled:**

COSTS
Tuition: $16,950
Average additional fees: $40-$650
Financial aid budget: $335,500
Average grant size: Varies
**% of Students receiving
financial aid:** Varies

NOTE: This data applies to the 2002–2003 school year.

ACADEMIC PROFILE

Number of faculty: 37 Full Time
15 Part Time
Languages and grades offered:
Spanish (5th-8th)
Number of AP classes offered:
Not applicable
Tutors/learning specialists:
None
Schools three or more graduates have attended over the past five years:

SPECIAL FEATURES

Progressive philosophy, child-centered approach

ENROLLMENT

Total number of students attending and graduating class size: 320 / Varies
Birthday cut-off: June 1 (guideline)
% Diversity: 24%
Grades with openings: PK (21), K (12), plus attrition

SUMMER PROGRAMS

Yes: 6 week summer camp

ART PROGRAMS

Extensive at all grade levels

SPORTS

Basketball, lacrosse, soccer, softball

LONG-RANGE PLANS

Complete phase three of a three phase facilities improvement plan

HISTORY AND MISSION STATEMENT

Throughout its history, Green Acres School has been dedicated to its progressive mission of fostering the natural curiosity of students, engaging them actively in the joy of learning, and facilitating problem solving. Based on an understanding of child development, the Green Acres program is cognitively, physically, and creatively challenging. An environment of trust, cooperation, mutual respect, and a valuing of diversity encourages students to become increasingly independent thinkers and responsible contributors to an ever-changing, multicultural world.

NOTE: This data applies to the 2002–2003 school year.

GREEN HEDGES SCHOOL

Year founded: 1942
415 Windover Avenue, NW
Vienna, VA 22180
Head of School:
Scott Votey

GENERAL
Grade range: N-8th   Coed
Religious affiliation: Nonsectarian
Average class size: 16
School day: 8:20-3:20
Morning or after-school care:
3:20-6:00

CAMPUS/CAMPUS LIFE
Facilities:
Village-like setting with new wing
and arts center, playing field,
administrative building
Lunch provided: No
Boarding option: No
Bus service: No
School uniform or dress code:
Dress code, uniform 3rd-8th for
special occasions
Handicapped access available: Yes
Community service requirement:
None

Director of Admission:
Leslie Dixon
Phone: 703-938-8323
Fax: 703-938-1485
E-mail:
ldixon@greenhedges.org
Website:
www.greenhedgesschool.org

ADMISSIONS
Application deadline: February 1
Application fee: $60
Application process: Application,
transcript, teacher recommendations,
applicant assessment, visit, recent
achievement test results (if available)
**Number of students
applied/enrolled:** 167 / 39

COSTS
Tuition: $8,848 (half day N-K),
$13,999 (full day K-8th)
Average additional fees:
Financial aid budget: 8.5% of budget
Average grant size: 40% of tuition
**% of Students receiving
financial aid:** 11%

NOTE: This data applies to the 2002–2003 school year.

ACADEMIC PROFILE

Number of faculty: 28

Languages and grades offered:
French (N-8th), Latin (5th-8th),
Spanish (5th-8th)

Number of AP classes offered:
Not applicable

Tutors/learning specialists:
None

Schools three or more graduates have attended over the past five years:
Bishop Ireton, Bullis, Edmund Burke, Flint Hill, Highland, Madeira, Paul VI, Potomac, St. Stephen's & St. Agnes, Thomas Jefferson

SPECIAL FEATURES
Montessori program for 3 to 5 year old children

ENROLLMENT

Total number of students attending and graduating class size: 190 / 17

Birthday cut-off: September 1

% Diversity: 30%

Grades with openings: N (12), 1st (8), plus attrition

SUMMER PROGRAMS
Yes: 6 week summer school drama, reading, math camp (2nd-6th)

ART PROGRAMS
Art, drama, music

SPORTS
Basketball (6th-8th)

LONG-RANGE PLANS
Build an endowment, redesign/ landscape grounds

HISTORY AND MISSION STATEMENT

Green Hedges School is an independent day school committed to providing a classical education in a relaxed, happy environment for children age 3 years through grade 8. GHS is a small school with a maximum of 190 students with a dedicated, talented teaching staff who demonstrate excellence in teaching. The Montessori preschool transitions to a spiral curriculum for the elementary grades 1-5 and a departmentalized middle school for grades 6-8. Music, art, drama, French, Spanish, Latin, and technology as well as character development and values are important parts of the Green Hedges program.

NOTE: This data applies to the 2002–2003 school year.

HARBOR SCHOOL (THE)

Year founded: 1972
7701 Bradley Boulevard
Bethesda, MD 20817
Head of School:
Carol Montag

GENERAL
Grade range: N-2nd   Coed
Religious affiliation: Nonsectarian
Average class size: 16
School day: 9:00-12:00 (N-PK),
8:45-3:00 (K-2nd), 8:45-12:00 F
(K-2nd)
Morning or after-school care:
8:00-4:15

CAMPUS/CAMPUS LIFE
Facilities:
Until new site is completed, located
within a church with a separate school
building, large gymnasium, playground
Lunch provided: No
Boarding option: No
Bus service: No
School uniform or dress code:
None
Handicapped access available: No
Community service requirement:
Yes: program includes children
and parents

Director of Admission:
Marti Jacobs
Phone: 301-365-1100
Fax: 301-365-7491
E-mail:
harbors172@aol.com
Website:
www.theharborschool.org

ADMISSIONS
Application deadline: February 1
Application fee: $50
Application process: School visit,
informal assessment
**Number of students
applied/enrolled:** 113 / 55

COSTS
Tuition: $6,514 (half day N-PK),
$12,584 (full day PK-2nd)
Average additional fees: $300
Financial aid budget:
Average grant size: Maximum of
50% of tuition
**% of Students receiving
financial aid:** 5%

NOTE: This data applies to the 2002–2003 school year.

ACADEMIC PROFILE
Number of faculty: 15 Full Time
12 Part Time
Languages and grades offered:
Number of AP classes offered:
Not applicable
Tutors/learning specialists:
Yes: reading, speech & language
pathologist
Schools three or more graduates have attended over the past five years:
Bullis, Holton-Arms, Landon

SPECIAL FEATURES
Movement/physical education
program, international student body,
strong parent involvement

ENROLLMENT
Total number of students attending and graduating class size: 130 / 17
Birthday cut-off: September 1
% Diversity: 16%
Grades with openings: N (28),
plus attrition

SUMMER PROGRAMS
Yes: camp for 3-5 year olds

ART PROGRAMS
Art, dance, music, story teller

SPORTS
Tennis (after school for children
5 years and older)

LONG-RANGE PLANS
Add 3rd, 4th, 5th grades at
new school site and building
to be announced

HISTORY AND MISSION STATEMENT

The Harbor School prepares children for life's journey. Children are encouraged to question, experiment, explore, take risks, and assume responsibility in the world around them. The school fosters a continuing love of learning and a respect for the uniqueness of each individual.

NOTE: This data applies to the 2002–2003 school year.

HEIGHTS SCHOOL (THE)

Year founded: 1969
10400 Seven Locks Road
Potomac, MD 20854
Head of School:
Alvaro DiVicente '83

GENERAL
Grade range: 3rd-12th   Boys
Religious affiliation: Catholic
Average class size: 19
School day: 8:20-3:00
Morning or after-school care:
No

CAMPUS/CAMPUS LIFE
Facilities:
20 acre suburban campus, 5 buidings,
new tennis and outdoor basketball courts
Lunch provided: Yes
Boarding option: No
Bus service: Yes
School uniform or dress code:
Dress code: shirt and tie 3rd-7th,
blazer and tie 8th-12th
Handicapped access available: Yes
Community service requirement:
No requirement, but active participation

Director of Admission:
Kevin Davern
Phone: 301-365-4300
Fax: 301-365-4303
E-mail:
kevindavern@mail.heights.edu
Website:
www.heights.edu

ADMISSIONS
Application deadline: January 31
Application fee: $40
Application process: Application,
teacher recommendation,
transcript, family interview,
applicant visit, informal assessment
(3rd-8th), SSAT (9th-12th)
**Number of students
applied/enrolled:** 240 / 76

COSTS
Tuition: $9,850 (3rd-5th), $11,200
(6th-8th), $11,800 (9th-12th)
Average additional fees: $150
Financial aid budget: $750,000
Average grant size: Varies
**% of Students receiving
financial aid:** 25%

NOTE: This data applies to the 2002–2003 school year.

ACADEMIC PROFILE
Number of faculty: 40 Full Time
5 Part Time
Languages and grades offered:
Greek (11th-12th), Latin (7th-12th),
Spanish (7th-12th)
Number of AP classes offered: 16
Tutors/learning specialists: None
Schools three or more graduates have attended over the past five years:
Columbia, Notre Dame, Princeton,
University of Maryland

SPECIAL FEATURES

ENROLLMENT
Total number of students attending and graduating class size: 460 / 50
Birthday cut-off: Not applicable
% Diversity: 15%
Grades with openings: 3rd (26),
6th (20), 9th (10), plus attrition

SUMMER PROGRAMS
Yes: summer school, math and
Latin summer camps, natural
history (2nd-5th), Civil War
(6th-8th)

ART PROGRAMS

SPORTS
Baseball, basketball, cross-country,
golf, lacrosse, soccer, swimming,
tennis

LONG-RANGE PLANS

HISTORY AND MISSION STATEMENT

The Heights, founded by a group of laymen, offers a rigorous and traditional liberal arts academic program as a means of working with parents to help form young men ready to succeed in college and professional work. Spiritual direction of the school is entrusted to Opus Dei, a prelature of the Catholic Church, which seeks to promote the pursuit of holiness through one's ordinary work and daily life.

NOTE: This data applies to the 2002–2003 school year.

HOLTON-ARMS SCHOOL

Year founded: 1901
7303 River Road
Bethesda, MD 20817
Head of School:
Diana Coulton Beebe

GENERAL
Grade range: 3rd-12th   Girls
Religious affiliation: Nonsectarian
Average class size: 15
School day: 8:10-3:30
Morning or after-school care:
3:30-6:00 (3rd-8th)

CAMPUS/CAMPUS LIFE
Facilities:
67 acre suburban campus with art
studio, child development center,
ceramics, darkroom and graphics
labs, greenhouse, indoor pool,
48,000 volume libraries, theater
Lunch provided: Yes
Boarding option: No
Bus service: Limited
School uniform or dress code:
Uniform: plaid jumpers or skirts, navy
or gray skirts or pants with white, navy
or gray shirts, sweaters or sweatshirts
Handicapped access available: Yes
Community service requirement:
Yes: 50 hours completed by beginning
of senior year

Director of Admission:
Sharron Rodgers
Phone: 301-365-5300
Fax: 301-365-6071
E-mail:
admit@holton-arms.edu
Website:
www.holton-arms.edu

ADMISSIONS
Application deadline: January 15
Application fee: $60 /$100 for
international applicants
Application process: School visit,
application, interview, WISC III
(3rd-5th), SSAT or ISEE (6th-12th),
transcript, teacher recommendations
**Number of students
applied/enrolled:**

COSTS
Tuition: $19,075
Average additional fees:
$700-$1,000
Financial aid budget: $1,245,000
Average grant size: $11,971
**% of Students receiving
financial aid:** 15%

NOTE: This data applies to the 2002–2003 school year.

ACADEMIC PROFILE
Number of faculty: 90 Full Time
4 Part Time
Languages and grades offered:
French (7th-12th), Latin (7th-12th),
Spanish (3rd-12th)
Number of AP classes offered: 12
Tutors/learning specialists:
Yes: learning specialists
Schools three or more graduates have attended over the past five years:
Brown, Columbia, Cornell, Duke,
George Washington, Harvard-Radcliffe,
Massachusetts Institute of Technology,
New York University, Princeton, Yale

SPECIAL FEATURES
Centennial Garden celebrates the past,
present, and future members of the
Holton community

ENROLLMENT
Total number of students attending and graduating class size: 650 / 72
Birthday cut-off: Not applicable
% Diversity: 28%
Grades with openings: 3rd (30),
6th (10), 7th (15), 9th (12),
plus attrition

SUMMER PROGRAMS
Yes: Creative Summer-coeducational
6 week camp for academics, arts,
computers, dance, drama, outdoor
exploration, sports, swimming
(ages 3-13)

ART PROGRAMS
Ceramics, drawing, painting,
photography, printmaking

SPORTS
Basketball, crew, cross-country,
diving, field hockey, ice hockey,
lacrosse, soccer, softball, swimming,
tennis, track & field, volleyball

LONG-RANGE PLANS
New science wing, synthetic track,
black box theater

HISTORY AND MISSION STATEMENT
The Holton-Arms School is dedicated "to the education not only of the mind, but of the soul and spirit." Our goals are to build the confidence, integrity, and love of learning that will prepare young women for a changing world and to endow each with a profound sense of respect and responsibility for herself and the community. Rigorous programs in academics, the arts, and athletics, and significant opportunities for leadership allow students to develop their full potential.

NOTE: This data applies to the 2002–2003 school year.

HOLY CROSS, ACADEMY OF THE

Year founded: 1868
4920 Strathmore Avenue
Kensington, MD 20895
Head of School:
Sister Katherine Kase, CSC

GENERAL
Grade range: 9th-12th   Girls
Religious affiliation: Catholic
Average class size: 20
School day: 7:55-2:55
Morning or after-school care:
No

CAMPUS/CAMPUS LIFE
Facilities:
28 acre suburban campus
Lunch provided: Yes
Boarding option: No
Bus service: No
School uniform or dress code:
Uniform: kilts, polo or oxford shirts,
sweaters
Handicapped access available: Yes
Community service requirement:
Yes

Director of Admission:
Patricia McGann
Phone: 301-942-2100
Fax: 301-942-6440
E-mail:
ahcadmin@erols.com
Website:
www.academyoftheholycross.org

ADMISSIONS
Application deadline: December 15
Application fee: $50
Application process: Terra Nova
(9th-12th)
**Number of students
applied/enrolled:** 355 / 140

COSTS
Tuition: $10,100
Average additional fees: $600
Financial aid budget:
Average grant size:
**% of Students receiving
financial aid:** 35%

NOTE: This data applies to the 2002–2003 school year.

ACADEMIC PROFILE
Number of faculty: 48
Languages and grades offered:
French, Latin, Spanish (9th-12th)
Number of AP classes offered: 9
Tutors/learning specialists:
Yes
Schools three or more graduates have attended over the past five years:
American, Boston University, Carnegie Mellon, Cornell, Duke, Georgetown, New York University, Pennsylvania State, Tufts, University of Virginia

SPECIAL FEATURES
New construction to be completed January, 2003

ENROLLMENT
Total number of students attending and graduating class size: 525 / 100
Birthday cut-off: Not applicable
% Diversity: 20%
Grades with openings: 9th (120)

SUMMER PROGRAMS
Yes: academic enrichment, sports

ART PROGRAMS

SPORTS
Basketball, cross-country, field hockey, lacrosse, soccer, swimming & diving, tennis, track & field

LONG-RANGE PLANS

HISTORY AND MISSION STATEMENT

NOTE: This data applies to the 2002–2003 school year.

HOLY TRINITY EPISCOPAL DAY SCHOOL

Year founded: 1963
13106 Annapolis Road
Bowie, MD 20720
Head of School:
Margaret Reiber

GENERAL
Grade range: N-8th   Coed
Religious affiliation: Episcopal
Average class size: 20
School day:
Morning or after-school care:
7:00-6:00

CAMPUS/CAMPUS LIFE
Facilities:
Preschool and Middle School
located at 11902 Daisey Ln.,
Glenn Dale, MD 20769
Lunch provided: Yes: additional fee
Boarding option: No
Bus service: No
School uniform or dress code:
Uniform
Handicapped access available: Yes
Community service requirement:
Yes: each grade level chooses a
service project

Director of Admission:
Suzanne Anderson
Phone: 301-262-5355
Fax: 301-262-9609
E-mail:
preiber@htrinity.org
Website:
www.htrinity.org

ADMISSIONS
Application deadline: Rolling
Application fee: $50
Application process: Informal
assessment, report cards, teacher
recommendations, transcript
Number of students
applied/enrolled:

COSTS
Tuition: $5,900 (PK),
$6,235 (K-4th), $7,535 (5th),
$7,700 (6th-8th)
Average additional fees:
Financial aid budget:
Average grant size:
% of Students receiving
financial aid:

NOTE: This data applies to the 2002–2003 school year.

ACADEMIC PROFILE
Number of faculty: 43 Full Time
9 Part Time
Languages and grades offered:
French (K-4th), Latin and Spanish
(5th-8th)
Number of AP classes offered:
Not applicable
Tutors/learning specialists:
Schools three or more graduates have
attended over the past five years:
Archbishop Spaulding, Bowie,
DeMatha, Eleanor Roosevelt, Pallotti,
St. John's College High

SPECIAL FEATURES

ENROLLMENT
Total number of students
attending and graduating
class size: 614 / 60
Birthday cut-off: September 30
% Diversity: 38%
Grades with openings:

SUMMER PROGRAMS
Yes: band, cheerleading, day camp,
environmental/ historical studies,
keyboarding, math, off campus
trips, soccer

ART PROGRAMS

SPORTS
Baseball, basketball, soccer, softball

LONG-RANGE PLANS
Build new gymnasium and
high school

HISTORY AND MISSION STATEMENT

NOTE: This data applies to the 2002–2003 school year.

HOLY TRINITY SCHOOL

Year founded: 1818
1325 36th Street, NW
Washington, DC 20007
Head of School:
Ann Marie Crowley

GENERAL
Grade range: N-8th   Coed
Religious affiliation: Roman Catholic,
Jesuit
Average class size: 12-15
School day: 8:20-3:00
Morning or after-school care:
7:30-6:00

CAMPUS/CAMPUS LIFE
Facilities:
2 large Federal style buildings spanning
a full city block in the heart of
Georgetown. Lower School (1st-4th)
cafeteria, health room, library,
media center, resource rooms; Upper
School (5th-8th) administrative offices,
art room, cafeteria, science lab, Spanish
room, theatre
Lunch provided: No
Boarding option: No
Bus service: No
School uniform or dress code:
Uniform: 1st-8th
Handicapped access available: No
Community service requirement:
Yes: for 8th

Director of Admission:
Kim Calnan Crismali
Phone: 202-337-2339
Fax: 202-337-0368
E-mail:
kcrismali@htsdc.org
Website:
www.htsdc.org

ADMISSIONS
Application deadline: Feb 1 for
priority status
Application fee: $60
Application process: Visit (N-1st),
in-house testing (2nd-7th),
transcripts, recommendations
**Number of students
applied/enrolled:** 230 / 61

COSTS
Tuition: $8,600-$10,000 (N-K),
$6,400-$8,700 (1st-8th)
Average additional fees: $150
Financial aid budget: $120,000
Average grant size: $3,000
**% of Students receiving
financial aid:** 15%

NOTE: This data applies to the 2002–2003 school year.

ACADEMIC PROFILE

Number of faculty: 60

Languages and grades offered:
Spanish (K-8th)

Number of AP classes offered:
Not applicable

Tutors/learning specialists:
Yes: reading, speech & language specialists

Schools three or more graduates have attended over the past five years:
Connelly School of the Holy Child, Georgetown Prep, Georgetown Visitation, Gonzaga, St. Albans, St. Anselm's, St. John's College High School, Sidwell Friends

SPECIAL FEATURES

ENROLLMENT

Total number of students attending and graduating class size: 340 / 45

Birthday cut-off: December 31

% Diversity: 29%

Grades with openings: N (14), K (10), 6th (12-15), plus attrition, no 8th grade applications accepted

SUMMER PROGRAMS
None

ART PROGRAMS

SPORTS
Baseball, basketball, softball

LONG-RANGE PLANS

HISTORY AND MISSION STATEMENT

Holy Trinity School is a Catholic School founded in the Jesuit tradition as an integral part of the mission of Holy Trinity Catholic Church. Holy Trinity School continues a 200 year old tradition of education and service. We work toward the development of skills, knowledge, character, and attitudes that reflect Christian responsibility.

NOTE: This data applies to the 2002–2003 school year.

IVYMOUNT SCHOOL

Year founded: 1961
11614 Seven Locks Road
Potomac, MD 20854
Head of School:
Janet Wintrol

GENERAL
Grade range: N-12th~ (ungraded) Coed
Religious affiliation: Nonsectarian
Average class size: 10
School day: 8:45-3:15
Morning or after-school care:
No

CAMPUS/CAMPUS LIFE
Facilities:
2 gymnasiums, occupational, music,
and art therapy rooms, 2 playgrounds,
playing field, assistive technology lab,
career center, library
Lunch provided: No
Boarding option: No
Bus service: Yes
School uniform or dress code:
None
Handicapped access available: Yes
Community service requirement:
None

Director of Admission:
Stephanie de Sibour
Phone: 301-469-0223
Fax: 301-469-0778
E-mail:
sdsibour@ivymount.org
Website:
www.ivymount.org

ADMISSIONS
Application deadline: Rolling
Application fee: $25
Application process: File review,
parent visit, student intake
**Number of students
applied/enrolled:** 190 / 26

COSTS
Tuition: $35,461, $52,752
for autism services (11 month
program)
Average additional fees: $75-$85/
hour for additional therapies
Financial aid budget: State funding
Average grant size:
**% of Students receiving
financial aid:** 99% state/county
funded

NOTE: This data applies to the 2002–2003 school year.

ACADEMIC PROFILE

Number of faculty: 163 Full Time
30 Part Time (includes therapists)

Languages and grades offered:
None

Number of AP classes offered:
Not applicable

Tutors/learning specialists:
Yes: clinical social workers, speech, reading, occupational, physical, behavioral, art, and music therapists, assistive technology team

Schools three or more graduates have attended over the past five years:
Not applicable

SPECIAL FEATURES
Non-diploma program, vocational training, after school therapeutic services, outreach/assessment

ENROLLMENT

Total number of students attending and graduating class size: 212 /

Birthday cut-off: Not applicable

% Diversity: 37%

Grades with openings: 5 openings per grade, 2-3 in Autism program

SUMMER PROGRAMS
Yes: extended school year for 4 weeks

ART PROGRAMS
Expressive arts program includes studio art, music, drama workshops

SPORTS
Baseball, basketball, volleyball

LONG-RANGE PLANS
Building expansion completed

HISTORY AND MISSION STATEMENT

Ivymount seeks to develop and refine innovative programs and services for students with disabilities so that, to the greatest extent possible, they can achieve productive and independent futures. Since 1961, Ivymount has served over 6,000 students from throughout the Washington Metropolitan area.

NOTE: This data applies to the 2002–2003 school year.

JEWISH PRIMARY DAY SCHOOL OF THE NATION'S CAPITAL

Year founded: 1988
2010 Linden Lane
Silver Spring, MD 20910
Head of School:
Susan Koss

GENERAL
Grade range: K-6th   Coed
Religious affiliation: Jewish
Average class size: 15
School day: 8:30-3:30, 8:30-2:15 F
Morning or after-school care:
2:15 or 3:30-6:30

CAMPUS/CAMPUS LIFE
Facilities:
New spacious campus includes art
studio, computer lab, gymnasium,
library, large multi-purpose room,
science lab
Lunch provided: Twice a month
Boarding option: No
Bus service: Yes
School uniform or dress code:
Handicapped access available: Yes
Community service requirement:
None required, but community service
is a large part of the JPDS culture

Director of Admission:
Elyse Rothschild
Phone: 301-578-4126
Fax: 301-578-4163
E-mail:
info@jpds.org
Website:
www.jpds.org

ADMISSIONS
Application deadline: February 1
Application fee: $50
Application process: Application,
recommendations, testing, records,
informal assessment
**Number of students
applied/enrolled:** 60 / 39

COSTS
Tuition: $10,650
Average additional fees: $300
Financial aid budget: $100,000
Average grant size: $5,500
**% of Students receiving
financial aid:** 15-17%

NOTE: This data applies to the 2002–2003 school year.

ACADEMIC PROFILE

Number of faculty: 22 Full Time
7 Part Time
Languages and grades offered:
Hebrew (K-6th)
Number of AP classes offered:
Not applicable
Tutors/learning specialists:
Schools three or more graduates have attended over the past five years:
Charles E. Smith Jewish Day School, Georgetown Day School, Lowell, Maret, Sheridan

SPECIAL FEATURES

Dual Judaic/Hebrew and general studies curriculum

ENROLLMENT

Total number of students attending and graduating class size: 145 / 21
Birthday cut-off: December 31
% Diversity: 8-9%
Grades with openings:

SUMMER PROGRAMS

None

ART PROGRAMS

Art, choir, music, drama

SPORTS

Ballet, basketball, gymnastics, karate

LONG-RANGE PLANS

HISTORY AND MISSION STATEMENT

Our mission is to provide our students with a firm foundation in Jewish and secular learning: to lay the groundwork for our children to become knowledgeable, responsible Jews and citizens. We foster in our students a deep respect for themselves and others, an appreciation of diversity, a strong commitment to Jewish living and Jewish values, and a lifelong love of learning.

NOTE: This data applies to the 2002–2003 school year.

KATHERINE THOMAS SCHOOL

Year founded: 1950
9975 Medical Center Drive
Rockville, MD 20850
Head of School:
Judith Zangwill

GENERAL
Grade range: PK-8th   Coed
Religious affiliation: Nonsectarian
Average class size: 10
School day: 9:00-3:30
Morning or after-school care:
8:15-5:30

CAMPUS/CAMPUS LIFE
Facilities:
2 story wing of Treatment and
Learning Center building
Lunch provided: No
Boarding option: No
Bus service: No
School uniform or dress code:
None
Handicapped access available: Yes
Community service requirement:
None

Director of Admission:
Ilana Egner
Phone: 301-738-9691 x164
Fax: 301-424-8063
E-mail:
IEGNER@ttlc.org
Website:
www.ttlc.org

ADMISSIONS
Application deadline: Rolling
Application fee: $50
Application process: Psychological,
educational, speech and language
testing
**Number of students
applied/enrolled:** 80 / 23

COSTS
Tuition: $19,368
Average additional fees: $5,000
Financial aid budget: $85,000
Average grant size: $10,000
**% of Students receiving
financial aid:** 5%

NOTE: This data applies to the 2002–2003 school year.

ACADEMIC PROFILE
Number of faculty: 12 Full Time
2 Part Time
Languages and grades offered:
None
Number of AP classes offered:
Not applicable
Tutors/learning specialists:
Yes: counseling, speech & language,
occupational, physical, auditory services
**Schools three or more graduates have
attended over the past five years:**
public schools, Nora, High Road
Academy, Lab School, Accotink
Achievement Center, Phillips SCE

SPECIAL FEATURES
Special needs program for moderate
to severe learning disabilities

ENROLLMENT
**Total number of students
attending and graduating
class size:** 100 / 12
Birthday cut-off: December 31
% Diversity: 37%
Grades with openings: All

SUMMER PROGRAMS
Yes: 7 week special needs program

ART PROGRAMS
Art, drama, music

SPORTS
None

LONG-RANGE PLANS
Develop extracurricular after-school
program, increase arts, sports,
technology programs

HISTORY AND MISSION STATEMENT
Founded to provide special education program for students with language-based
learning disabilities.

NOTE: This data applies to the 2002–2003 school year.

KINGSBURY DAY SCHOOL (THE)

Year founded: 1984
5000 14th Street, NW
Washington, DC 20011
Head of School:
Marlene S. Gustafson

GENERAL
Grade range: K-8th (ungraded)   Coed
Religious affiliation: Nonsectarian
Average class size: 8-10 with 2 teachers
School day: 8:15-3:00
Morning or after-school care:
3:00-6:00

CAMPUS/CAMPUS LIFE
Facilities:
Urban setting
Lunch provided: No
Boarding option: No
Bus service: No
School uniform or dress code:
None
Handicapped access available: Yes
Community service requirement:
None

Director of Admission:
Karen Soltes & Alex McCarthy
Phone: 202-722-5555
Fax: 202-667-2290
E-mail:
center@kingsbury.org
Website:
www.kingsbury.org

ADMISSIONS
Application deadline: February 1
Application fee: $50
Application process: Psycho-educational or neuropsychological evaluation, psychological, speech and language, or occupational evaluations (if applicable), school visit, parent interview, teacher recommendation, application
Number of students applied/enrolled: 75 / 37

COSTS
Tuition: $21,200
Average additional fees: $500
Financial aid budget: $20,000
Average grant size: $5,000
% of Students receiving financial aid: Most students funded through public school system

NOTE: This data applies to the 2002–2003 school year.

ACADEMIC PROFILE

Number of faculty: 34 Full Time
5 Part Time
Languages and grades offered:
None
Number of AP classes offered:
Not applicable
Tutors/learning specialists:
Yes: speech & language, learning
differences, occupational therapy,
psychologist
**Schools three or more graduates have
attended over the past five years:**
Capitol Hill Day School, Chelsea, Field,
Holy Trinity, Lab, Lowell, Maret,
McLean, Owl, Parkmont, Thornton
Friends, Washington Episcopal

SPECIAL FEATURES

After school enrichment program,
in-school clubs: community service,
sign language, crafts, sports,
pastry making

ENROLLMENT

**Total number of students
attending and graduating
class size:** 151 / 8
Birthday cut-off: December 1
% Diversity: 50%
Grades with openings: PK (12),
plus spaces at all levels

SUMMER PROGRAMS

Yes: academic classes,
summer camp

ART PROGRAMS

Art, drama, music

SPORTS

Physical education

LONG-RANGE PLANS

Expand to an Upper School in
September 2002, develop
sports progam

HISTORY AND MISSION STATEMENT

The Kingsbury Day School is an independent school which is part of The Kingsbury Center. The School is dedicated to serving children with learning disabilities and their families. Our goal is to provide educational intervention for children ages 5-15. We teach academic skills and concepts, facilitate self-esteem, social and emotional growth. Teachers and specialists work together to provide an integrated program for children and foster staff development.

NOTE: This data applies to the 2002–2003 school year.

LAB SCHOOL OF WASHINGTON (THF)

Year founded: 1967
4759 Reservoir Road, NW
Washington, DC 20007
Head of School:
Sally L. Smith

Director of Admission:
Susan Feeley
Phone: 202-965-6600
Fax: 202-944-3088
E-mail:

GENERAL
Grade range: K-12th   Coed
Religious affiliation: Nonsectarian
Average class size: 6-8
School day: 8:30-3:25
Morning or after-school care:
8:00-5:30

Website:
www.labschool.org

ADMISSIONS
Application deadline: February 1
Application fee: $100
Application process: WISC III,
Woodcock-Johnson Revised

CAMPUS/CAMPUS LIFE
Facilities:
New gym, Olympic size swimming
pool, performing arts center;
new campus in Baltimore, MD
Lunch provided: No
Boarding option: No
Bus service: No
School uniform or dress code:
Dress code: 7th-12th
Handicapped access available: Yes
Community service requirement:
Yes: 100 hours in Upper School

Number of students
applied/enrolled: 400+ / 48

COSTS
Tuition: $19,525 (K-6th), $20,225
(7th-8th), $21,120 (9th-12th)
Average additional fees: Dependent
upon number of related services
Financial aid budget: Most students
funded through public school system
Average grant size:
% of Students receiving
financial aid:

NOTE: This data applies to the 2002–2003 school year.

ACADEMIC PROFILE
Number of faculty: 102
Languages and grades offered:
Spanish (11th-12th)
Number of AP classes offered:
None
Tutors/learning specialists:
Yes: psychologist, speech & language, occupational therapists, social workers
Schools three or more graduates have attended over the past five years:
American, Bard, Brown, Emory, James Madison, Oberlin, Rhode Island School of Design, Syracuse, Smith, Drexel, University of Colorado, University of Virginia

SPECIAL FEATURES
College and career counseling

ENROLLMENT
Total number of students attending and graduating class size: 310 / 35
Birthday cut-off:
% Diversity: 30%
Grades with openings:

SUMMER PROGRAMS
Yes: 6 week academic, remedial arts-based program, Shakespeare Summer Theater (7th-12th)

ART PROGRAMS
The arts employed at the Lab School enhance the process of neural maturation, increase attention, and build organizational skills and competencies leading to scholarly pursuits and a strong sense of self-worth.

SPORTS
Basketball, soccer, softball, swimming & diving, track & field

LONG-RANGE PLANS
Third campus

HISTORY AND MISSION STATEMENT
The Lab School of Washington is a special education program for students of at least average intelligence with specific learning disabilities. It is an arts-based program which teaches in a multi-sensory manner.

NOTE: This data applies to the 2002–2003 school year.

LANDON SCHOOL

Year founded: 1929
6101 Wilson Lane
Bethesda, MD 20817
Head of School:
Damon F. Bradley

GENERAL
Grade range: 3rd-12th   Boys
Religious affiliation: Nonsectarian
Average class size: 15
School day: 8:10-3:40 (3rd-8th),
8:10-4:30 (9th-12th)
Morning or after-school care:
4:00-6:00 (3rd-8th)

CAMPUS/CAMPUS LIFE
Facilities:
75 acre Bethesda campus, Lower
School, Middle and Upper School
buildings, Banfield Academic Center,
Barton Alumni Sports Center, Mondzac
Performing Arts Center
Lunch provided: Yes
Boarding option: No
Bus service: Limited
School uniform or dress code:
Dress code: 3rd-5th - button-down
shirt, khakis, leather shoes; 6th-12th -
jacket and tie
Handicapped access available: Yes
Community service requirement:
No requirement, but active
participation

Director of Admission:
Russell L. Gagarin
Phone: 301-320-3200
Fax: 301-320-1133
E-mail:
russ_gagarin@landon.net
Website:
www.landon.net

ADMISSIONS
Application deadline: February 1
Application fee: $50
Application process: Internal
assessment (3rd-4th) using ERB
CTP III and our own tests given in
early January, ISEE (5th-12th)
**Number of students
applied/enrolled:** 450 / 112

COSTS
Tuition: $18,600 (3rd-5th),
$20,200 (6th-12th)
Average additional fees: $600
Financial aid budget: $1,600,000
Average grant size: $11,000
**% of Students receiving
financial aid:** 16%

NOTE: This data applies to the 2002–2003 school year.

ACADEMIC PROFILE

Number of faculty: 104 Full Time
1 Part Time
Languages and grades offered:
Chinese, French, Latin, Spanish
(5th-12th)
Number of AP classes offered: 16
Tutors/learning specialists:
None
Schools three or more graduates have attended over the past five years:
Amherst, Duke, Harvard, Princeton,
University of Pennsylvania, University
of Virginia, Vanderbilt

SPECIAL FEATURES

Only all-boys, non-denominational day
school between Baltimore & Richmond,
Upper School cross-registered classes
with Holton-Arms.

ENROLLMENT

Total number of students attending and graduating class size: 660 / 75
Birthday cut-off: Generally
8 years old when entering 3rd grade
% Diversity: 23%
Grades with openings: 3rd (30),
4th (15), 5th (attrition), 6th (15),
7th (15), 8th (attrition), 9th (15),
10th (attrition)

SUMMER PROGRAMS

Yes: coed preschool, academic,
art, athletic, and music day camps

ART PROGRAMS

Art, chorus, concert band, drama,
handbells, jazz band, music,
painting, photography, sculpture,
string orchestra; drama production
in cooperation with Holton-Arms

SPORTS

Baseball, basketball, cross-country,
football, golf, ice hockey, lacrosse,
soccer, swimming & diving, tennis,
track & field, wrestling

LONG-RANGE PLANS

Addition to Lower School

HISTORY AND MISSION STATEMENT

Landon School prepares talented boys for productive lives as accomplished,
responsible, and caring men whose actions are guided by the principles of perse-
verance, teamwork, honor, and fair play.

NOTE: This data applies to the 2002–2003 school year.

LANGLEY SCHOOL (THE)

Year founded: 1942
1411 Balls Hill Road
McLean, VA 22101
Head of School:
Doris Cottam

GENERAL
Grade range: N-8th   Coed
Religious affiliation: Nonsectarian
Average class size: 4-15
School day: 8:00-3:00 (K-8th),
8:00-11:00 or 12:00-3:00 (N-PK)
Morning or after-school care:
3:00-6:00

CAMPUS/CAMPUS LIFE
Facilities:
Primary, Lower, and Upper School
buildings, new athletic center, gym,
library, media center with TV
production facilities, new resource
center, science labs
Lunch provided: No
Boarding option: No
Bus service: Yes
School uniform or dress code:
Dress code
Handicapped access available: Yes
Community service requirement:
Yes: all grade levels participate in age
appropriate ways

Director of Admission:
Holly Hartge
Phone: 703-356-1920 x882
Fax: 703-790-9712
E-mail:
hhartge@langley.edu.net
Website:
www.langley.edu.net

ADMISSIONS
Application deadline: January 15
Application fee: $60
Application process: Parent tour and
interview, recommendation,
transcript (1st-8th), Detroit (PK*),
WPPSI-R (K-1st), WISC III
(2nd-5th), SSAT or ISEE (6th-8th),
applicant visit (*Subject to change)
**Number of students
applied/enrolled:** 350 / 74

COSTS
Tuition: $9,646 (N-PK),
$16,281 (K-5th), $16,932
(6th-8th)
Average additional fees: $250
Financial aid budget: $500,000
Average grant size: $8,500
**% of Students receiving
financial aid:** 7%

NOTE: This data applies to the 2002–2003 school year.

ACADEMIC PROFILE

Number of faculty: 56 Full Time
14 Part Time

Languages and grades offered:
French, Spanish (K-8th)

Number of AP classes offered:
Not applicable

Tutors/learning specialists:
Yes: reading

Schools three or more graduates have attended over the past five years:
Flint Hill, Georgetown Day, Georgetown Prep, Gonzaga, Langley High, Madeira, Maret, National Cathedral, St. Albans, Thomas Jefferson

SPECIAL FEATURES

Media center with full video and cable TV capacity, science with lab 1st-8th, algebra and geometry 7th-8th

ENROLLMENT

Total number of students attending and graduating class size: 475 / 47

Birthday cut-off: September 30

% Diversity: 20%

Grades with openings: N (18), PK (10-12), K (4), 6th (2-6), 7th (1-4), 8th (1-2)

SUMMER PROGRAMS

Yes: Langley Summer Studio, academics, arts, humanities, preschool camp

ART PROGRAMS

band (4th-8th), ceramics, drawing, graphic design, mixed media, music appreciation, photography

SPORTS

Basketball, lacrosse, soccer, track

LONG-RANGE PLANS

Build fine arts center

HISTORY AND MISSION STATEMENT

The Langley School is committed to the pursuit of excellence offering a challenging and enriching curriculum geared towards attracting students with promise and potential from diverse backgrounds throughout the greater Washington area who demonstrate the ability and readiness to participate and progress within Langley's curriculum. Emphasis is placed on educating the whole child in a comprehensive, well-rounded program that helps each child reach his/her full potential in a nurturing and stimulating environment where learning is enjoyed and sharing is commonplace. Students leave Langley feeling good about themselves and on their way to becoming contributing members of their adult communities.

NOTE: This data applies to the 2002–2003 school year.

LOUDOUN COUNTRY DAY SCHOOL

Year founded: 1953
237 Fairview Street, NW
Leesburg, VA 20176
Head of School:
E. Randall Hollister

GENERAL
Grade range: PK-8th   Coed
Religious affiliation: Nonsectarian
Average class size: 16
School day: 8:30-3:20
Morning or after-school care:
7:00-6:00

CAMPUS/CAMPUS LIFE
Facilities: 4 main buildings, 1 home
with offices, 2 temporary classroom
buildings
Lunch provided: No
Boarding option: No
Bus service: Yes
School uniform or dress code:
Uniform: Land's End
Handicapped access available: Yes
Community service requirement:
Yes

Director of Admission:
Pam Larimer
Phone: 703-777-3841
Fax: 703-771-1346
E-mail:
lcdsinfo@aol.com
Website:
www.lcds.org

ADMISSIONS
Application deadline: March 1
Application fee: $60
Application process: Informal
assessment, developmental
screening, speech and language
evaluation, WISC III, school
visit, transcript
**Number of students
applied/enrolled:** 260 / 60

COSTS
Tuition: $7,300 (PK), $11,000
(K-5th), $11,400 (6th-8th)
Average additional fees:
Financial aid budget:
Average grant size:
**% of Students receiving
financial aid:**

NOTE: This data applies to the 2002–2003 school year.

ACADEMIC PROFILE
Number of faculty: 48 Full Time
6 Part Time
Languages and grades offered:
French (PK-8th), Spanish (6th-8th)
Number of AP classes offered:
Not applicable
Tutors/learning specialists:
Yes: speech pathology, occupational
therapy
Schools three or more graduates have attended over the past five years:
Foxcroft, Georgetown Prep, Hill,
Madeira, Notre Dame,
Thomas Jefferson, Wakefield

SPECIAL FEATURES
Library science, music and movement
program, technology

ENROLLMENT
Total number of students attending and graduating class size: 260 / 20
Birthday cut-off: September 1
% Diversity:
Grades with openings: PK (24),
plus attrition

SUMMER PROGRAMS
Yes: French, lacrosse, summer
camps

ART PROGRAMS
Chorus, instruments, music,
visual arts

SPORTS
Basketball, cross-country, field
hockey, flag football, lacrosse,
soccer, swimming, track & field

LONG-RANGE PLANS
Move to new campus in 2004,
expand to high school

HISTORY AND MISSION STATEMENT

NOTE: This data applies to the 2002–2003 school year.

LOWELL SCHOOL

Year founded: 1965
1640 Kalmia Road, NW
Washington, DC 20012
Head of School:
Abigail Wiebenson

GENERAL
Grade range: N-6th   Coed
Religious affiliation: Nonsectarian
Average class size: 15
School day: 8:15-3:15, 8:15-12:15 F
Morning or after-school care:
After school until 6:00 PM

CAMPUS/CAMPUS LIFE
Facilities: 8 acre campus with stream,
art workshop, computer lab, indoor
pool, library, 3 playgrounds
Lunch provided: No
Boarding option: No
Bus service: No
School uniform or dress code:
None
Handicapped access available: Yes
Community service requirement:
None

Director of Admission:
Michelle Belton
Phone: 202-577-2000
Fax: 202-577-2001
E-mail:
mbelton@lowellschool.org
Website:
www.lowellschool.org

ADMISSIONS
Application deadline: February 7
Application fee: $60
Application process: Tour, applicant
visit, informal assessment
(PK-2nd), WISC III (3rd-6th)
Number of students
applied/enrolled: 218 / 58

COSTS
Tuition: $9,575 (PK half day),
$15,150 (PK full day), $15,990
(K-6th)
Average additional fees: $550
Financial aid budget: $453,790
Average grant size: $8,169
% of Students receiving
financial aid: 18%

NOTE: This data applies to the 2002–2003 school year.

ACADEMIC PROFILE

Number of faculty: 51 Full Time
9 Part Time
Languages and grades offered:
Spanish (1st-6th)
Number of AP classes offered:
Not applicable
Tutors/learning specialists: None
Schools three or more graduates have attended over the past five years:
Edmund Burke, Field, Georgetown Day, Holton-Arms, Maret, St. Albans, Sidwell Friends

SPECIAL FEATURES

ENROLLMENT

Total number of students attending and graduating class size: 310 / 18
Birthday cut-off: September 30
% Diversity: 22%
Grades with openings:

SUMMER PROGRAMS

Yes: nonacademic day camp, swimming

ART PROGRAMS

Art workshop, creative movement, music

SPORTS

Physical education

LONG-RANGE PLANS

HISTORY AND MISSION STATEMENT

Learning at Lowell encourages adventurous and disciplined thinking, develops social and intellectual competence, teaches global and environmental responsibility, and values an optimistic zest for life. With a broad range of families, Lowell seeks, respects, and honors differences and individuality.

NOTE: This data applies to the 2002–2003 school year.

MADEIRA SCHOOL (THE)

Year founded: 1906
8328 Georgetown Pike
McLean, VA 22102
Head of School:
Elisabeth Griffith, PhD.

GENERAL
Grade range: 9th-12th   Girls
Religious affiliation: Nonsectarian
Average class size: 13
School day: 7:50-3:30
Morning or after-school care:
No

CAMPUS/CAMPUS LIFE
Facilities: 400 acre Potomac riverfront
campus, extensive arts facilities, indoor
pool, stables, theater
Lunch provided: Yes
Boarding option: Yes / 163
Bus service: No
School uniform or dress code:
Dress code: neat and clean
Handicapped access available: Yes
Community service requirement:
Yes: 10th grade co-curriculum

Director of Admission:
Cheryl Plummer
Phone: 703-556-8273
Fax: 703-821-2845
E-mail:
admissions@madeira.org
Website:
www.madeira.org

ADMISSIONS
Application deadline: January 31
Application fee: $50
Application process: Application,
applicant and parent written
statements, English, math,
counselor/head of school
recommendations, transcript,
current grades, SSAT or PSAT
(9th-12th), TOFL (for international
students), interview
**Number of students
applied/enrolled:** 375 / 84

COSTS
Tuition: $20,500 day,
$31,000 boarding
Average additional fees: $1,000
Financial aid budget: $1,123,125
Average grant size: $16,000
**% of Students receiving
financial aid:** 21%

NOTE: This data applies to the 2002–2003 school year.

ACADEMIC PROFILE
Number of faculty: 39 Full Time
14 Part Time
Languages and grades offered:
French, Latin, Spanish (9th-12th)
Number of AP classes offered:
17
Tutors/learning specialists:
Yes
Schools three or more graduates have attended over the past five years:
Boston College, Boston University, Brown, Cornell, Georgetown, Harvard, Princeton, University of Pennsylvania, University of Virginia, William & Mary

SPECIAL FEATURES
Co-curriculum Experiential Learning Program. ⅕ of academic program is dedicated to work opportunities of the DC metro area, internships

ENROLLMENT
Total number of students attending and graduating
class size: 308 / 81
Birthday cut-off: Not applicable
% Diversity: 30%
Grades with openings: 9th (70-75), 10th (10-15), 11th (2-5), 12th (0)

SUMMER PROGRAMS

ART PROGRAMS
Ceramics, chorus, computer graphic design, drama, drawing, orchestra, painting, photography, printmaking, sculpture

SPORTS
Basketball, cross-country, diving, equestrian sports, field hockey, lacrosse, soccer, softball, squash, swimming, tennis, volleyball

LONG-RANGE PLANS
Madeira will celebrate its centennial in 2006 with building projects and increased endowment

HISTORY AND MISSION STATEMENT

The Madeira School believes in the lasting value of single-sex education for girls. Young women expect more of themselves and learn to take pride in their individual effort when their community focuses solely on them and on their success. In this natural setting of woods and fields above the Potomac River, boarders and day students from ninth to twelfth grades prepare to take their place in the wider world. The Madeira education occurs in three arenas simultaneously: the classroom, the workplace, and the international community of the campus.

NOTE: This data applies to the 2002–2003 school year.

MARET SCHOOL

Year founded: 1911
3000 Cathedral Avenue, NW
Washington, DC 20008
Head of School:
Marjo Talbott

GENERAL
Grade range: K-12th   Coed
Religious affiliation: Nonsectarian
Average class size: 12-15
School day: 8:15-3:10, 8:15-1:30 W
Morning or after-school care:
3:00-6:00

CAMPUS/CAMPUS LIFE
Facilities: 7½ acres, 6 buildings,
auditorium, 3 computer labs,
2 gyms, kindergarten cottage,
movement studio, weight room
Lunch provided: Yes
Boarding option: No
Bus service: No
School uniform or dress code:
None
Handicapped access available: Yes
Community service requirement:
Yes: 30 hours (9th-12th)

Director of Admission:
Annie Farquhar
Phone: 202-939-8814
Fax: 202-939-8884
E-mail:
admissions@maret.org
Website:
www.maret.org

ADMISSIONS
Application deadline:
December 30 (4th),
January 10 (all other grades)
Application fee: $50
Application process: WPPSI-R
(K-1st), WISC III (2nd-5th), SSAT,
ISEE (6-10th), PSAT (11th)
**Number of students
applied/enrolled:** 928 / 85

COSTS
Tuition: $16,725 (K), $17,240
(1st-4th), $18,695 (5th-8th),
$19,850 (9th-12th)
Average additional fees: $500
Financial aid budget: $1,254,504
Average grant size: $13,376
**% of Students receiving
financial aid:** 15%

NOTE: This data applies to the 2002–2003 school year.

ACADEMIC PROFILE
Number of faculty: 86 Full Time
6 Part Time
Languages and grades offered:
French (K-12th), Latin (5th-12th),
Spanish (1st-12th)
Number of AP classes offered: 15
Tutors/learning specialists:
Yes: learning skills specialist, tutors
Schools three or more graduates have attended over the past five years:
Bowdoin, Brown, Colgate, Columbia,
Davidson, Emory, Harvard, Kenyon,
Princeton, Tulane, University of
Pennsylvania, University of Wisconsin,
Vanderbilt, Yale

SPECIAL FEATURES
Intensive study week, senior projects,
independent studies

ENROLLMENT
Total number of students attending and graduating class size: 600 / 73
Birthday cut-off: October 1 (K-4th)
% Diversity: 23%
Grades with openings: K (18-20),
1st (6-8), 4th (4-6), 7th (20-25),
9th (10-15), 10th (2-3), 11th (1-2)

SUMMER PROGRAMS
Yes: academic courses, athletic
clinics (2nd-12th), language
immersion camp, travel programs

ART PROGRAMS
Studio-focused art, drama, music,
integration of computer technology
and music compostition, advanced
and independent study

SPORTS
Aerobics, baseball, basketball,
cross-country, dance, football, golf,
kickboxing, lacrosse, martial arts,
pilates, soccer, softball, tennis,
track & field, ultimate frisbee,
volleyball, weight training, wrestling

LONG-RANGE PLANS
Renovate Lower School building

HISTORY AND MISSION STATEMENT
Maret School joins with parents to galvanize the intellectual and creative capabilities of each student, to equip each to excel in future academic endeavors, and to instill in each the self-reliance and moral awareness to identify and work through life's challenges. Maret prepares our students to be healthy, responsible, and informed adults who will play an active role in improving the world they will inherit.

NOTE: This data applies to the 2002–2003 school year.

MATER DEI SCHOOL

Year founded: 1960
9600 Seven Locks Road
Bethesda, MD 20817
Head of School:
Edward N. Williams

GENERAL

Grade range: 1st-8th   Boys
Religious affiliation: Catholic
Average class size: 20
School day:
Morning or after-school care:
No

CAMPUS/CAMPUS LIFE

Facilities: 20 acre newly renovated
campus with art room, chapel, 2 gyms,
music room, library, science lab
Lunch provided:
Boarding option: No
Bus service: No
School uniform or dress code:
Uniform
Handicapped access available: Yes
Community service requirement:
Yes

Director of Admission:
Edward N. Williams
Phone: 301-365-2700
Fax: 301-365-2710
E-mail:
nwilliams@materdeischool.net
Website:

ADMISSIONS

Application deadline: December 15
Application fee: $50
Application process:
Informal assessment
**Number of students
applied/enrolled:** 60 / 20

COSTS

Tuition: $8,700
Average additional fees: $400
Financial aid budget:
Average grant size:
**% of Students receiving
financial aid:**

NOTE: This data applies to the 2002–2003 school year.

ACADEMIC PROFILE

Number of faculty:

Languages and grades offered:
Spanish (after school), Latin (8th)

Number of AP classes offered:
Not applicable

Tutors/learning specialists:
Yes: phonics, reading specialists

Schools three or more graduates have attended over the past five years:
Georgetown Prep, Gonzaga, Landon, St. Albans

SPECIAL FEATURES
Fall outdoor week (5th-8th), spring DC week (5th-8th)

ENROLLMENT

Total number of students attending and graduating class size: 225 /

Birthday cut-off:

% Diversity: 9%

Grades with openings: 1st (20), 6th (20)

SUMMER PROGRAMS
Yes: lacrosse, summer camps

ART PROGRAMS
Art, music

SPORTS
Baseball, basketball, football, lacrosse, soccer, wrestling

LONG-RANGE PLANS

HISTORY AND MISSION STATEMENT

NOTE: This data applies to the 2002–2003 school year.

MCLEAN SCHOOL OF MARYLAND

Year founded: 1954
8224 Lochinver Lane
Potomac, MD 20854
Head of School:
Darlene B. Pierro

GENERAL
Grade range: K-12th   Coed
Religious affiliation: Nonsectarian
Average class size: 15
School day: 8:15-3:00
Morning or after-school care:
No

CAMPUS/CAMPUS LIFE
Facilities: Newly renovated building
and addition
Lunch provided: Yes: optional
Boarding option: No
Bus service: Yes
School uniform or dress code:
Uniform: boys - khakis, navy blue/white
collared shirt; girls - school plaid
skirt/jumper or khakis.
Handicapped access available: Yes
Community service requirement:
No: opportunities available

Director of Admission:
Catherine A. Biern
Phone: 301-299-8277
Fax: 301-299-8638
E-mail:
admission@mcleanschool.org
Website:
www.mcleanschool.org

ADMISSIONS
Application deadline: February 14
Application fee: $100
Application process: WPPSI-R
(K-1st), WISC III (2nd-12th), SSAT
or equivalent (9th-12th),
Woodcock-Johnson III (2nd - 8th),
open house or personal interview,
application, transcript, teacher
recommendations, applicant visit
**Number of students
applied/enrolled:** 400 / 100

COSTS
Tuition: $15,700-$19,900
Average additional fees: $900
Financial aid budget: $540,000
Average grant size: $12,500
**% of Students receiving
financial aid:** 9%

NOTE: This data applies to the 2002–2003 school year.

ACADEMIC PROFILE

Number of faculty: 100 Full Time
9 Part Time
Languages and grades offered:
Latin, Spanish (7th-12th)
Number of AP classes offered:
Not applicable at this time
Tutors/learning specialists:
Yes: learning specialist, 3 school
counselors, speech & language
pathologist; tutors at additional cost
Schools three or more graduates have attended over the past five years:
No graduates yet

SPECIAL FEATURES

Each division has its own science labs,
art, computer, and music rooms

ENROLLMENT

Total number of students attending and graduating class size: 449 /
Birthday cut-off: September
% Diversity: 23%
Grades with openings: K (12-14),
2nd (12-14), 3rd (12-14), 7th (5),
9th (5), plus attrition

SUMMER PROGRAMS

Yes: 3rd-4th

ART PROGRAMS

Extensive

SPORTS

Basketball, cross-country, field
hockey, lacrosse, soccer

LONG-RANGE PLANS

First graduating class 2003

HISTORY AND MISSION STATEMENT

Through all of our growth, it is important to underscore that the core beliefs of this school have not changed. We remain true to our Mission - to recognize and foster the unique learning style of each student, to help each student explore and discover that style, and to develop appropriate teaching methods and programs that respect and encourage individual, cultural, and intellectual diversity. We offer programs designed to provide active participation and learning, supported by small classes, a low student to teacher ratio, and a nurturing environment.

NOTE: This data applies to the 2002–2003 school year.

NATIONAL CATHEDRAL SCHOOL

Year founded: 1900
Mount Saint Alban
Washington, DC 20016
Head of School:
Agnes C. Underwood

GENERAL
Grade range: 4th-12th   Girls
Religious affiliation: Episcopal
Average class size: 15
School day: 8:00-3:15
Morning or after-school care:
3:30-6:00 (4th-8th)

CAMPUS/CAMPUS LIFE
Facilities: 57 acre close of Washington
National Cathedral, 4 interconnected
academic buildings, historic Hearst
Hall with auditorium and dining
room, new athletic and fitness center
Lunch provided: Yes
Boarding option: No
Bus service: Limited: AM metro pick-up
School uniform or dress code:
Uniform: 4th-6th
Handicapped access available: Yes
Community service requirement:
Yes: 60 hours

Director of Admission:
Denise Buchanan
Phone: 202-537-6374
Fax: 202-537-2382
E-mail:
ncs.admission@cathedral.org
Website:
www.ncs.cathedral.org

ADMISSIONS
Application deadline: February 1
Application fee: $60
Application process: School visit
(4th-6th), interview (7th-11th),
English and math teacher
recommendations, WISC III
(4th-6th), SSAT (6th-11th)
or ISEE (5th-11th)
**Number of students
applied/enrolled:** 318 / 91

COSTS
Tuition: $20,225 (4th-12th)
Average additional fees: $225-$475
Financial aid budget: $1,220,000
Average grant size: $13,600
**% of Students receiving
financial aid:** 16%

NOTE: This data applies to the 2002–2003 school year.

ACADEMIC PROFILE

Number of faculty: 69 Full Time
17 Part Time
Languages and grades offered:
Chinese (9th-12th), French (4th-12th),
German (9th-12th), Greek (9th-12th),
Japanese (9th-12th), Latin (7th-12th),
Spanish (4th-12th)
Number of AP classes offered: 16
Tutors/learning specialists:
Yes: study skills department with
diagnostician, individual short-term
tutoring
**Schools three or more graduates have
attended over the past five years:**
Brown, Columbia, Cornell, Duke,
Georgetown, Harvard, Princeton,
Stanford, University of Chicago,
University of Pennsylvania, University
of Virginia, Yale

SPECIAL FEATURES

Coordinant program with St. Albans
School for Boys, girl chorister program
with Washington National Cathedral

ENROLLMENT

**Total number of students
attending and graduating
class size:** 565 / 71
Birthday cut-off: December 30
% Diversity: 28%
Grades with openings: 4th (48:
$\frac{2}{3}$ of spaces reserved for Beauvoir),
7th (14-18), 9th (10-15),
plus attrition

SUMMER PROGRAMS

Yes: math, science, technology

ART PROGRAMS

Extensive offerings in all areas of
studio art, music

SPORTS

Basketball, crew, cross-country, field
hockey, gymnastics, ice hockey,
lacrosse, soccer, softball, swimming
& diving, tae-bo, tennis, track &
field, volleyball

LONG-RANGE PLANS

Redesign and renovate former
athletic space

HISTORY AND MISSION STATEMENT

National Cathedral School is an independent Episcopal day school for girls that
offers a rigorous college-preparatory program for grades 4 through 12. NCS provides an ideal environment for girls to develop integrity, respect, and responsibility. NCS believes that diversity enhances and strengthens the community and seeks
students and faculty from different racial, religious, cultural, and economic backgrounds. Some classes and activities are coordinated with boys from St. Albans.

NOTE: This data applies to the 2002–2003 school year.

NATIONAL PRESBYTERIAN SCHOOL

Year founded: 1969
4121 Nebraska Avenue, NW
Washington, DC 20016
Head of School:
Jay R. Roudebush

GENERAL
Grade range: N-6th   Coed
Religious affiliation: Presbyterian
Average class size: 14
School day: 8:30-3:15
Morning or after-school care:
8:00-6:00

CAMPUS/CAMPUS LIFE
Facilities: 12 acre campus, newly
renovated building
Lunch provided: No
Boarding option: No
Bus service: No
School uniform or dress code:
None
Handicapped access available: Yes
Community service requirement:
Yes

Director of Admission:
Stephanie Ball
Phone: 202-537-7504
Fax: 202-537-7568
E-mail:
sball@nps-dc.org
Website:
www.nps-dc.org/school

ADMISSIONS
Application deadline: February 1
Application fee: $50
Application process: Parent
interview and tour, applicant visit,
teacher recommendations,
transcript, Detroit (PK*), WPPSI-R
(K-1st), WISC III (2nd-6th)
(*Subject to change)
**Number of students
applied/enrolled:** 160 / 43

COSTS
Tuition: $7,350-$9,100 (N),
$9,750-$12,500 (PK),
$13,950 (K-6th)
Average additional fees:
$100-$2,000
Financial aid budget: $300,000
Average grant size: $8,795
**% of Students receiving
financial aid:** 13%

NOTE: This data applies to the 2002–2003 school year.

ACADEMIC PROFILE
Number of faculty: 35 Full Time
10 Part Time
Languages and grades offered:
French (PK-6th)
Number of AP classes offered:
Not applicable
Tutors/learning specialists:
Yes: reading, math specialists
Schools three or more graduates have attended over the past five years:
Bullis, Holton-Arms, Landon, Maret, National Cathedral, Potomac, St. Albans, St. Andrew's, Sidwell Friends

SPECIAL FEATURES

ENROLLMENT
Total number of students attending and graduating class size: 244 / 25
Birthday cut-off: Sept 1
% Diversity: 17%
Grades with openings: N (16), PK (16), K-6 (attrition only)

SUMMER PROGRAMS
Yes: camp

ART PROGRAMS
Art, chorus, drama, handbells, music

SPORTS
Basketball, lacrosse, soccer, softball

LONG-RANGE PLANS

HISTORY AND MISSION STATEMENT
NPS is a school for and about children. As one of the few independent schools in the Washington, DC, metropolitan area dedicated exclusively to primary and elementary education, its focus and mission are clear and distinct. NPS is dedicated to the proposition that different children learn in different ways, but that all children benefit from a learning environment that is safe, wholesome, joyful, challenging, and supportive.

NOTE: This data applies to the 2002–2003 school year.

NEW SCHOOL OF NORTHERN VIRGINIA (THE)

Year founded: 1989
9431 Silver King Court
Fairfax, VA 22031
Head of School:
John Potter

GENERAL
Grade range: 3rd-12th   Coed
Religious affiliation: Nonsectarian
Average class size: 9
School day: 9:00-4:00
Morning or after-school care:
4:00-5:30

CAMPUS/CAMPUS LIFE
Facilities: 3 acres, 2 buildings, athletic
fields, basketball & volleyball courts,
wooded play area
Lunch provided: No
Boarding option: No
Bus service: Limited: to Metro
School uniform or dress code:
None
Handicapped access available: Yes
Community service requirement:
Yes: 30 hours a year plus school
work program

Director of Admission:
John Potter / Denise Jones
Phone: 703-691-3040
Fax: 703-691-3041
E-mail:
jpotter@nsnva.pvt.k12.va.us
Website:
www.nsnva.pvt.k12.va.us

ADMISSIONS
Application deadline: March
Application fee: $75
Application process: Interview with
Head, application, recommendations,
school visit
**Number of students
applied/enrolled:** 70 / 35

COSTS
Tuition: $12,600 (3rd-6th),
$14,075 (7th-8th), $15,475
(9th-12th)
Average additional fees: $350
Financial aid budget:
Average grant size: $3,000
**% of Students receiving
financial aid:** 5%

NOTE: This data applies to the 2002–2003 school year.

ACADEMIC PROFILE

Number of faculty: 25 Full Time

Languages and grades offered:
French, German, Spanish (7th-12th)

Number of AP classes offered: 7

Tutors/learning specialists:
Yes: at an additional fee

Schools three or more graduates have attended over the past five years:
Bryn Mawr, Colorado College, Hampshire, Marlboro, Mary Washington, Maryland Institute of Art, New York University, Rochester Institute of Technology, University of Virginia, Virginia Technology

SPECIAL FEATURES

Only school in area belonging to Coalition of Essential Schools, Socratic seminars, exhibitions, several domestic & overseas travel courses, school actively employs Howard Gardner's multiple intelligence theory in all classes

ENROLLMENT

Total number of students attending and graduating class size: 130 / 17

Birthday cut-off: Not applicable

% Diversity: 30%

Grades with openings: 3rd (6), 4th-6th (2 each), 7th (6), 8th (5), 9th (7), plus attrition

SUMMER PROGRAMS

Yes: academics, computer camps

ART PROGRAMS

Drama, fine arts, music

SPORTS

Basketball, soccer, swimming, volleyball

LONG-RANGE PLANS

Purchase campus, expand buildings, add interscholastic sports, senior independent exhibition

HISTORY AND MISSION STATEMENT

Our central academic goal is to prepare students to enter college as self-motivated and accomplished thinkers, writers, collaborators and communicators.

NOTE: This data applies to the 2002–2003 school year.

NEWPORT SCHOOL

Year founded: 1930
10914 Georgia Avenue
Silver Spring, MD 20902
Head of School:
Ronald W. Stephens

GENERAL
Grade range: N-12th   Coed
Religious affiliation: Nonsectarian
Average class size: 13
School day: 8:30-3:30
Morning or after-school care:
7:00-6:00

CAMPUS/CAMPUS LIFE
Facilities:
Lunch provided: Yes
Boarding option: No
Bus service: No
School uniform or dress code:
Uniform: 1st-8th, variation 9th-12th
Handicapped access available: No
Community service requirement:
None

Director of Admission:
Marilyn Grossblatt
Phone: 301-942-4550
Fax: 301-949-2654
E-mail:

Website:

ADMISSIONS
Application deadline: Rolling
Application fee: $50
Application process:
Informal assessment
Number of students
applied/enrolled:

COSTS
Tuition: $8,500–$10,600 (N-PK)
$12,700 (K), $13,300–$13,800
(1st-4th), $14,400 (5th-6th),
$15,300 (7th-8th),
$16,700 (9th-12th)
Average additional fees: None
Financial aid budget:
Average grant size:
% of Students receiving
financial aid:

NOTE: This data applies to the 2002–2003 school year.

ACADEMIC PROFILE
Number of faculty: 25
Languages and grades offered:
French (7th-12th), Spanish (N-12th)
Number of AP classes offered: 5
Tutors/learning specialists: None
Schools three or more graduates have attended over the past five years:
Elon, High Point, University of Maryland

SPECIAL FEATURES
Strong academics with individual attention, can accomodate some learning differences

ENROLLMENT
Total number of students attending and graduating class size: 105 / 5
Birthday cut-off: December 31
% Diversity:
Grades with openings: Most

SUMMER PROGRAMS
N-3rd

ART PROGRAMS
Drama, music, visual arts

SPORTS
No inter-scholastic

LONG-RANGE PLANS

HISTORY AND MISSION STATEMENT
Our mission is to provide a learning environment that challenges students to reach their maximum development as rapidly as their talents permit. Combining a rigorous curriculum with highest educational standards, Newport is committed to graduating well-rounded, responsible young students.

NOTE: This data applies to the 2002–2003 school year.

NORA SCHOOL (THE)

Year founded: 1964
955 Sligo Avenue
Silver Spring, MD 20910
Head of School:
David Mullen

GENERAL
Grade range: 9th-12th   Coed
Religious affiliation: Nonsectarian
Average class size: 10
School day: 8:45-2:35
Morning or after-school care:
No

CAMPUS/CAMPUS LIFE
Facilities: New facility with art studio, computer and science labs
Lunch provided: No
Boarding option: No
Bus service: No
School uniform or dress code:
None
Handicapped access available: Yes
Community service requirement:
Yes: one day per month

Director of Admission:
Elaine Mack
Phone: 301-495-6672
Fax: 301-495-7829
E-mail:
elaine@nora-school.org
Website:
www.nora-school.org

ADMISSIONS
Application deadline: Rolling
Application fee: $50
Application process: Application, transcript, references, parent and applicant interview
Number of students
applied/enrolled: 57 / 25

COSTS
Tuition: $15,365
Average additional fees: $600
Financial aid budget: $72,000
Average grant size: $7,500
% of Students receiving
financial aid: 30%

NOTE: This data applies to the 2002–2003 school year.

ACADEMIC PROFILE
Number of faculty: 11 Full Time
3 Part Time
Languages and grades offered:
Spanish (9th-12th)
Number of AP classes offered:
Tutors/learning specialists:
Yes: learning disabilities specialists
contracted through Kingsbury Center
Schools three or more graduates have
attended over the past five years:
Boston University, Dickinson,
Goucher, Guilford, Hofstra,
New York University, Syracuse,
University of Maryland, Wittenberg

SPECIAL FEATURES
Overnight camping, day hikes,
rafting trips, ropes courses, ski trips,
foreign travel

ENROLLMENT
Total number of students
attending and graduating
class size: 62 / 17
Birthday cut-off: Not applicable
% Diversity: 34%
Grades with openings: 9th (12),
10th (3), 11th (2)

SUMMER PROGRAMS
None

ART PROGRAMS
Art, crafts, drama, music,
photography

SPORTS
Basketball, soccer, softball

LONG-RANGE PLANS

HISTORY AND MISSION STATEMENT

The Nora School continues the tradition of the Washington Ethical High School as a college preparatory school where small classes and individual attention help students work up to their potential. Our mission is to help students who struggle in traditional environments.

NOTE: This data applies to the 2002–2003 school year.

NORWOOD SCHOOL

Year founded: 1952
8821 River Road
Bethesda, MD 20817
Head of School:
Richard T. Ewing, Jr.

GENERAL
Grade range: K-8th   Coed
Religious affiliation: Nonsectarian
Average class size: 12
School day: 8:10-2:30 or 3:30
or 4:10 (M-Th), 8:10-12:30 or
2:30 or 3:30 (F)
Morning or after-school care:
3:30-5:50

CAMPUS/CAMPUS LIFE
Facilities: Newly renovated 40 acre
campus, art and music studios, athletic
fields, 3 gyms, science labs
Lunch provided: Yes: Middle School
Boarding option: No
Bus service: No
School uniform or dress code:
Dress code: appropriate
Handicapped access available: Yes
Community service requirement:
Yes

Director of Admission:
Reneé Johnson
Phone: 301-365-2595
Fax: 301-365-9693
E-mail:

Website:
www.norwoodschool.org

ADMISSIONS
Application deadline: January 17
Application fee: $50
Application process: WPPSI-R (K),
WISC III (1st-5th), SSAT or ISEE
(6th-8th), (ERB 5th-8th), parent
tour, applicant visit, transcript
Number of students
applied/enrolled: 329 / 83

COSTS
Tuition: $15,640 (K-2nd),
$16,180 (3rd-4th), $16,240
(5th-6th), $16,740 (7th-8th)
Average additional fees:
$550-$1,700
Financial aid budget:
Average grant size:
% of Students receiving
financial aid:

NOTE: This data applies to the 2002–2003 school year.

ACADEMIC PROFILE

Number of faculty: 80

Languages and grades offered:
French (2nd-8th), Latin (7th-8th),
Spanish (2nd-8th)

Number of AP classes offered:
Not applicable

Tutors/learning specialists:
Yes: reading, math, psychologist

Schools three or more graduates have attended over the past five years:
Bullis, Georgetown Prep, Holton-Arms,
Landon, Madeira, National Cathedral,
Potomac, St. Albans, St. Andrew's,
Sidwell Friends

SPECIAL FEATURES

ENROLLMENT

Total number of students attending and graduating class size: 505 / 54

Birthday cut-off: None

% Diversity: 19%

Grades with openings: K (54),
plus attrition

SUMMER PROGRAMS
Yes: Summer at Norwood

ART PROGRAMS
Art, dance, drama, music

SPORTS
Baseball, basketball, field hockey,
fitness, lacrosse, outdoor education,
soccer, softball, track & field

LONG-RANGE PLANS

HISTORY AND MISSION STATEMENT

"The School's mission is to assure that each of its children grows intellectually, morally, physically and socially. The School provides outstanding instruction in fundamental skills and logical and analytical thinking, while encouraging independence of mind, intellectual curiosity, moral growth, and creative self-expression." Norwood's curriculum and pedagogy are specifically aimed toward the realization of these goals. The School seeks to graduate confident, independent learners who are well prepared for the challenges that await them.

NOTE: This data applies to the 2002–2003 school year.

NYSMITH SCHOOL FOR THE GIFTED

Year founded: 1983
13625 EDS Drive
Herndon, VA 20171
Head of School:
Carole Nysmith

GENERAL
Grade range: PK-8th   Coed
Religious affiliation: Nonsectarian
Average class size: 18
School day: 8:30-3:00
Morning or after-school care:
6:30-6:30

CAMPUS/CAMPUS LIFE
Facilities: New spacious, state-of-the-art facility
Lunch provided: Yes
Boarding option: No
Bus service: Yes
School uniform or dress code:
Dress code: no jeans or sweats, plain shirts with collar, plain dresses or jumpers
Handicapped access available: Yes
Community service requirement:
Yes: monthly community projects

Director of Admission:
Jody Amberly
Phone: 703-713-3332
Fax: 703-713-3336
E-mail:
knysmith@nysmith.com
Website:
www.nysmith.com

ADMISSIONS
Application deadline: Rolling
Application fee: $250
Application process: WISC III, Otis Lennon, teacher recommendations, 2-day applicant visit, parent tour
Number of students applied/enrolled:

COSTS
Tuition: $11,420 (PK), $15,700 (K-3rd), $17,730 (4th-8th)
Average additional fees: $100
Financial aid budget:
Average grant size: Varies
% of Students receiving financial aid:

NOTE: This data applies to the 2002–2003 school year.

ACADEMIC PROFILE
Number of faculty: 78 Full Time
27 Part Time
Languages and grades offered:
French (PK-8th), Latin (6th)
Number of AP classes offered:
Not applicable
Tutors/learning specialists:
None
Schools three or more graduates have attended over the past five years:
Episcopal High, Flint Hill, Madeira, Maret, Paul VI, Potomac, St. Anslem's, St. Stephen's & St. Agnes, Thomas Jefferson

SPECIAL FEATURES
In classes with peers, students work up to five grade levels ahead, innovative technology, K-8th change classes for different subjects

ENROLLMENT
Total number of students attending and graduating class size: 625 / 40
Birthday cut-off: September 30
% Diversity:
Grades with openings: PK (68), plus attrition

SUMMER PROGRAMS
Yes: academic programs, day camp, swimming

ART PROGRAMS
Art, drama, music including Orff program, piano lab

SPORTS
Baseball, fencing, golf, karate, lacrosse, soccer, softball, tennis, volleyball

LONG-RANGE PLANS
Add second gym/stage and 8 more classrooms

HISTORY AND MISSION STATEMENT
We as educators believe we should challenge our students to perform to the best of their abilities. We have provided a unique environment with highly intelligent and creative teachers. We offer a strong technology program, literature and writing and the arts.

NOTE: This data applies to the 2002–2003 school year.

OAKCREST SCHOOL

Year founded: 1976
850 Balls Hill Road
McLean, VA 22102
Head of School:
Ellen M. Cavanagh

GENERAL
Grade range: 7th-12th   Girls
Religious affiliation: Catholic
Average class size: 12-18
School day: 8:10-2:50
Morning or after-school care:
No

CAMPUS/CAMPUS LIFE
Facilities: New campus, state-of-the-art
science lab and computer program
Lunch provided: No
Boarding option: No
Bus service: No
School uniform or dress code:
Uniform
Handicapped access available: Yes
Community service requirement:
No requirement, but active participation

Director of Admission:
Amy Jolly
Phone: 703-790-5450
Fax: 703-790-5380
E-mail:
admissions@oakcrest.org
Website:
www.oakcrest.org

ADMISSIONS
Application deadline: February 1
Application fee: $50
Application process: Informal
assessment, application, Oakcrest
Entrance Exam, transcript,
applicant and parent interviews,
current principal and teacher
recommendations
**Number of students
applied/enrolled:** 106 / 63

COSTS
Tuition: $8,700 (7th-8th),
$9,800 (9th-12th)
Average additional fees: $350
Financial aid budget:
Average grant size: $2,000
**% of Students receiving
financial aid:** 20%

NOTE: This data applies to the 2002–2003 school year.

ACADEMIC PROFILE
Number of faculty: 20 Full Time
5 Part Time
Languages and grades offered:
Latin (8th), French and Spanish I,II,III
Number of AP classes offered: 8
Tutors/learning specialists: Yes

Schools three or more graduates have attended over the past five years:
James Madison, Notre Dame, Princeton, Providence, University of Dallas, University of Maryland, William and Mary

SPECIAL FEATURES
Study skills class for 7th grade; food technology class

ENROLLMENT
Total number of students attending and graduating class size: 170 / 22
Birthday cut-off: Not applicable
% Diversity: 15%
Grades with openings: 7th (40), plus attrition

SUMMER PROGRAMS
No

ART PROGRAMS
Art, art history, musical

SPORTS
Basketball, cross-country, intramural lacrosse, soccer, softball, tennis, track & field

LONG-RANGE PLANS
Expand new facility, sports, chapel, classrooms

HISTORY AND MISSION STATEMENT

Oakcrest is founded on the conviction that women make a unique contribution to our families, professions, and communities. We believe young women thrive from an education that develops the whole person—one that encompasses academic excellence and character development, as well as cultural, athletic, and community service opportunities. At Oakcrest, this educational vision is achieved through a partnership between faculty and parents. Oakcrest School is inspired by the teachings of the Catholic Church and the spirit of the Prelature of Opus Dei, which seeks to promote the vocation to holiness in the midst of daily activities.

NOTE: This data applies to the 2002–2003 school year.

OAKWOOD SCHOOL

Year founded: 1971
7210 Braddock Road
Annandale, VA 22003
Head of School:
Robert C. McIntyre

GENERAL
Grade range: 1st-8th   Coed
Religious affiliation: Nonsectarian
Average class size: 12
School day: 8:30-3:00
Morning or after-school care:
No

CAMPUS/CAMPUS LIFE
Facilities:
Lunch provided: No
Boarding option: No
Bus service: No
School uniform or dress code:
None
Handicapped access available: Yes
Community service requirement:
None

Director of Admission:
Muriel Jedlicka
Phone: 703-941-5788
Fax: 703-941-4186
E-mail:

Website:
www.oakwoodschool.com

ADMISSIONS
Application deadline: Rolling
Application fee: $50
Application process: Educational
and pychological reports and other
pertinent information; as openings
occur, applicants invited for
interview, Educational Evaluation
(fee of $250)
**Number of students
applied/enrolled:**

COSTS
Tuition: $19,900
Average additional fees:
Financial aid budget:
Average grant size:
**% of Students receiving
financial aid:**

NOTE: This data applies to the 2002–2003 school year.

ACADEMIC PROFILE
Number of faculty: 28 Full Time
8 Part Time
Languages and grades offered:
Number of AP classes offered:
Not applicable
Tutors/learning specialists:
Yes: speech & language,
occupational therapy
Schools three or more graduates have
attended over the past five years:
Bishop O'Connell, Field, McLean,
Paul VI

SPECIAL FEATURES
Special needs support

ENROLLMENT
Total number of students
attending and graduating
class size: 110 / 16
Birthday cut-off:
% Diversity:
Grades with openings: 1st, plus
most other grades

SUMMER PROGRAMS
None

ART PROGRAMS
Art, music

SPORTS

LONG-RANGE PLANS

HISTORY AND MISSION STATEMENT

It is the mission of Oakwood School to provide the highest quality educational opportunities for learning disabled students of average to gifted potential. To accomplish the goal of preparing young people for their future, the school's professional staff combines proven educational strategies of the past with effective, innovative methods and technologies of the present, in a nurturing environment that builds good character.

NOTE: This data applies to the 2002–2003 school year.

ONENESS-FAMILY SCHOOL

Year founded: 1988
6701 Wisconsin Avenue
Chevy Chase, MD 20815
Head of School:
Andrew Kutt

GENERAL
Grade range: PN-8th   Coed
Religious affiliation: Nonsectarian
Average class size: 25
School day: 9:00-3:40
Morning or after-school care:
7:30-6:00

CAMPUS/CAMPUS LIFE
Facilities: PK-K on second campus
located at 7750 16th St., NW,
Washington, DC 20012
Lunch provided: No
Boarding option: No
Bus service: No
School uniform or dress code:
Dress code: casual, no violent images
Handicapped access available: Yes
Community service requirement:
Yes

Director of Admission:
Maria Leon
Phone: 301-652-7751
Fax: 301-718-6214
E-mail:
admissions@onenessfamily.org
Website:
www.onenessfamily.org

ADMISSIONS
Application deadline: Rolling
Application fee: $50
Application process: Parent tour or
open house, application, applicant
visit, parent interview, teacher
recommendations, transcript
Number of students
applied/enrolled:

COSTS
Tuition: $8,500–$9,750 (PK-K),
$10,500 (1st-3rd),
$10,750–$10,950 (4th-8th)
Average additional fees: $500
Financial aid budget: $75,000
Average grant size: $2,000
% of Students receiving
financial aid: 20%

NOTE: This data applies to the 2002–2003 school year.

ACADEMIC PROFILE

Number of faculty: 10 Full Time
8 Part Time
Languages and grades offered:
DC campus (preschool)-Italian, Spanish;
MD campus-Spanish, French
Number of AP classes offered:
Not applicable
Tutors/learning specialists:
Yes: counselor, speech pathologist
Schools three or more graduates have attended over the past five years:
Barrie, Edmund Burke, Field,
Washington Waldorf

SPECIAL FEATURES

2 campuses

ENROLLMENT

Total number of students attending and graduating class size: 100 /
Birthday cut-off: September 1
% Diversity: 25%
Grades with openings: PK (10),
1st-8th (7 per grade)

SUMMER PROGRAMS

Yes: art, drama, nature,
self-expression

ART PROGRAMS

Art, creative movement, drama,

SPORTS

Basketball, soccer

LONG-RANGE PLANS

Integrate new educational
knowledge into our Montessori-
based program.

HISTORY AND MISSION STATEMENT

The Oneness-Family School is an eclectic Montessori school, dedicated to world peace and personal excellence. We believe that peace begins with each individual, and that successful academic achievement must be balanced by comprehensive personal growth.

Every child deserves to be acknowledged as a unique, growing individual. The years of childhood are vastly enriched by a school where students are treated with dignity, given a sense of safety, inspired, and stimulated to learn.

NOTE: This data applies to the 2002–2003 school year.

OWL SCHOOL (THE)

Year founded: 1972
6045 16th Street, NW
Washington, DC 20011
Head of School:
Margaret G. Harris

GENERAL
Grade range: N-8th   Coed
Religious affiliation: Nonsectarian
Average class size: 18
School day:
Morning or after-school care:
7:45-6:00

CAMPUS/CAMPUS LIFE
Facilities: Dance studio, gymnasium,
library, science labs
Lunch provided:
Boarding option: No
Bus service: Yes
School uniform or dress code:
Handicapped access available: No
Community service requirement:
Yes

Director of Admission:
Margaret G. Harris
Phone: 202-722-6957
Fax: 202-722-7945
E-mail:
mharris@owlschool.com
Website:
www.owlschool.com

ADMISSIONS
Application deadline: Rolling
Application fee: $60
Application process:
Informal assessment
Number of students
applied/enrolled:

COSTS
Tuition: $9,300 (N-PK),
$10,750 (K-3rd), $11,460 (4th-8th)
Average additional fees: $300
Financial aid budget: $38,000
Average grant size:
% of Students receiving
financial aid:

NOTE: This data applies to the 2002–2003 school year.

ACADEMIC PROFILE

Number of faculty:

Languages and grades offered:
French (N-8th), Latin (6th-8th)

Number of AP classes offered:
Not applicable

Tutors/learning specialists:
None

Schools three or more graduates have attended over the past five years:
Barrie, Edmund Burke, Georgetown Day, Good Counsel, Landon, Maret, National Cathedral, Newport, St. Anselm's, Sandy Spring Friends, Sidwell Friends, Washington International

SPECIAL FEATURES

ENROLLMENT

Total number of students attending and graduating class size: 197/

Birthday cut-off: October 1

% Diversity: 98%

Grades with openings:

SUMMER PROGRAMS
Yes: camp, European travel/study

ART PROGRAMS

SPORTS
Baseball, basketball, golf, soccer

LONG-RANGE PLANS

HISTORY AND MISSION STATEMENT

NOTE: This data applies to the 2002–2003 school year.

PALADIN ACADEMY

Year founded: 1964
3753 Centreview Drive
Chantilly, VA 20151
Head of School:
Connie Jackson

GENERAL
Grade range: K-8th   Coed
Religious affiliation: Nonsectarian
Average class size: 7
School day: 9:00-4:00
Morning or after-school care:
6:30-6:30

CAMPUS/CAMPUS LIFE
Facilities: Computer lab, large gym,
large outdoor area
Lunch provided: Yes
Boarding option: No
Bus service: No
School uniform or dress code:
Uniform: khakis and blue/white polos
Handicapped access available: Yes
Community service requirement:
Yes: 1 hour per week in Middle School

Director of Admission:
Connie Jackson
Phone: 703-397-0520
Fax: 703-397-0565
E-mail:
Connie.Jackson@nlcinc.com
Website:

ADMISSIONS
Application deadline: Rolling
Application fee: None
Application process: WISC III,
Woodcock-Johnson Revised, review
records, school visit, conference
Number of students
applied/enrolled: 35 / 30

COSTS
Tuition: $15,000
Average additional fees: $600
Financial aid budget:
Average grant size: $1,000
% of Students receiving
financial aid:

NOTE: This data applies to the 2002–2003 school year.

ACADEMIC PROFILE
Number of faculty: 6 Full Time
2 Part Time
Languages and grades offered:
Spanish (K-8th)
Number of AP classes offered:
Not applicable
Tutors/learning specialists:
Yes: tutoring, outside contracts with
speech language, occupational, physical
therapists, counseling
**Schools three or more graduates have
attended over the past five years:**
Accotink, Chesterbrook Academy,
public schools

SPECIAL FEATURES
Exceptional LD, ADD/ADHD, and
dyslexia programs

ENROLLMENT
**Total number of students
attending and graduating
class size:** 30 / 7
Birthday cut-off:
% Diversity:
Grades with openings: K-2nd (3),
3rd & 4th (4), 5th & 6th (attrition),
7th & 8th (2)

SUMMER PROGRAMS
Yes: academic courses,
summer camp

ART PROGRAMS
Art

SPORTS
Karate, soccer

LONG-RANGE PLANS

HISTORY AND MISSION STATEMENT
Our mission at Paladin is to provide a specialized school with individual educational programs for learning challenged children and to foster their willingness to take responsibility as active and independent learners - to become their own advocates in society.

PARKMONT SCHOOL

Year founded: 1972
4842 16th Street, NW
Washington, DC 20011
Head of School:
Ron McClain

GENERAL
Grade range: 6th-12th   Coed
Religious affiliation: Nonsectarian
Average class size: 10
School day: 8:30-3:30
Morning or after-school care:
No

CAMPUS/CAMPUS LIFE
Facilities: Large house in residential
community in NW, DC
Lunch provided: No
Boarding option: No
Bus service: No
School uniform or dress code:
None
Handicapped access available: No
Community service requirement:
Yes: internship program, 180 hours
per year for Upper School students

Director of Admission:
Jenny Chung
Phone: 202-726-0740
Fax: 202-726-0748
E-mail:
jchung@parkmont.org
Website:
www.parkmont.org

ADMISSIONS
Application deadline: Rolling
Application fee: $50
Application process: Informal
assessment, parent interview,
applicant visit
**Number of students
applied/enrolled:**

COSTS
Tuition: $17,200
Average additional fees: None
Financial aid budget: $200,000
Average grant size: $14,000
**% of Students receiving
financial aid:** 31%

NOTE: This data applies to the 2002–2003 school year.

ACADEMIC PROFILE
Number of faculty: 8 Full Time
6 Part Time
Languages and grades offered:
Spanish (9th-12th)
Number of AP classes offered:
None
Tutors/learning specialists:
Yes
Schools three or more graduates have
attended over the past five years:
Antioch, Columbia, Emerson,
Georgetown, Johns Hopkins, Spellman,
Wesleyan, University of Miami

SPECIAL FEATURES
Modular scheduling allows three
courses at a time and field trips,
small classes, multi-age groups with
diverse learning styles, internships
for Upper School students

ENROLLMENT
Total number of students
attending and graduating
class size: 65 / 8
Birthday cut-off: Not applicable
% Diversity: 40%
Grades with openings: 6th-8th (20),
9th-12th (20)

SUMMER PROGRAMS
Yes: summer school

ART PROGRAMS
Art, ceramics, dance, photography

SPORTS
Basketball, soccer, softball, tennis,
volleyball

LONG-RANGE PLANS

HISTORY AND MISSION STATEMENT

We help adolescents develop the confidence and skills they need to move ahead energetically with their lives. We create a community where students ally themselves with creative adults whose driving concern is their success and well-being. We provide them with substantial experience in the world beyond school that invites them to see more clearly the possibilities ahead. We challenge them with an academic program that fuses adolescent interests with traditional disciplines and respects the variety of their talents and motivations. They get ready to chart their own course; we make sure they are prepared for the journey.

NOTE: This data applies to the 2002–2003 school year.

PAUL VI CATHOLIC HIGH SCHOOL

Year founded: 1983
10675 Lee Highway
Fairfax, VA 22030
Head of School:
Philip Robey

GENERAL
Grade range: 9th-12th   Coed
Religious affiliation: Catholic
Average class size: 24
School day: 7:50-2:40
Morning or after-school care:
No

CAMPUS/CAMPUS LIFE
Facilities: 16.4 acres, baseball/football
and practice fields
Lunch provided: Yes: additional cost
Boarding option: No
Bus service: Yes: limited
School uniform or dress code:
Uniform: girls - kilt, shirt; boys -
khaki pants
Handicapped access available: No
Community service requirement:
Yes

Director of Admission:
Eileen Hanley
Phone: 703-352-0925 x331
Fax: 703-273-9845
E-mail:
admissions@paulvi.net
Website:
www.paulvi.net

ADMISSIONS
Application deadline: December 1
Application fee: $50
Application process: Transcript,
teacher recommendations,
entrance test (9th)
Number of students
applied/enrolled: 500 / 270

COSTS
Tuition: $6,690 (diocese),
$8,750 (nondiocese)
Average additional fees: $700
Financial aid budget: $374,000
Average grant size: $2,000
% of Students receiving
financial aid: 10%

NOTE: This data applies to the 2002–2003 school year.

ACADEMIC PROFILE
Number of faculty: 96
Languages and grades offered:
French, German, Latin, Spanish
(9th-12th)
Number of AP classes offered: 11
Tutors/learning specialists:
Yes: DeSales Academic Support
Program, special education teacher
Schools three or more graduates have
attended over the past five years:
Auburn, Boston College, Cornell,
George Mason, Holy Cross, James
Madison, Notre Dame, University of
Virginia, Wake Forest, William & Mary

SPECIAL FEATURES
Academic Support Program, Options
Program for developmentally delayed
students (limited enrollment)

ENROLLMENT
Total number of students
attending and graduating
class size: 1200 / 295
Birthday cut-off: Not applicable
% Diversity: 15%
Grades with openings:

SUMMER PROGRAMS
Yes: enrichment, remediation,
study skills

ART PROGRAMS
Art, band, chorus, drama

SPORTS
Baseball, basketball, cross-country,
drill team, football, golf, ice hockey,
lacrosse, soccer, softball, swimming,
tennis, track & field, volleyball,
wrestling

LONG-RANGE PLANS
Build activity center

HISTORY AND MISSION STATEMENT
The mission of Paul VI High School is to provide an excellent Catholic education
to young men and women in Northern Virginia by affording them the means to
achieve spiritual, intellectual, personal, social and physical development according to the teachings of the Gospel and St. Francis de Sales. Paul VI High School is
devoted to graduating responsible, moral young adults so that they will continue
to "grow in grace and wisdom."

NOTE: This data applies to the 2002–2003 school year.

POTOMAC SCHOOL (THE)

Year founded: 1904
1301 Potomac School Road; PO Box 430
McLean, VA 22101
Head of School:
Geoffrey Jones

GENERAL
Grade range: K-12th   Coed
Religious affiliation: Nonsectarian
Average class size: 15
School day: 8:15-3:10 (K-8th),
8:15-5:30 (9th-12th)
Morning or after-school care:
3:10-6:00

CAMPUS/CAMPUS LIFE
Facilities: 82 acre campus, 3 gyms,
3 libraries, new performing arts center
Lunch provided: Yes: Upper School
Boarding option: No
Bus service: Yes
School uniform or dress code:
Dress code: Lower and
Upper Schools, Uniform: 4th-8th
Handicapped access available: Yes
Community service requirement:
Yes: school-wide community service
with Community Service Coordinator

Director of Admission:
Charlotte Nelsen
Phone: 703-749-6313
Fax: 703-356-1764
E-mail:

Website:
www.potomacschool.org

ADMISSIONS
Application deadline: January 15
Application fee: $60
Application process: WPPSI-R
(K-1st), WISC III (2nd-6th),
SSAT or ISEE (7th-12th)
**Number of students
applied/enrolled:** 900 / 102

COSTS
Tuition: $16,290 (K-3rd),
$17,375 (4th-6th),
$18,960 (7th-12th)
Average additional fees: Varies
Financial aid budget: $1,400,000
Average grant size:
**% of Students receiving
financial aid:** 13%

NOTE: This data applies to the 2002–2003 school year.

ACADEMIC PROFILE
Number of faculty: 106 Full Time
30 Part Time
Languages and grades offered:
French, Japanese, Latin, Spanish
(7th-12th)
Number of AP classes offered: 14
Tutors/learning specialists:
Yes: math, language arts resource
teachers, counselors
Schools three or more graduates have attended over the past five years:
Brown, Duke, Harvard, James Madison, Princeton, University of Pennsylvania, University of Virginia, Vanderbilt, William and Mary, Yale

SPECIAL FEATURES
18 bus routes to VA, MD, DC, variety of field trips, long-standing traditions and events

ENROLLMENT
Total number of students
attending and graduating
class size: 875 / 74
Birthday cut-off: September 1
(K only)
% Diversity: 24%
Grades with openings: K (48),
1st (6), 4th (12), 7th (15), 9th (15)

SUMMER PROGRAMS
Yes: day camps, outdoor and academic programs, specialty camps (ages 3-17)

ART PROGRAMS
Art, drama, music, photography

SPORTS
Baseball, basketball, cross-country, field hockey, football, lacrosse, outdoor education, soccer, softball, squash, swimming, tennis, track & field, wrestling, weight training and conditioning

LONG-RANGE PLANS
New field house, new tennis courts, additional athletic fields

HISTORY AND MISSION STATEMENT
Potomac seeks to provide an atmosphere which encourages high academic achievement, love of learning, caring for others, delight in creative expression, satisfaction of accomplishment, and an appreciation for diversity among students, faculty, administration, and trustees. The School promotes a firm sense of personal integrity, a solid commitment to high ethical and moral values, and a strong social conscience.

NOTE: This data applies to the 2002–2003 school year.

PRIMARY DAY SCHOOL (THE)

Year founded: 1944
7300 River Road
Bethesda, MD 20817
Head of School:
Louise Plumb

Director of Admission:
Ivy Velte
Phone: 301-365-4355
Fax: 301-469-8611
E-mail:

GENERAL
Grade range: PK-2nd   Coed
Religious affiliation: Nonsectarian
Average class size: 20
School day: 8:45-12:45 (PK),
8:45-2:45 (K-2nd)
8:45-12:45
Morning or after-school care:
No

Website:

ADMISSIONS
Application deadline: January 15
Application fee: $50
Application process: Developmental
assessment (informal)
**Number of students
applied/enrolled:** 156 / 45

CAMPUS/CAMPUS LIFE
Facilities: Art/music room, auditorium,
library, playground, science, math,
and computer labs, soccer field,
sport court
Lunch provided: No
Boarding option: No
Bus service: No
School uniform or dress code:
None
Handicapped access available: Yes
Community service requirement:
No requirement, but active
participation

COSTS
Tuition: $7,500 (PK), $10,200 (K),
$10,500 (1st), $11,000 (2nd)
Average additional fees: None
Financial aid budget:
Average grant size:
**% of Students receiving
financial aid:** 9.3%

NOTE: This data applies to the 2002–2003 school year.

ACADEMIC PROFILE
Number of faculty: 19 Full Time
2 Part Time
Languages and grades offered:
None
Number of AP classes offered:
Not applicable
Tutors/learning specialists:
Yes: reading, math specialists
Schools three or more graduates have attended over the past five years:
Bullis, Georgetown Day, Holton-Arms, Landon, Sidwell Friends, Stone Ridge

SPECIAL FEATURES
Phonovisual teaching method (phonics)

ENROLLMENT
Total number of students attending and graduating class size: 162 / 42
Birthday cut-off: September 1
% Diversity: 18%
Grades with openings: PK (36), K (2), plus attrition

SUMMER PROGRAMS
None

ART PROGRAMS
Art, music

SPORTS
Physical education

LONG-RANGE PLANS
Expand science and technology program

HISTORY AND MISSION STATEMENT

The Primary Day School was founded as a demonstration school for the Phonovisual Method, a multi-sensory approach to word recognition. A diverse, coeducational school, Primary Day offers instruction for children in Pre-Kindergarten through 2nd grade. The school's warm and supportive atmosphere encourages the development of students intellectually, physically and emotionally according to each child's gifts and talent.

NOTE: This data applies to the 2002–2003 school year.

QUEEN ANNE SCHOOL

Year founded: 1964
14111 Oak Grove Road
Upper Marlboro, MD 20772
Head of School:
J. Temple Blackwood

GENERAL
Grade range: 6th-12th   Coed
Religious affiliation: Episcopal
Average class size: 15
School day: 8:00-3:30
Morning or after-school care:
3:30-5:00

CAMPUS/CAMPUS LIFE
Facilities: 60 acre campus with
8 buildings
Lunch provided: Yes
Boarding option: No
Bus service: Yes
School uniform or dress code:
Dress code
Handicapped access available: Yes
Community service requirement:
Yes: 100 hours in 9th-12th

Director of Admission:
Brenda B. Walker
Phone: 301-249-5000 x310
Fax: 301-249-3838
E-mail:
bwalker@queenanne.org
Website:
www.queenanne.org

ADMISSIONS
Application deadline: Rolling
Application fee: $50
Application process: English, math
teachers and administrator
recommendations, writing sample,
ISEE, transcript, interview
**Number of students
applied/enrolled:** 102 / 79

COSTS
Tuition: $12,800 (6th-8th),
$14,300 (9th-12th)
Average additional fees: $250
Financial aid budget: $168,000
Average grant size: $4,200
**% of Students receiving
financial aid:** 27%

NOTE: This data applies to the 2002–2003 school year.

ACADEMIC PROFILE

Number of faculty: 32 Full Time
11 Part Time
Languages and grades offered:
French (9th-12th), Latin
(6th-8th), Spanish (9th-12th)
Number of AP classes offered: 9
Tutors/learning specialists:
None
Schools three or more graduates have attended over the past five years:
Brown, Bucknell, Dickinson, Duke, Georgetown, Howard, Middlebury, Princeton, University of Chicago, University of Maryland, University of Pennsylvania, University of Richmond, University of Virginia

SPECIAL FEATURES

College style campus, rigorous academic program, strong technology and arts program

ENROLLMENT

Total number of students attending and graduating class size: 282 / 27
Birthday cut-off: Not applicable
% Diversity: 50%
Grades with openings: 6th (32), plus attrition

SUMMER PROGRAMS

Yes: enrichment, sports

ART PROGRAMS

Art, ceramics, photography

SPORTS

Baseball, basketball, cross-country, lacrosse, soccer, softball, tennis, track & field

LONG-RANGE PLANS

Add 2 academic buildings and increase enrollment

HISTORY AND MISSION STATEMENT

Queen Anne School, founded and sponsored within the Episcopal tradition by St. Barnabas' Church, encourages expansion of academic and artistic horizons while promoting moral, physical, social and spiritual growth in each student.

NOTE: This data applies to the 2002–2003 school year.

RIVENDELL

Year founded: 1989
5700 North Lee Highway
Arlington, VA 22207
Head of School:
Bentley Craft & Byron List

GENERAL
Grade range: K-8th   Coed
Religious affiliation: Christian
Average class size: 16
School day: 9:00-3:00, 9:00-1:00 W
Morning or after-school care:
No

CAMPUS/CAMPUS LIFE
Facilities: 3 floor building with large all
purpose room, lunch room w/stage,
Chapel building, playground area,
county parks across street for recess
Lunch provided: No
Boarding option: No
Bus service: No
School uniform or dress code:
Uniform: plaid jumpers/skirts, navy
pants/shorts, white/blue oxford shirts
Handicapped access available: No
Community service requirement:
Yes: 20 hours for 8th

Director of Admission:
Lyle Peterson
Phone: 703-532-1200
Fax: 703-532-3003
E-mail:

Website:

ADMISSIONS
Application deadline: January 31
Application fee: $35
Application process: Application,
recommendations, parent
interview, applicant interview
for upper grades, transcript
**Number of students
applied/enrolled:** 58 / 25
(sibling priority given)

COSTS
Tuition: $4,750 (K), $6,000
(1st-8th)
Average additional fees: None
Financial aid budget: 20% of tuition
Average grant size:
**% of Students receiving
financial aid:**

NOTE: This data applies to the 2002–2003 school year.

ACADEMIC PROFILE
Number of faculty: 11 Full Time
2 Part Time
Languages and grades offered:
Latin (4th-8th), Spanish (1st-2nd)
Number of AP classes offered:
Not applicable
Tutors/learning specialists:
**Schools three or more graduates have
attended over the past five years:**
Bishop O'Connell, Field, George Mason
High, McLean High, St. Stephen's &
St. Agnes, Trinity Christian, Washington
Lee High, Yorktown High

SPECIAL FEATURES
Parent involvement required

ENROLLMENT
**Total number of students
attending and graduating
class size:** 146 / 17
Birthday cut-off: September 1
% Diversity: 10%
Grades with openings: K (16),
plus attrition

SUMMER PROGRAMS
None

ART PROGRAMS
Art

SPORTS

LONG-RANGE PLANS

HISTORY AND MISSION STATEMENT

Rivendell School is Christ-centered. Our goal is to help children explore God's world and discover their place in it. Our primary commitment is to nurture children toward responsible maturity through academic excellence and we strive to prepare children for their calling in God's creation.

NOTE: This data applies to the 2002–2003 school year.

RIVER SCHOOL (THE)

Year founded: 1998
4880 MacArthur Boulevard, NW
Washington, DC 20007
Head of School:
Nancy Mellon

GENERAL
Grade range: PN-3rd   Coed
Religious affiliation: Nonsectarian
Average class size: 10
School day: 8:30-12:00 (half day),
8:30-3:00 (full day)
Morning or after-school care:
8:00-5:00

CAMPUS/CAMPUS LIFE
Facilities: 4 story building,
2 playgrounds, gym
Lunch provided: No
Boarding option: No
Bus service: No
School uniform or dress code:
None
Handicapped access available: Yes
Community service requirement:
None

Director of Admission:
Sarah Wainscott
Phone: 202-337-3554
Fax: 202-337-3534
E-mail:

Website:
www.riverschool.net

ADMISSIONS

Application deadline: February 15
Application fee: $50
Application process:
Informal assessment
**Number of students
applied/enrolled:** 180 / 70

COSTS
Tuition: $5,500-$12,000
(base tuition), $7,750-$23,000
(tuition with related services)
Average additional fees:
Financial aid budget:
Average grant size: Maximum of
50% of tuition
**% of Students receiving
financial aid:** 15%

NOTE: This data applies to the 2002–2003 school year.

ACADEMIC PROFILE

Number of faculty: 25 Full Time

Languages and grades offered:
None

Number of AP classes offered:
Not applicable

Tutors/learning specialists:
Yes: speech & language therapists, consulting occupational therapist

Schools three or more graduates have attended over the past five years:
Georgetown Day School

SPECIAL FEATURES

Eleven month school year starting in September and ending in July;
Focus on language and literacy;
Infant and toddler program

ENROLLMENT

Total number of students attending and graduating class size: 100 / 10

Birthday cut-off:

% Diversity: 30%

Grades with openings: PN (16), N (10), PK (12), K (14)

SUMMER PROGRAMS
None

ART PROGRAMS
Art, creative movement, drama, music

SPORTS

LONG-RANGE PLANS
Expand school size

HISTORY AND MISSION STATEMENT

River School is a national model for the education of young deaf children alongside their hearing peers. The mission of the school is to provide successful educational experiences for children and their families by uniting best practices of early childhood education and oral deaf education, and to promote clinical research and training in child language and literacy. The curriculum is designed and implemented by master's level professionals from the fields of early childhood, elementary, and deaf education, speech-language pathology, developmental psychology and audiology.

NOTE: This data applies to the 2002–2003 school year.

ROCK CREEK INTERNATIONAL SCHOOL

Year founded: 1988
1550 Foxhall Road, NW
Washington, DC 20007
Head of School:
J. Daniel Hollinger

GENERAL
Grade range: N-6th   Coed
Religious affiliation: Nonsectarian
Average class size: 15
School day: 8:30-3:30
Morning or after-school care:
8:00-6:00

CAMPUS/CAMPUS LIFE
Facilities: Remodeled 1940's school
building, art and music rooms,
basketball and tennis courts, library,
2 playgrounds, soccer field,
technology lab
Lunch provided: No
Boarding option: No
Bus service: Yes
School uniform or dress code:
None
Handicapped access available: No
Community service requirement:
None

Director of Admission:
Alejandra Maudet
Phone: 202-965-8700
Fax: 202-965-8973
E-mail:
a.maudet@rcis.org
Website:
www.rcis.org

ADMISSIONS
Application deadline: February 20
Application fee: $60
Application process: Informal
assessment, class visit, teacher
recommendation
**Number of students
applied/enrolled:** 120 / 63

COSTS
Tuition: $15,500
Average additional fees: $50
Financial aid budget: 30% of budget
Average grant size: $5,000-$7,000
**% of Students receiving
financial aid:** 25%

NOTE: This data applies to the 2002–2003 school year.

ACADEMIC PROFILE
Number of faculty: 26
Languages and grades offered:
Arabic, French, Spanish (N-5th)
Number of AP classes offered:
Not applicable
Tutors/learning specialists:
Yes: languages and math, some reading
Schools three or more graduates have
attended over the past five years:
Holton-Arms, Georgetown Day, Maret,
St. Albans, Washington International

SPECIAL FEATURES
Dual-Language immersion

ENROLLMENT
Total number of students
attending and graduating
class size: 180 / 17
Birthday cut-off: September 1
% Diversity: 30%
Grades with openings:

SUMMER PROGRAMS
Yes: language immersion camps

ART PROGRAMS
Art, drama, music

SPORTS
Soccer

LONG-RANGE PLANS
Add middle school

HISTORY AND MISSION STATEMENT

The mission of Rock Creek International School is to educate young people to high academic performance, proficiency in two languages, in-depth knowledge and appreciation of diverse peoples and cultures, responsible participation in local, national and global communities, and pursuit of life-long commitment to personal development and service to others. Rock Creek's educational format is unique in the Washington, DC area. Our curriculum, taught in English and either French or Spanish on alternate days, creates a high level of fluency in both languages.

NOTE: This data applies to the 2002–2003 school year.

SANDY SPRING FRIENDS SCHOOL

Year founded: 1961
16923 Norwood Road
Sandy Spring, MD 20860
Head of School:
Kenneth W. Smith

GENERAL
Grade range: PK-12th   Coed
Religious affiliation: Society of Friends
(Quaker)
Average class size: 15
School day: 8:10-3:20
Morning or after-school care:
7:30-6:00 (PK-4th)

CAMPUS/CAMPUS LIFE
Facilities: 140 acre rural campus with
11 buildings, dorms, library, Meeting
House, observatory, performing arts
center, science center
Lunch provided: Yes
Boarding option: Yes /45 (5 and 7-day)
Bus service: Yes
School uniform or dress code:
Dress code: can wear jeans, sneakers
and appropriate t-shirts
Handicapped access available: No
Community service requirement:
Yes: community service coordinator,
stewardship campus work program

Director of Admission:
Mecha Inman
Phone: 301-774-7455
Fax: 301-924-1115
E-mail:
apply@ssfs.org
Website:
www.ssfs.org

ADMISSIONS
Application deadline: January 15
Application fee: $50
Application process: Informal and
standardized assessment (PK-5th),
SSAT (6th-12th)
**Number of students
applied/enrolled:** 576 / 88

COSTS
Tuition: $11,625-$13,400 (PK-6th)
$14,800 (7th-8th), $16,225-
$16,725 (9th-12th day), $22,775-
$27,900 (9th-12th boarding)
Average additional fees: $500
Financial aid budget: $659,000
Average grant size: $8,000
**% of Students receiving
financial aid:** 16%

NOTE: This data applies to the 2002–2003 school year.

ACADEMIC PROFILE

Number of faculty: 63 Full Time

Languages and grades offered:
French (5th-12th), Spanish (K-12th)

Number of AP classes offered: 9

Tutors/learning specialists:
Yes: learning specialist

Schools three or more graduates have attended over the past five years:
Cornell, Georgetown, George Washington, Guilford, Johns Hopkins, Princeton, Smith, University of Maryland

SPECIAL FEATURES

Friends Meeting for Worship, a no-cut policy in sports

ENROLLMENT

Total number of students attending and graduating class size: 513 / 56

Birthday cut-off:

% Diversity: 30%

Grades with openings: PK (12), K (16), 1st-8th (attrition), 9th (15)

SUMMER PROGRAMS

Yes: arts & crafts, computer, drama, rocketry, sports camps

ART PROGRAMS

Art, ceramics, dance, drama, music, painting, photography

SPORTS

Baseball, basketball, cross-country, golf, lacrosse, soccer, tennis, track & field, volleyball,

LONG-RANGE PLANS

Major building expansion

HISTORY AND MISSION STATEMENT

The Religious Society of Friends, also known as Quakers, cherishes the worth and dignity of each individual because we believe there is that of God in every person. Sandy Spring Friends School develops the trained mind, the skilled hand, and the healthy body within a nurturing community centered in the Life of the Spirit. We provide a challenging academic program combined with stimulating opportunities in the arts, athletics, and community service. Our mission is most clearly stated in our motto "Let Your Lives Speak."

NOTE: This data applies to the 2002–2003 school year.

SHERIDAN SCHOOL

Year founded: 1927
4400 36th Street, NW
Washington, DC 20008
Head of School:
C. Randall Plummer

GENERAL

Grade range: K-8th   Coed
Religious affiliation: Nonsectarian
Average class size: 23 with 2 teachers
(3 for K)
School day: 8:25-3:30, 8:25-2:30 W
Morning or after-school care:
7:45- 6:00

CAMPUS/CAMPUS LIFE

Facilities: City campus central building;
Mountain campus 130 acres in the
Shenandoah Mountains
Lunch provided: Yes
Boarding option: No
Bus service: No
School uniform or dress code: None
Handicapped access available: No
Community service requirement:
Yes: each class actively participates
in school-wide, student-generated
projects

Director of Admission:
Julie Calloway Lewis
Phone: 202-362-7900 x103
Fax: 202-244-9696
E-mail:
admission@sheridanschool.org
Website:
www.sheridanschool.org

ADMISSIONS

Application deadline: January 17
Application fee: $50
Application process: Parent
tour, application, teacher
recommendations, transcript,
applicant visit, WPPSI-R (K),
WISC III (1st-5th), SSAT or ISEE
(6th-8th)
**Number of students
applied/enrolled:** 140 / 42

COSTS

Tuition: $16,555 (K-3rd),
$17,576 (4th), $18,383 (5th-8th)
Average additional fees: $35-$100
Financial aid budget: $280,000
Average grant size: $9,300
**% of Students receiving
financial aid:** 13%

NOTE: This data applies to the 2002–2003 school year.

ACADEMIC PROFILE
Number of faculty: 28 Full Time
4 Part Time
Languages and grades offered:
French, Spanish (K-8th)
Number of AP classes offered:
Not applicable
Tutors/learning specialists:
Yes: learning specialist; tutors at
an additional fee
Schools three or more graduates have attended over the past five years:
Bullis, Edmund Burke, Georgetown
Day, Georgetown Prep, Landon, Madeira,
Maret, National Cathedral, St. Albans,
Sidwell Friends, Washington
International, boarding, public
magnet schools

SPECIAL FEATURES
Central Subject approach to social
studies; mountain campus

ENROLLMENT
**Total number of students
attending and graduating
class size:** 215 / 20
Birthday cut-off: September 1
% Diversity: 24%
Grades with openings: K (24),
plus attrition

SUMMER PROGRAMS
Yes: "Shenandoah Summer" sleep
away camp at mountain campus;
Creative Arts & Summer Adventure
day camp at city campus (ages 3-14)

ART PROGRAMS
Art, music, performing arts

SPORTS
Basketball, soccer, softball,
track & field

LONG-RANGE PLANS
Renovate space to accommodate
current program

HISTORY AND MISSION STATEMENT
Sheridan School's mission is to educate confident, responsible, and kind children who are well-prepared to meet the challenges of a complex and changing world. We believe this is best accomplished by faculty, staff, and parents working together as a community, emphasizing high academic standards in a small, diverse, nurturing and learning-centered environment. The school's two campuses provide a unique opportunity for its students and their families to combine academic and experiential learning.

NOTE: This data applies to the 2002–2003 school year.

SIDWELL FRIENDS SCHOOL

Year founded: 1883
3825 Wisconsin Avenue, NW
Washington, DC 20016
Head of School:
Bruce B. Stewart

GENERAL
Grade range: PK-12th   Coed
Religious affiliation: Society of Friends
(Quaker)
Average class size: 24 (PK-4th with
2 teachers), 17 (5th-12th)
School day: 8:45-3:00 (Lower School),
8:00-3:15 (Middle and Upper Schools)
Morning or after-school care:
3:00-6:00 (PK-8th)

CAMPUS/CAMPUS LIFE
Facilities: 15 acre Upper and Middle
School campus; 5 acre Lower School
campus on Edgemoor Lane in
Bethesda, MD
Lunch provided: Yes
Boarding option: No
Bus service: Yes: PreK-4th
School uniform or dress code:
None
Handicapped access available: Yes
Community service requirement:
Yes

Director of Admission:
Joshua Wolman
Phone: 202-537-8111
Fax: 202-537-2401
E-mail:
admissions@sidwell.edu
Website:
www.sidwell.edu

ADMISSIONS
Application deadline: January 10
Application fee: $50
Application process: Application
including parent's statement,
applicant visit, teacher
recommendations, transcript,
Detroit (PK*), WPPSI-R (K),
WISC III (1st-5th), SSAT or ISEE
(7th-12th) (*Subject to change)
**Number of students
applied/enrolled:** 950 / 145

COSTS
Tuition: $17,600 (PK-4th), $19,700
(5th-8th), $19,990 (9th-12th)
Average additional fees:
$500 (5th-12th), $650 (9th-12th)
Financial aid budget: $2,950,000
Average grant size: $13,100
**% of Students receiving
financial aid:** 20%

NOTE: This data applies to the 2002–2003 school year.

ACADEMIC PROFILE

Number of faculty: 123 Full Time
26 Part Time

Languages and grades offered:
Chinese (7th-12th), French (7th-12th),
Latin (7th-12th), Spanish (PK-12th)

Number of AP classes offered:
11

Tutors/learning specialists:
Yes: 3 full time learning specialists

Schools three or more graduates have attended over the past five years:
Columbia, Duke, Harvard, Haverford,
Princeton, Stanford, University of
Pennsylvania, Yale, Oberlin,
Washington University

SPECIAL FEATURES

Quaker Meeting for Worship,
Chinese begins 7th grade

ENROLLMENT

Total number of students attending and graduating class size: 1,090 / 115

Birthday cut-off: September 1
(PK-4th) October 1 (5th-6th)

% Diversity: 34%

Grades with openings: PK (34),
K (15), 3rd (10), 5th (10), 7th (30),
9th (20)

SUMMER PROGRAMS

Yes: Alaska travel camp, day camp,
enrichment classes, remediation,
sports camps

ART PROGRAMS

Performing and visual arts facilities
for chorus, drama, music

SPORTS

Baseball, basketball, crew, cross-
country, diving, field hockey,
football, lacrosse, indoor soccer,
soccer, softball, squash, swimming,
tennis, track & field, ultimate
frisbee, volleyball, wrestling

LONG-RANGE PLANS

HISTORY AND MISSION STATEMENT

Embracing the Quaker belief in the unique worth of each individual, we seek students of diverse cultural, racial, religious and economic backgrounds — students of ability and promise whose qualities of mind and heart indicate that they will thrive in an atmosphere of intellectual, creative and physical vitality intended to foster strength of character and concern for others.

NOTE: This data applies to the 2002–2003 school year.

ST. ALBANS SCHOOL

Year founded: 1909
Mount St. Alban
Washington, DC 20016
Head of School:
Vance Wilson

GENERAL
Grade range: 4th-12th   Boys
Religious affiliation: Episcopal
Average class size: 13
School day: 7:55-3:30 (Lower School),
7:55-5:30 (Upper School)
Morning or after-school care:
No

CAMPUS/CAMPUS LIFE
Facilities: 60 acre campus with
7 buildings including 2 gyms,
indoor pool, theater
Lunch provided: Yes
Boarding option: Yes / 30
Bus service: No
School uniform or dress code:
Dress code: coat and tie
Handicapped access available: Yes
Community service requirement:
Yes: 60 hours by start of senior year

Director of Admission:
Andrew M. Rodin
Phone: 202-537-6440
Fax: 202-537-5288
E-mail:
sta_admission@cathedral.org
Website:
www.sta.cathedral.org

ADMISSIONS
Application deadline: January 15
Application fee: $75
Application process: Informal
assessment (4th-5th), SSAT
(6th-12th), interview, tour
**Number of students
applied/enrolled:** 104 / 20 (9th)

COSTS
Tuition: $20,408 (4th-12th),
$28,868 (9th-12th boarding)
Average additional fees: $500
Financial aid budget: $1,800,000
Average grant size: $12,000
**% of Students receiving
financial aid:** 25%

NOTE: This data applies to the 2002–2003 school year.

ACADEMIC PROFILE
Number of faculty: 75
Languages and grades offered:
Chinese (9th-12th), French (7th-12th),
German (9th-12th), Greek (9th-12th),
Japanese (7th-12th), Latin (5th-12th),
Spanish (4th-12th)
Number of AP classes offered: 13
Tutors/learning specialists:
Yes: including study skills
Schools three or more graduates have attended over the past five years:
Bowdoin, Brown, Columbia, Duke,
Georgetown, Harvard, Princeton,
Stanford, University of Pennsylvania,
Vanderbilt, University of Virginia, Yale

SPECIAL FEATURES

ENROLLMENT
Total number of students attending and graduating class size: 563 / 77
Birthday cut-off: Not applicable
% Diversity: 25%
Grades with openings: 4th (35-40),
7th (15-20), 9th (15-20),
plus attrition

SUMMER PROGRAMS
Yes: sports camp, summer school

ART PROGRAMS
Extensive

SPORTS
Baseball, basketball, canoeing/
kayaking, climbing, crew, cross-
country, diving, football, golf, ice
hockey, lacrosse, running, indoor
soccer, soccer, swimming, tennis

LONG-RANGE PLANS

HISTORY AND MISSION STATEMENT

St. Albans School is a college preparatory school for boys which challenges its students to achieve excellence and to embrace responsibility. It expects them to act always with honor and to respect and care for others.

St. Albans School is a diverse family that welcomes and values individuals from all backgrounds. Such diversity is essential to a vital community of learning and growth. In nurturing the hearts, minds, and bodies of students, St. Albans prepares boys for fulfilling lives of responsibility, leadership, and service to others. Classes and activities may be coordinated with girls from National Cathedral School, which is located next to St. Albans on the Cathedral Close.

NOTE: This data applies to the 2002–2003 school year.

ST. ANDREW'S EPISCOPAL SCHOOL

Year founded: 1978
8804 Postoak Road
Potomac, MD 20854
Head of School:
Robert F. Kosasky

GENERAL
Grade range: 6th-12th   Coed
Religious affiliation: Episcopal
Average class size: 15
School day: 8:25-3:25 (6th-8th),
8:25-3:05 (9th-12th)
Morning or after-school care:
3:25-6:00 (6th-8th)

CAMPUS/CAMPUS LIFE
Facilities: Beautiful 19.2 acre campus
features a 75,000 sq. ft. state-of-the-art
classroom facility with science and
technology laboratories, 14,000 volume
library, and theater/assembly hall;
gymnasium; athletic center; tennis
courts; and athletic fields.
Lunch provided: Yes
Boarding option: No
Bus service: Yes
School uniform or dress code:
Dress code
Handicapped access available: Yes
Community service requirement:
Yes: 20 hours annually in 9th-11th,
60 hours in 12th

Director of Admission:
Julie Jameson
Phone: 301-983-5200
Fax: 301-983-4620
E-mail:
admission@saes.org
Website:
www.saes.org

ADMISSIONS
Application deadline: February 1
Application fee: $50
Application process: Application,
interview, tour, transcript, teacher
recommendations, SSAT (6th-12th),
optional half day visit
**Number of students
applied/enrolled:** 400 / 90

COSTS
Tuition: $19,145 (6th-8th),
$20,365 (9th-12th)
Average additional fees: $500
Financial aid budget: $540,000
Average grant size:
**% of Students receiving
financial aid:** 10%

NOTE: This data applies to the 2002–2003 school year.

ACADEMIC PROFILE
Number of faculty: 64
Languages and grades offered:
French, Latin, Spanish (7th-12th)
Number of AP classes offered: 8
Tutors/learning specialists:
Yes: full time learning specialist, part
time school psychologist, tutoring
facilities on site
**Schools three or more graduates have
attended over the past five years:**
Boston College, Bowdoin, Duke,
Kenyon, New York University,
Oberlin, Tufts, University of Maryland,
University of Pennsylvania, William
and Mary

SPECIAL FEATURES
Advanced Placement economics, civil
rights, and media studies consortiums.
Student exchange program with
Honduras, France, and China.
Numerous curricular-related and
athletic team trips (USA and abroad)

ENROLLMENT
**Total number of students
attending and graduating
class size:** 450 / 71
Birthday cut-off: Not applicable
% Diversity: 14%
Grades with openings: 6th (30-35),
7th (25-30), 9th (20), plus attrition

SUMMER PROGRAMS
Yes: camp, summer school

ART PROGRAMS
Students take 2 trimesters per
year, 30 visual arts classes,
30 performing arts classes

SPORTS
Baseball, basketball, cross-country,
equestrian, fitness, golf, lacrosse,
outdoor program, soccer, softball,
tennis, track & field, volleyball,
wrestling

LONG-RANGE PLANS

HISTORY AND MISSION STATEMENT

Founded in 1978, St. Andrew's is an independent, coeducational, college preparatory school for a diverse group of students in grades 6 through 12. Our mission
is to nurture each student's intellectual development, personal integrity and sense
of self-worth in a cooperative environment that embodies the faith and perspective of the Episocopal Church.

NOTE: This data applies to the 2002–2003 school year.

ST. ANSELM'S ABBEY SCHOOL

Year founded: 1942
4501 South Dakota Avenue, NE
Washington, DC 20017
Head of School:
Father Peter Weigand, OSB, MTS

GENERAL
Grade range: 6th-12th   Boys
Religious affiliation: Catholic
Average class size: 17
School day: 8:00-3:20
Morning or after-school care:
No

CAMPUS/CAMPUS LIFE
Facilities: 40 acre urban campus with
new gym and performing arts center
Lunch provided: No
Boarding option: No
Bus service: Limited: to Metro
School uniform or dress code:
Dress code: coat, tie, dress pants,
dress shoes
Handicapped access available: No
Community service requirement:
Yes: Tuesday mornings for 11th-12th

Director of Admission:
Patrick I. Parsons
Phone: 202-269-2379
Fax: 202-269-2373
E-mail:
admissions@saintanselms.org
Website:
www.saintanselms.org

ADMISSIONS
Application deadline: Rolling
Application fee: $35
Application process: Application,
in-house testing, interview,
writing sample
**Number of students
applied/enrolled:** 136 / 61

COSTS
Tuition: $12,600-$13,100
(6th-12th)
Average additional fees: $650-$900
Financial aid budget: $350,000
Average grant size: $4,500
**% of Students receiving
financial aid:** 24%

NOTE: This data applies to the 2002–2003 school year.

ACADEMIC PROFILE
Number of faculty: 55
Languages and grades offered:
French (8th-12th), Ancient Greek
(11th-12th), Latin (7th-12th),
Spanish (8th-12th)
Number of AP classes offered: 22
Tutors/learning specialists:
Yes
Schools three or more graduates have attended over the past five years:
Columbia, Georgetown, Johns Hopkins, Notre Dame, Princeton, Rice, University of Chicago, University of Maryland, University of Virginia, Yale

SPECIAL FEATURES

ENROLLMENT
Total number of students attending and graduating class size: 255 / 28
Birthday cut-off: Not applicable
% Diversity: 24%
Grades with openings: 6th (30), 7th (10-15), 9th (8-10)

SUMMER PROGRAMS
Yes: academics, sports

ART PROGRAMS
Art, chorus, computer graphics, drama, jazz band, music, orchestra

SPORTS
Baseball, basketball, cross-country, fencing, soccer, tennis, track & field, wrestling

LONG-RANGE PLANS

HISTORY AND MISSION STATEMENT
St. Anselm's Abbey is a small, independent college preparatory school for academically gifted young men. Rooted in the Gospel and guided Benedictine tradition of 1500 years, we foster within the entire school community an awareness of the sacredness of creation and a desire to live within a covenant of peace. We strive to engender a love of truth, a vital intellectual curiosity, and a profound respect for prayer and work, virtue and service. With a zeal for learning and commitment for personal integrity our students develop balance in body, mind, and spirit.

NOTE: This data applies to the 2002–2003 school year.

ST. FRANCIS EPISCOPAL DAY SCHOOL

Year founded: 1988
10033 River Road
Potomac, MD 20854
Head of School:
Walter T. McCoy

GENERAL
Grade range: PN-5th   Coed
Religious affiliation: Episcopal
Average class size: 12 (PN-PK),
15 (K-5th)
School day: 8:30-12:00 or 11:30-3:00
(PN-PK), 8:15-3:15 (K-5th)
Morning or after-school care:
3:15-5:30

CAMPUS/CAMPUS LIFE
Facilities: New wing
Lunch provided: No
Boarding option: No
Bus service: No
School uniform or dress code:
Dress code: PN-PK appropriate
Uniform: K-5th
Handicapped access available: Yes
Community service requirement:
Yes

Director of Admission:
Joanne Zinsmeister
Phone: 301-365-2642
Fax: 301-299-0412
E-mail:
zinsmeisterj@sfeds.org
Website:
www.sfeds.org

ADMISSIONS
Application deadline: February 15
Application fee: $50
Application process: Application,
open house, pre-school playgroups,
informal assessment
**Number of students
applied/enrolled:** 120 / 57

COSTS
Tuition: $3,761-$8,137 (PN-PK),
$11,989 (K-5th)
Average additional fees: $250
Financial aid budget: $77,000
Average grant size: 49-100% of
tuition
**% of Students receiving
financial aid:** 3%

NOTE: This data applies to the 2002–2003 school year.

ACADEMIC PROFILE

Number of faculty: 36 Full Time
7 Part Time

Languages and grades offered:
Spanish (K-5th)

Number of AP classes offered:
Not applicable

Tutors/learning specialists:
Yes: reading, speech and language

Schools three or more graduates have attended over the past five years:
Bullis, Connelly School of the Holy
Child, Holton-Arms, Landon,
St. Albans, Stone Ridge

SPECIAL FEATURES
Suburban school in urban environment

ENROLLMENT

Total number of students attending and graduating class size: 240 / 15

Birthday cut-off: September 1
(N -5th), March 1 (PN)

% Diversity: 14%

Grades with openings: PN (20),
N (18), PK (5), plus attrition

SUMMER PROGRAMS
Yes: "Summer Journeys"

ART PROGRAMS
Art, chorus, creative movement,
music

SPORTS
Basketball, soccer

LONG-RANGE PLANS
Be a model parish school, increase
need-based financial aid, strengthen
school, home, church collaboration

HISTORY AND MISSION STATEMENT

The St. Francis Episcopal Day School opened in response to the need for a quality Christian education program. The school has expanded from a preschool with 48 students to Grade 5 with a current enrollment of 240. As SFEDS begins its 13th year of operation it is committed to abide by its identity as a Christian mission and to carry out the plans of our vision statement.

NOTE: This data applies to the 2002–2003 school year.

ST. JOHN'S COLLEGE HIGH SCHOOL

Year founded: 1851
2607 Military Road, NW
Washington, DC 20015
Head of School:
Jeffrey W. Mancabelli

GENERAL
Grade range: 9th-12th   Coed
Religious affiliation: Catholic
Average class size: 22
School day:
Morning or after-school care:
No

CAMPUS/CAMPUS LIFE
Facilities:
27 acre urban campus adjacent
to Rock Creek Park with new
athletic center
Lunch provided: Yes
Boarding option: No
Bus service: Yes
School uniform or dress code:
Uniform
Handicapped access available: No
Community service requirement:
Yes

Director of Admission:
Edward A. Miehle
Phone: 202-363-2316
Fax: 202-686-5162
E-mail:
admissions@stjohns-chs.org
Website:
www.stjohns-chs.org

ADMISSIONS
Application deadline:
January 10
Application fee: $35
Application process: Terra Nova
(9th-12th)
**Number of students
applied/enrolled:**

COSTS
Tuition: $9,000
Average additional fees: $400
Financial aid budget:
Average grant size:
**% of Students receiving
financial aid:**

NOTE: This data applies to the 2002–2003 school year.

ACADEMIC PROFILE
Number of faculty:
Languages and grades offered:
French, Spanish (9th-12th)
Number of AP classes offered:
Tutors/learning specialists:
Yes: Benilde Learning Differences
Program
Schools three or more graduates have
attended over the past five years:
Boston College, Catholic, Fordham,
LaSalle, University of Maryland

SPECIAL FEATURES

ENROLLMENT
Total number of students
attending and graduating
class size: 950 /
Birthday cut-off: Not applicable
% Diversity: 40%
Grades with openings:

SUMMER PROGRAMS
Yes

ART PROGRAMS

SPORTS
Baseball, basketball, cross-country,
football, lacrosse, golf, soccer,
softball, swimming & diving,
track & field, wrestling

LONG-RANGE PLANS

HISTORY AND MISSION STATEMENT

NOTE: This data applies to the 2002–2003 school year.

ST. JOHN'S EPISCOPAL SCHOOL

Year founded: 1961
3427 Olney-Laytonsville Road
Olney, MD 20832
Head of School:
John H. Zurn

GENERAL
Grade range: K-8th   Coed
Religious affiliation: Episcopal
Average class size: 18
School day: 8:25-3:15, 8:25-1:50 F
Morning or after-school care:
7:00-6:00

CAMPUS/CAMPUS LIFE
Facilities:
New Lower School building, arts center,
gymnasium
Lunch provided: No
Boarding option: No
Bus service: No
School uniform or dress code:
Uniform
Handicapped access available: Yes
Community service requirement:
Yes

Director of Admission:
John H. Zurn
Phone: 301-774-6804
Fax: 301-774-2375
E-mail:
tiffney.brockway@
stjohnsepiscopalschool.com
Website:
www.stjohnsepiscopalschool.com

ADMISSIONS
Application deadline: February 1
Application fee: $50
Application process:
Informal assessment
Number of students
applied/enrolled: 125 / 52

COSTS
Tuition: $9,100
Average additional fees:
$245 (K-5th), $475 (6th-8th)
Financial aid budget: $145,000
Average grant size: $2,500
% of Students receiving
financial aid: 12%

NOTE: This data applies to the 2002–2003 school year.

ACADEMIC PROFILE
Number of faculty: 35 Full Time
Languages and grades offered:
French (7th-8th), Latin (7th-8th),
Spanish (K-8th)
Number of AP classes offered:
Not applicable
Tutors/learning specialists:
Yes: reading, counseling, resource
specialists
Schools three or more graduates have attended over the past five years:
Georgetown Prep, Good Counsel,
Holy Cross, Landon, National Cathedral,
St. Andrew's, Stone Ridge

SPECIAL FEATURES

ENROLLMENT
Total number of students attending and graduating class size: 323 / 36
Birthday cut-off: October 1
% Diversity: 11%
Grades with openings: K (36),
plus attrition

SUMMER PROGRAMS
Yes: academics, day camp, sports

ART PROGRAMS
Art, drama, music

SPORTS
Basketball, lacrosse, running, soccer

LONG-RANGE PLANS
Build arts center

HISTORY AND MISSION STATEMENT
To provide a structured and challenging academic program; an everyday focus on Christian values and moral character; a community centered approach to learning.

NOTE: This data applies to the 2002–2003 school year.

ST. PATRICK'S EPISCOPAL DAY SCHOOL

Year founded: 1956
4700 Whitehaven Parkway, NW
Washington, DC 20007
Head of School:
Peter A. Barrett

GENERAL
Grade range: N-8th   Coed
Religious affiliation: Episcopal
Average class size: 15
School day: 9:00-12:00 or 2:50 (N)
8:15-2:50 M-Th, 8:15-12:00 F (K-3rd)
8:00-2:50 M-Th, 8:00-12:00 F (4th-6th)
8:00-4:00 M, T, W, F, 8:00-2:30 Th
(7th-8th)
Morning or after-school care:
Until 6:00

CAMPUS/CAMPUS LIFE
Facilities:
2 campuses, 34 classrooms, 2 art
studios, cafeteria, chapel, gymnasium/
performance center, 2 libraries,
3 music rooms, 3 playgrounds,
2 acre playing field, 3 science labs,
3 technology centers
Lunch provided: No
Boarding option: No
Bus service: No
School uniform or dress code:
None
Handicapped access available: Yes
Community service requirement:
None

Director of Admission:
Jennifer Danish
Phone: 202-342-2805
Fax: 202-342-7001
E-mail:
danish@stpatsdc.org
Website:
www.stpatsdc.org

ADMISSIONS
Application deadline: January 31,
December 13 (siblings, parishioners)
Application fee: $50
Application process: Informal
assessment (N-PK), WPPSI-R (K),
WISC III (1st-5th), SSAT or ISEE
(6th-8th)
**Number of students
applied/enrolled:**

COSTS
Tuition: $8,600-$13,150 (N-PK),
$16,150 (K-6th), $16,950
(7th-8th)
Average additional fees: $680
Financial aid budget: $810,000
Average grant size: $10,509
**% of Students receiving
financial aid:** 16%

NOTE: This data applies to the 2002–2003 school year.

ACADEMIC PROFILE

Number of faculty: 70 Full Time
14 Part Time
Languages and grades offered:
French, Spanish in after school program
Number of AP classes offered:
Not applicable
Tutors/learning specialists:
Yes: resource teachers
Schools three or more graduates have attended over the past five years:
Bullis, Holton-Arms, Landon, Maret,
National Cathedral, St. Albans,
St. Andrew's, Sidwell Friends

SPECIAL FEATURES

ENROLLMENT

Total number of students attending and graduating class size: 457 / 44
Birthday cut-off: September 1
% Diversity: 21%
Grades with openings: N (28),
PK (23), K (5-12), 7th (10-15),
plus attrition

SUMMER PROGRAMS
Yes: day program

ART PROGRAMS
Art, drama, handbells

SPORTS
Basketball, cross-country,
lacrosse, soccer

LONG-RANGE PLANS
Consider extending program
through 12th grade making
St. Patrick's the only coeducational,
Episcopal secondary school in the
nation's capital

HISTORY AND MISSION STATEMENT

St. Patrick's Episcopal Day School educates children in Nursery through Grade 8.
The active, growing, changing individuals within this diverse learning community
- students, teachers, parents - recognize the infinite value of every participant as a
child of God. We strive to create an atmosphere of trust and cooperation in which
to nourish each child's growth toward personal integrity and a lifetime of service.

NOTE: This data applies to the 2002–2003 school year.

ST. STEPHEN'S & ST. AGNES SCHOOL

Year founded: 1924
400 Fontaine Street
Alexandria, VA 22302
Head of School:
Joan G. Ogilvy Holden

GENERAL
Grade range: K-12th   Coed
Religious affiliation: Episcopal
Average class size: 16
School day: 8:00-3:00
Morning or after-school care:
7:00-6:00 (Lower School),
3:00-6:00 (Middle School)

CAMPUS/CAMPUS LIFE
Facilities: 35 acre Upper School campus
at 1000 St. Stephen's Rd.; 16 acre Lower
School campus at 400 Fontaine St.;
7 acre Middle School campus at
4401 West Braddock Rd.
Lunch provided: Yes
Boarding option: No
Bus service: Yes
School uniform or dress code:
Uniform: K-5th - khaki or navy
shorts/long pants/skirts or plaid
skirt/jumper and collared shirts.
Dress Code: Middle/Upper -
no jeans or t-shirts. Sunday
dress for chapel (6th-12th)
Handicapped access available:
Yes: Middle and Upper Schools
Community service requirement:
Yes: 40 hours before senior year,
opportunities at all grades

Director of Admission:
Diane Dunning
Phone: Lower: 703-212-2705
Middle/Upper: 703-212-2706
Fax: Lower: 703-838-0032
Middle/Upper: 703-751-7142
E-mail:
DDunning@sssas.org (K-12th)
TDoyle@sssas.org (Middle/Upper)
Website:
www.sssas.org

ADMISSIONS
Application deadline: January 15
Application fee: $60
Application process: Parent
interview, applicant interview
(2nd-12th), play date (K-1st),
WPPSI-R (K), WISC III (1st-5th),
achievement testing (2nd-5th)
SSAT or ISEE (6th-12th), teacher
recommendations, application,
transcripts,
**Number of students
applied/enrolled:**

COSTS
Tuition: $12,000-$16,400 (K-5th),
$17,400 (6th-8th)
$18,400 (9th-12th)
Average additional fees: Varies
Financial aid budget: $2,000,000
Average grant size: 10-90% of
tuition
**% of Students receiving
financial aid:** 19%

NOTE: This data applies to the 2002–2003 school year.

ACADEMIC PROFILE
Number of faculty: 170
Languages and grades offered:
French (4th-12th), Latin (6th-12th),
Spanish (4th-12th)
Number of AP classes offered: 20
Tutors/learning specialists:
Yes: organizational skills,
language/writing
Schools three or more graduates have attended over the past five years:
Columbia, Duke, James Madison,
Princeton, University of Virginia,
Virginia Polytechnic Institute and State
University, William and Mary

SPECIAL FEATURES
Single gender math and science classes
(6th-8th), interdisciplinary history
program in Upper School, Junior
Kindergarten for "young" 5 year olds
who progress to Kindergarten

ENROLLMENT
Total number of students attending and graduating class size: 1,150 / 110
Birthday cut-off:
September 1 (K)
October 1 ("young" K class)
% Diversity: 20%
Grades with openings: JK (12),
K (48-52), 4th (6-8), 6th (20),
7th (20), 9th (20), plus attrition

SUMMER PROGRAMS
Yes: art/fine arts, computers, day
camp, enrichment, sports

ART PROGRAMS
New Performing Arts
Center/Chapel, extensive art,
music, drama

SPORTS
Baseball, basketball, cross-country,
diving, field hockey, football, golf,
ice hockey, lacrosse, soccer, softball,
swimming, tennis, track & field,
volleyball, wrestling

LONG-RANGE PLANS

HISTORY AND MISSION STATEMENT

St. Stephen's & St. Agnes School is a college preparatory Episcopal Church School in the Diocese of Virginia that educates boys and girls from junior kindergarten through twelfth grade. To help our students succeed in a complex and changing world, we seek to inspire a passion for learning, an enthusiasm for athletic and artistic endeavors, a striving for excellence, a celebration of diversity and a commitment to service. Our mission is to pursue goodness as well as knowledge and to honor the unique value of each of our members as a child of God in a caring community.

NOTE: This data applies to the 2002–2003 school year.

STONE RIDGE SCHOOL OF THE SACRED HEART

Year founded: 1923
9101 Rockville Pike
Bethesda, MD 20814
Head of School:
Sister Anne Dyer

GENERAL
Grade range: PK-12th (Girls),
PK-K (Boys)
Religious affiliation: Catholic
Average class size: 16
School day: 8:00-3:00
Morning or after-school care:
3:00-6:00

CAMPUS/CAMPUS LIFE
Facilities:
35 acre campus, new Upper School
building and competition size
swimming pool
Lunch provided: Yes
Boarding option: No
Bus service: No
School uniform or dress code:
Uniform: 1st-12th
Handicapped access available: Yes
Community service requirement:
Yes

Director of Admission:
Andrea R. Williams
Phone: 301-657-4322 x321
Fax: 301-657-4393
E-mail:
admissions@stoneridge.org
Website:
www.stoneridge.org

ADMISSIONS
Application deadline: January 15
Application fee: $50
Application process: WPPSI-R
(K-1st), WISC III and ERB
(2nd-6th), SSAT, ISEE, or ERB
(6th-12th)
**Number of students
applied/enrolled:** / 121

COSTS
Tuition: $8,460 (half day PK),
$13,660 (full day PK-6th),
$14,610 (7th-8th),
$16,010 (9th-12th)
Average additional fees: $300
Financial aid budget: $1,000,000
Average grant size: $7,800
**% of Students receiving
financial aid:** 21%

NOTE: This data applies to the 2002–2003 school year.

ACADEMIC PROFILE

Number of faculty: 132

Languages and grades offered:

French (5th-12th), Latin (8th-12th),
Spanish (5th-12th)

Number of AP classes offered: 10

Tutors/learning specialists:

Yes: learning, reading

Schools three or more graduates have attended over the past five years:

SPECIAL FEATURES

Independent study, career internships,
exchange program, Coed program PK-K
New competition size swimming pool

ENROLLMENT

Total number of students attending and graduating class size: 808 / 78

Birthday cut-off: September 1

% Diversity: 21%

Grades with openings:

PK, K, 3, 5, 7, 9

SUMMER PROGRAMS

Yes

ART PROGRAMS

Art, dance, drama, music

SPORTS

Basketball, cross-country, diving,
field hockey, lacrosse, soccer,
softball, swimming, tennis, track &
field, volleyball

LONG-RANGE PLANS

HISTORY AND MISSION STATEMENT

Stone Ridge is a Catholic, independent, college preparatory school for girls rooted in the tradition of Sacred Heart education around the world and committed to the contemporary expression of Sacred Heart values. A Stone Ridge education enables young women to develop a personal faith and prepares them to take their places as informed and active members of the Church and society. Consequently, the school provides programs that expose students to the needs of the world, awaken their sense of personal responsibility, and equip them with leadership skills.

NOTE: This data applies to the 2002–2003 school year.

THORNTON FRIENDS UPPER SCHOOL (MD)

Year founded: 1973
13925 New Hampshire Avenue
Silver Spring, MD 20904
Head of School:
Michael DeHart

GENERAL
Grade range: 9th-12th   Coed
Religious affiliation: Society of Friends
(Quaker)
Average class size: 9
School day: 8:30-2:45, 8:30-12:25 W
Morning or after-school care:
No

CAMPUS/CAMPUS LIFE
Facilities:
3 campuses: MD 6th-8th
11612 New Hampshire Ave.;
MD 9th-12th 13925 New
Hampshire Ave.; VA 9th-12th
3830 Seminary Rd. Alexandria, VA
Lunch provided: No
Boarding option: No
Bus service: No
School uniform or dress code:
Dress code: appropriate
Handicapped access available: Yes
Community service requirement:
Yes: 40 hours per year

Director of Admission:
Norman Maynard
Phone: 301-384-0320
Fax: 301-236-9481
E-mail:
admissions@thorntonfriends.org
Website:
www.thorntonfriends.org

ADMISSIONS
Application deadline: Rolling
Application fee: $50
Application process: Interview with
Principal during day-long visit,
4 references, transcript, essay
questions
**Number of students
applied/enrolled:** 45 / 16

COSTS
Tuition: $15,295 (9th-12th)
Average additional fees: $400
Financial aid budget: $101,740
Average grant size: $6,359
**% of Students receiving
financial aid:** 30%

NOTE: This data applies to the 2002–2003 school year.

ACADEMIC PROFILE

Number of faculty: 10 Full Time

Languages and grades offered:
Spanish I and II (9th-12th)

Number of AP classes offered:
None

Tutors/learning specialists:
None

Schools three or more graduates have attended over the past five years:
Davis & Elkins, Earlham, Eckerd, Frostburg State, Guilford, Mitchell, Montgomery, New England, Temple

SPECIAL FEATURES

ENROLLMENT

Total number of students attending and graduating class size: 54 / 12

Birthday cut-off: Not applicable

% Diversity: 15%

Grades with openings: 9th (4-6), 10th (3-4), 11th (2-3), 12th (rarely)

SUMMER PROGRAMS
None

ART PROGRAMS
Drama, drawing, painting, stained glass making

SPORTS
Basketball, soccer, softball

LONG-RANGE PLANS
Thornton's belief that quality education can only happen in a small, personal setting, leads to the creation of small, cluster campuses in which every individual is known.

HISTORY AND MISSION STATEMENT

Thornton Friends Schools' mission is to provide a school in which students who have not previously done well might have their interest in learning reinvigorated. Thornton seeks to allow teachers and students to learn cooperatively through relationships based on trust, respect and shared excitement for learning. A middle school and a second upper school opened in 1993 and 1997. All three campuses form the present day Thornton Friends School.

NOTE: This data applies to the 2002–2003 school year.

THORNTON FRIENDS SCHOOL (VA)

Year founded: 1997
3830 Seminary Road
Alexandria, VA 22304
Head of School:
Michael DeHart

GENERAL
Grade range: 9th-12th   Coed
Religious affiliation: Society of Friends
(Quaker)
Average class size: 9
School day: 8:15-2:55, 8:15-12:25 W
Morning or after-school care:
No

CAMPUS/CAMPUS LIFE
Facilities:
3 campuses:
MD 6th-8th 11612 New Hampshire Ave.;
MD 9th-12th 13925 New Hampshire Ave.;
VA 9th-12th 3830 Seminary Rd.
Alexandria, VA
Lunch provided: No
Boarding option: No
Bus service: No
School uniform or dress code:
None
Handicapped access available: No
Community service requirement:
Yes: 40 hours per year

Director of Admission:
Gail Miller
Phone: 703-461-8880
Fax: 703-461-3697
E-mail:
admissions@thorntonfriends.org
Website:
www.thorntonfriends.org

ADMISSIONS
Application deadline: Rolling
Application fee: $50
Application process: Interview with
Principal during day-long visit,
4 references, transcript, essay
questions
**Number of students
applied/enrolled:** 22 / 15

COSTS
Tuition: $15,395 (9th-12th)
Average additional fees: $400
Financial aid budget: $50,995
Average grant size: $10,199
**% of Students receiving
financial aid:** 14%

NOTE: This data applies to the 2002–2003 school year.

ACADEMIC PROFILE
Number of faculty: 8 Full Time
1 Part Time
Languages and grades offered:
Spanish (9th-12th)
Number of AP classes offered:
None
Tutors/learning specialists:
None
Schools three or more graduates have attended over the past five years:
Antioch, Auburn, Bard, Beloit, Case Western Reserve, Colorado College, Dartmouth, Guilford, Earlham, New College of South Florida

SPECIAL FEATURES
New building, performance hall, technology curriculum, writing center

ENROLLMENT
Total number of students attending and graduating class size: 41 / 12
Birthday cut-off: Not applicable
% Diversity: 18%

Grades with openings: 9th (5), 10th (5), 11th (4), 12th (rarely)

SUMMER PROGRAMS
None

ART PROGRAMS
Music appreciation, studio art, theater arts

SPORTS
Basketball, coed soccer, coed softball

LONG-RANGE PLANS
Thornton's belief that quality education can only happen in a small, personal setting, leads to the creation of small, cluster campuses in which every individual is known.

HISTORY AND MISSION STATEMENT

Thornton Friends Schools' mission is to provide a school in which students who have not previously done well might have their interest in learning reinvigorated. Thornton seeks to allow teachers and students to learn cooperatively through relationships based on trust, respect and shared excitement for learning. A middle school and a second upper school opened in 1993 and 1997. All three campuses form the present day Thornton Friends School.

NOTE: This data applies to the 2002–2003 school year.

THORNTON FRIENDS MIDDLE SCHOOL (MD)

Year founded: 1994
11612 New Hampshire Avenue
Silver Spring, MD 20904
Head of School:
Michael DeHart

GENERAL
Grade range: 6th-8th   Coed
Religious affiliation: Society of Friends
(Quaker)
Average class size: 9
School day: 8:30-3:00, 8:30-2:30 W
Morning or after-school care:
3:00-5:00 (except W)

CAMPUS/CAMPUS LIFE
Facilities:
3 campuses:
MD 6th-8th 11612 New Hampshire Ave.;
MD 9th-12th 13925 New Hampshire Ave.;
VA 9th-12th 3830 Seminary Rd.
Alexandria, VA
Lunch provided: No
Boarding option: No
Bus service: No
School uniform or dress code:
None
Handicapped access available: No
Community service requirement:
Yes: 3 hours per week

Director of Admission:
Benj Thomas
Phone: 301-622-9033
Fax: 301-622-4786
E-mail:
admissions@thorntonfriends.org
Website:
www.thorntonfriends.org

ADMISSIONS
Application deadline: Rolling
Application fee: $50
Application process: Interview with
Principal during day-long visit,
4 references, transcript, essay
questions
**Number of students
applied/enrolled:** 24 / 18

COSTS
Tuition: $14,095 (6th-8th)
Average additional fees: $450
Financial aid budget: $57,985
Average grant size: $7,248
**% of Students receiving
financial aid:** 22%

NOTE: This data applies to the 2002–2003 school year.

ACADEMIC PROFILE

Number of faculty: 7 Full Time
1 Part Time
Languages and grades offered:
Spanish (6th-8th)
Number of AP classes offered:
Not applicable
Tutors/learning specialists:
None
Schools three or more graduates have attended over the past five years:
Barrie, Edmund Burke, Sandy Spring Friends School, Thornton Upper School, public

SPECIAL FEATURES

Regular community service, hands-on, interdisciplinary

ENROLLMENT

Total number of students attending and graduating class size: 37 / 17
Birthday cut-off: Not applicable
% Diversity: 30%
Grades with openings: 6th (11), 7th (11), 8th (5-10)

SUMMER PROGRAMS

None

ART PROGRAMS

Drama, visual arts

SPORTS

Basketball, soccer, softball

LONG-RANGE PLANS

Thornton's belief that quality education can only happen in a small, personal setting, leads to the creation of small, cluster campuses in which every individual is known.

HISTORY AND MISSION STATEMENT

Thornton Friends Schools' mission is to provide a school in which students who have not previously done well might have their interest in learning reinvigorated. Thornton seeks to allow teachers and students to learn cooperatively through relationships based on trust, respect and shared excitement for learning. A middle school and a second upper school opened in 1993 and 1997. All three campuses form the present day Thornton Friends School.

NOTE: This data applies to the 2002–2003 school year.

TOWN AND COUNTRY SCHOOL OF VIENNA

Year founded: 1971
9525 Leesburg Pike
Vienna, VA 22182
Head of School:
Barbara Logan

GENERAL
Grade range: N-6th   Coed
Religious affiliation: Nonsectarian
Average class size: 15
School day: 9:00-3:45
Morning or after-school care:
7:00-6:00

CAMPUS/CAMPUS LIFE
Facilities:
6 acre networked campus, art studio,
basketball court, computer lab, fields,
library, 2 playgrounds, pool
Lunch provided: Yes
Boarding option: No
Bus service: Yes
School uniform or dress code:
Dress code: boys - khakis and polo
shirts; girls - jumpers, skirts, pants, shirts
Handicapped access available: Limited
Community service requirement:
No requirement, but active participation

Director of Admission:
Barbara Logan
Phone: 703-759-3000
Fax: 703-759-5526
E-mail:
townandcountry@yahoo.com
Website:
www.tcvienna.com

ADMISSIONS
Application deadline: January 30
Application fee: $50
Application process: Parent tour,
application, transcript, teacher
recommendation, applicant visit
Number of students
applied/enrolled:

COSTS
Tuition: $6,600 (N-PK half day),
$9,500 (PK-1st), $9,700 (2nd-6th)
Average additional fees: $430
Financial aid budget:
Average grant size:
% of Students receiving
financial aid:

NOTE: This data applies to the 2002–2003 school year.

ACADEMIC PROFILE
Number of faculty: 20 Full Time
5 Part Time
Languages and grades offered:
Spanish (N-6th)
Number of AP classes offered:
Not applicable
Tutors/learning specialists:
Yes: tutors, speech therapists at an
additional fee
**Schools three or more graduates have
attended over the past five years:**
Flint Hill, Loudoun Country Day,
public schools

SPECIAL FEATURES
After school program includes Spanish,
karate, arts, sports, gymnastics,
piano, science, book club;
networked campus

ENROLLMENT
**Total number of students
attending and graduating
class size:** 200 /
Birthday cut-off: September 30
% Diversity: 27 different countries
Grades with openings: N (20),
PK (20), K (14), 1st (6),
plus attrition

SUMMER PROGRAMS
Yes: day camp (ages 3-12), sports,
pool on campus, recreational

ART PROGRAMS
Art, drama, music

SPORTS
Physical fitness—aerobics,
basketball, running, soccer,
softball, volleyball

LONG-RANGE PLANS
Build new gymnasium and
classrooms, add 7th and 8th grades

HISTORY AND MISSION STATEMENT
Our vision is to create a unique educational environment built on sound research,
qualified instruction and a sense of community that fosters academic excellence,
instills a love of active learning, and provides experiences that enable all students
to acquire a firm foundation of skills for lifelong achievement. We work with the
whole child for a balanced education.

NOTE: This data applies to the 2002–2003 school year.

WASHINGTON EPISCOPAL SCHOOL

Year founded: 1985
5600 Little Falls Parkway
Bethesda, MD 20816
Head of School:
Stuart Work

GENERAL
Grade range: N-8th   Coed
Religious affiliation: Episcopal
Average class size: 16
School day: 8:25-3:25
Morning or after-school care:
3:30-6:00

CAMPUS/CAMPUS LIFE
Facilities:
6 acre newly renovated campus
with art and music rooms, gym,
sports field, theater
Lunch provided: No
Boarding option: No
Bus service: No
School uniform or dress code:
Uniform: girls - plaid jumper or skirt,
white blouse; boys - tan pants,
white shirt, tie 7th-8th only
Handicapped access available: Yes
Community service requirement:
Yes: 10 hours in 7th-8th

Director of Admission:
Kathleen Herman
Phone: 301-652-7878
Fax: 301-652-7255
E-mail:
kherman@w-e-s.org
Website:
www.w-e-s.org

ADMISSIONS
Application deadline: February 1
Application fee: $50
Application process: Informal
assessment (N-PK), WPPSI-R (K),
WISC III (1st-6th), ISSE or SSAT
(7th-8th)
Number of students
applied/enrolled: 250 / 50

COSTS
Tuition: $8,600-$10,750 (N),
$16,595 (PK), $16,995 (K-8th)
Average additional fees:
$350 (7th-8th)
Financial aid budget: $500,000
Average grant size: $10,000
% of Students receiving
financial aid: 10%

NOTE: This data applies to the 2002–2003 school year.

ACADEMIC PROFILE

Number of faculty: 60

Languages and grades offered:

French (PK-8th), Latin (5th-8th)

Number of AP classes offered:

Not applicable

Tutors/learning specialists:

Yes: psychologist, resource teachers, tutors at an additional fee

Schools three or more graduates have attended over the past five years:

Bullis, Connelly School of the Holy Child, Georgetown Prep, Georgetown Visitation, Gonzaga, Madeira, Maret, St. Albans, St. Andrew's, St. John's College High, Sidwell Friends

SPECIAL FEATURES

Pentanque team

ENROLLMENT

Total number of students attending and graduating class size: 325 / 36

Birthday cut-off: September 1

% Diversity: 7%

Grades with openings: N (14), PK (14-16), K (6-10), plus attrition

SUMMER PROGRAMS

Yes: academic, sports day programs, sleep away camp

ART PROGRAMS

Movement class (N-2nd), band (4th-8th), chorus (5th-8th)

SPORTS

Basketball, lacrosse, soccer, softball, track & field

LONG-RANGE PLANS

HISTORY AND MISSION STATEMENT

Washington Episcopal School's focus is on helping students to become confident, happy, respectful, loving people. We build a strong partnership among the students and their families, the faculty and staff, and a network of fellow professionals. The WES program is rich in content and discipline to create a firm educational foundation. Our children work hard, have fun together, and enjoy one another in their daily living and growing.

NOTE: This data applies to the 2002–2003 school year.

WASHINGTON INTERNATIONAL SCHOOL

Year founded: 1966
3100 Macomb Street, NW
Washington, DC 20008
Head of School:
Richard P. Hall

GENERAL
Grade range: N-12th   Coed
Religious affiliation: Nonsectarian
Average class size: 16
School day: 8:45-3:00 (PK-K),
8:30-3:30 (1st-5th), 8:15-2:50
(6th-12th)
Morning or after-school care:
8:00-6:00

CAMPUS/CAMPUS LIFE
Facilities:
7 acre Middle and Upper School
campus with 2 art studios, auditorium,
darkroom, 2 libraries, 7 science labs;
PK-5th campus occupies a city block
on 36th Street, NW
Lunch provided: Yes: optional
Boarding option: No
Bus service: Limited
School uniform or dress code:
Dress code: neat and appropriate
Handicapped access available: Yes
Community service requirement:
Yes: active participation at all
grade levels

Director of Admission:
Dorrie Fuchs
Phone: 202-243-1815
Fax: 202-243-1807
E-mail:
admissions@wis.edu
Website:
www.wis.edu

ADMISSIONS
Application deadline: January 15
Application fee: $50
Application process: Application,
teacher recommendation,
transcript, informal assessment
(PK-1st), in-house testing
(2nd-12th)
**Number of students
applied/enrolled:** 655 / 149

COSTS
Tuition: $13,690 (PK), $16,500
(K-5th), $18,380 (6th-12th)
Average additional fees: $400-$600
Financial aid budget: $980,000
Average grant size: $10,500
**% of Students receiving
financial aid:** 12%

NOTE: This data applies to the 2002–2003 school year.

ACADEMIC PROFILE
Number of faculty: 95 Full Time
18 Part Time
Languages and grades offered:
Dutch (1st-12th for native speakers),
French (PK-12th), Spanish (PK-12th)
Number of AP classes offered:
International Baccalaureate
Tutors/learning specialists:
Yes: tutorial support for ESL
Schools three or more graduates have attended over the past five years:
Cornell, George Washington, London School of Economics, McGill, Oberlin, Princeton, University of Bristol (UK), University of Toronto, University of Virginia, Vassar

SPECIAL FEATURES
Culturally and racially diverse, ESL, bilingual curriculum

ENROLLMENT
Total number of students attending and graduating class size: 820 / 58
Birthday cut-off: September 1
% Diversity: 12%
plus 21% international students
Grades with openings: PK (35-45), K (25-30), 6th (12-16), 7th (6-10), 9th (8-10)

SUMMER PROGRAMS
Yes: academic review, bilingual summer camp, ESL courses, summer language institute

ART PROGRAMS
Art, chorus, instrumental music, theater arts

SPORTS
Baseball, basketball, cross-country, golf, soccer, softball, tennis, track & field, volleyball

LONG-RANGE PLANS

HISTORY AND MISSION STATEMENT

Unique among Washington's independent schools, unusual even among international schools worldwide, WIS offers a demanding, globally focused academic program in an environment that prizes respect for individuals and individual differences. Our students, their families, and the faculty and staff represent nearly ninety countries and bring to the School a breadth of experience and an array of talents. WIS also enrolls American children drawn by the bilingual curriculum, the strength of the academic program, and the rich diversity of the community.

NOTE: This data applies to the 2002–2003 school year.

WASHINGTON WALDORF SCHOOL

Year founded: 1969
4800 Sangamore Road
Bethesda, MD 20816
Head of School:
Brian J. Lake

GENERAL
Grade range: N-12th   Coed
Religious affiliation: Nonsectarian
Average class size: 26 (N-8th), 23 (9th-12th)
School day: 8:30-3:00 (N-8th), 8:15-3:00 (9th-12th)
Morning or after-school care: 3:00-6:00 (1st-6th)

CAMPUS/CAMPUS LIFE
Facilities:
2 art studios, auditorium, computer lab, crafts room, library, music room, playground, 2 science labs, playing fields, tennis courts, woodworking shop
Lunch provided: No
Boarding option: No
Bus service: No
School uniform or dress code:
None
Handicapped access available: Yes
Community service requirement:
None, but active participation in Upper School

Director of Admission:
Ed Buckley
Phone: 301-229-6107 x154
Fax: 301-229-9379
E-mail:
info@washingtonwaldorf.org
Website:
www.washingtonwaldorf.org

ADMISSIONS
Application deadline: Rolling
Application fee: $40
Application process: In-house assessment (9th-12th)
Number of students applied/enrolled: 168 / 76

COSTS
Tuition: $2,490-$12,450 (N-8th), $13,050 (9th-12th)
Average additional fees: $400
Financial aid budget: $380,000
Average grant size: Maximum of 75% of tuition
% of Students receiving financial aid: 24%

NOTE: This data applies to the 2002–2003 school year.

ACADEMIC PROFILE

Number of faculty: 33 Full TIme
8 Part Time
Languages and grades offered:
German, Spanish (1st-12th)
Number of AP classes offered: 1
Tutors/learning specialists:
Yes: math, German, Spanish
Schools three or more graduates have attended over the past five years:
Bates, Colorado College, George Washington, Goucher, New York University, Oberlin, Syracuse, University of Maryland, University of Michigan, University of Virginia, Yale

SPECIAL FEATURES

3½ to 6 year old program called "Children's Garden" for 50 students, can accommodate a limited number of ESL students, primary teacher remains with same class from 1st-8th, movement education, and Eurythmy

ENROLLMENT

Total number of students attending and graduating class size: 334 / 20
Birthday cut-off: September (N-K)
May 31 (1st-8th)
% Diversity:
Grades with openings: N (7), PK (7), K (7), 1st (5), 2nd (7), plus attrition

SUMMER PROGRAMS

Yes: camp (5-6 year olds)

ART PROGRAMS

Art, crafts, handwork, metalwork, music, students create Main Lesson books, woodwork

SPORTS

Baseball, basketball, cross-country, soccer, softball, track & field

LONG-RANGE PLANS

The Washington Waldorf School has purchased Chestnut Lodge, a 20 acre site in Rockville, Maryland, move by September 2004

HISTORY AND MISSION STATEMENT

The Washington Waldorf School has been a vital member of the international Waldorf School movement, founded by Rudolf Steiner. We are dedicated to inspiring these qualities in our students: a clear-thinking mind; a warm, compassionate heart; an appreciation of artistic life and form; a purposeful, creative, productive will; a sense of trust in and joy for the evolving human story; and a sense of unity with all life. Our aim is to kindle within each student capacities for articulate self-expression, service to the world, and life long learning and growth.

NOTE: This data applies to the 2002–2003 school year.

WESTMINSTER SCHOOL

Year founded: 1962
3819 Gallows Road
Annandale, VA 22003
Head of School:
Ellis Glover

GENERAL
Grade range: K-8th   Coed
Religious affiliation: Nonsectarian
Average class size: 18
School day: 8:30-3:00
Morning or after-school care:
3:00-5:30

CAMPUS/CAMPUS LIFE
Facilities:
Single-story building, 23 classrooms,
art and music studios, gymnasium,
library
Lunch provided: No
Boarding option: No
Bus service: Yes
School uniform or dress code:
Uniform
Handicapped access available: Yes
Community service requirement:
None

Director of Admission:
Nancy Schuler
Phone: 703-256-3620
Fax: 703-256-9621
E-mail:
admissions@westminsterschool.com
Website:
www.westminsterschool.com

ADMISSIONS
Application deadline: Rolling
Application fee: $100
Application process: In-house
testing, applicant visit, transcript,
teacher recommendation
**Number of students
applied/enrolled:**

COSTS
Tuition: $9,952-$12,284 (K-8th)
Average additional fees:
Financial aid budget:
Average grant size: Not available
to families new to the school
**% of Students receiving
financial aid:**

NOTE: This data applies to the 2002–2003 school year.

ACADEMIC PROFILE
Number of faculty: 28 Full Time
Languages and grades offered:
Latin (7th-8th), French (K-8th)
Number of AP classes offered:
Not applicable
Tutors/learning specialists:
Yes: tutors, teachers available after school
Schools three or more graduates have attended over the past five years:
Bishop Ireton, Bishop O'Connell, Flint Hill, Gonzaga, Madeira, Marshall High (IB), Paul VI St. Stephen's & St. Agnes, Thomas Jefferson

SPECIAL FEATURES
Classical style education in a traditional setting

ENROLLMENT
Total number of students attending and graduating class size: 307 / 26
Birthday cut-off: October 31
% Diversity:
Grades with openings: K (32), 1st (2), 2nd (2), plus attrition, no 8th applicants

SUMMER PROGRAMS
Yes: basketball, English, enrichment courses, French, math, science, summer fun camp, theater

ART PROGRAMS
Art, music, performing arts

SPORTS
Basketball, cross-country, soccer, softball, track & field

LONG-RANGE PLANS
Fine and performing arts center, computer center, and classrooms, library, gymnasium

HISTORY AND MISSION STATEMENT

Westminster provides a superior elementary education based on a structured, classical curriculum; rigorous academic standards; and an emphasis on personal responsiblity, courtesy, and upright conduct. Its well-rounded program both nurtures and challenges children's development in all areas: intellectual, physical, and—with its emphais on the arts—spiritual. With its classical curriculum, challenging academics, and old-fashioned insistence on genuine effort and good manners, Westminster turns out graduates distiguished by their knowledge, study habits, maturity, and self-confidence.

NOTE: This data applies to the 2002–2003 school year.

WOODS ACADEMY (THE)

Year founded: 1975
6801 Greentree Road
Bethesda, MD 20817
Head of School:
Mary C. Worch

GENERAL
Grade range: N-8th   Coed
Religious affiliation: Catholic
Average class size: 30 (N-K),
20 (1st-5th), 12-15 (6th-8th)
School day: 8:25-11:30 (N),
8:25-3:10 (K-8)
Morning or after-school care:
7:15-6:00

CAMPUS/CAMPUS LIFE
Facilities:
6 acre campus, basketball courts,
computer lab, library, playing fields,
science lab, tennis courts
Lunch provided: No
Boarding option: No
Bus service: No
School uniform or dress code:
Dress code: girls - jumpers, skirts,
skorts, white blouse; boys - shorts,
khakis, white button down shirt, tie,
blazer for dress uniform
Handicapped access available: Yes
Community service requirement:
No requirement, but active
participation

Director of Admission:
Barbara B. Snyder
Phone: 301-365-3080
Fax: 301-469-6439
E-mail:
admissions@woodsacademy.org
Website:
www.woodsacademy.org

ADMISSIONS
Application deadline: February 15
Application fee: $50
Application process: Application,
applicant visit, recommendation,
transcript, informal assessment for
Montessori applicants, standardized
testing (1st-4th), ISEE or SSAT
(5th-8th), parent visit
**Number of students
applied/enrolled:** 237 / 43

COSTS
Tuition: $7,225 (half day N),
$9,745 (K-5th), $10,365 (6th-8th)
Average additional fees: $50
Financial aid budget: Limited
Average grant size:
**% of Students receiving
financial aid:**

NOTE: This data applies to the 2002–2003 school year.

ACADEMIC PROFILE

Number of faculty: 32 Full Time
4 Part Time
Languages and grades offered:
French (K-8th)
Number of AP classes offered:
Not applicable
Tutors/learning specialists:
Yes: math and reading specialists (Lower School to facilitate small instructional groups), enrichment teacher, guidance counselors
Schools three or more graduates have attended over the past five years:
Connelly School of the Holy Child, Episcopal High, Georgetown Prep, Georgetown Visitation, Gonzaga, Good Counsel, Heights, Holy Cross, St. Andrew's, St. Anselm's, St. John's College High, Stone Ridge, public IB programs

SPECIAL FEATURES

Montessori program for 3 to 6 year olds, after school study-hall, French instruction beginning with 5-year olds, guitars for all Upper School students, curriculum integration, library theatre (1st-2nd)

ENROLLMENT

Total number of students attending and graduating class size: 240 / 29
Birthday cut-off: September
% Diversity: 10-15%
Grades with openings: N (14), 1st (4), 3rd (4), 6th (9), plus attrition

SUMMER PROGRAMS

None

ART PROGRAMS

Drama, fine arts, guitar, music, public speaking

SPORTS

Basketball, cross-country, soccer, softball, track & field

LONG-RANGE PLANS

New facility to be completed by January 2003, including 10 new classrooms, chapel, music studio, student actvity center with regulation size gym, stage, courtyards

HISTORY AND MISSION STATEMENT

An independent, Catholic school, offering boys and girls from Montessori pre-school through traditional grades one to eight, a challenging and supportive educational program that encourages all students to reach their full intellectual, spiritual, emotional, social, and physical potential.

NOTE: This data applies to the 2002–2003 school year.

Independent School
Maps, Charts, and Worksheet

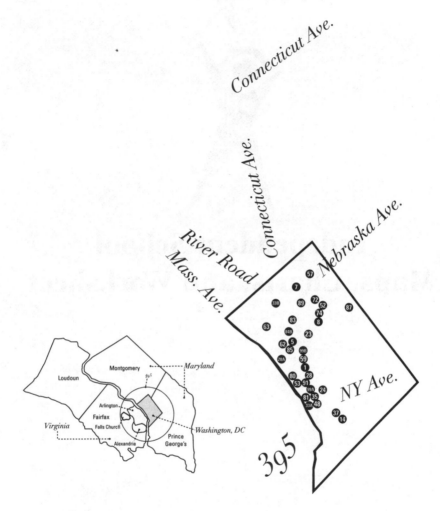

DC Independent Schools

1 Aidan Montessori	37 Gonzaga College High	81 Rock Creek
5 Beauvoir	48 Holy Trinity School	International
7 Blessed Sacrament	52 Kingsbury Day	83 Sheridan School
8 British School	School	Sidwell Friends School
14 Capitol Hill Day School	53 Lab School of	84B Middle/Upper
23 Edmund Burke School	Washington	Lower in Maryland
24 Emerson Preparatory	57 Lowell School	85 St. Albans School
28 Field School (The)	59 Maret School	87 St. Anselm's Abbey
28A New Field site	62 National Cathedral	89 St. John's College High
Georgetown Day School	63 National Presbyterian	91 St. Patrick's
33A Lower/Middle School	72 Owl School (The)	Washington International
33B Upper	74 Parkmont School	99A Lower
35 Georgetown Visitation	80 River School (The)	99B Middle/Upper

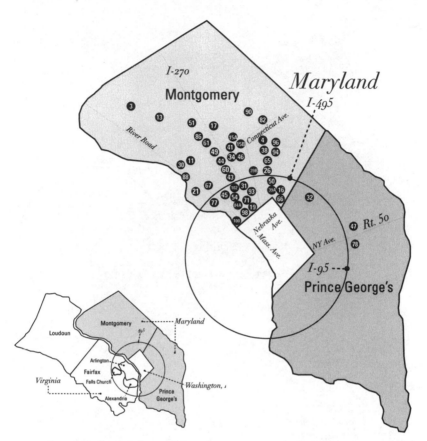

Maryland Independent Schools

Montgomery County
3   Barnesville School
4   Barrie School
11   Bullis School (The)
13   Butler School
Charles E. Smith Jewish
Day School
15A   Lower
15B   Middle/Upper
16   Chelsea School (The)
17   Christ Episcopal
19   Concord Hill School
21   Connelly School
26   Evergreen School
30   Fourth Presbyterian
31   French International
34   Georgetown Preparatory
38   Good Counsel High
Grace Episcopal Day School

39A   Silver Spring
39B   Kensington
41   Green Acres School
43   Harbor School (The)
44   Heights School (The)
45   Holton-Arms School
46   Holy Cross Academy
49   Ivymount School
50   Jewish Primary Day
51   Katherine Thomas
54   Landon School
60   Mater Dei School
61   McLean School of
     Maryland
65   Newport School
66   Nora School (The)
67   Norwood School
71   Oneness-Family School
77   Primary Day School
82   Sandy Spring Friends

Sidwell Friends School
84A   Lower
86   St. Andrew's Episcopal
88   St. Francis Episcopal
90   St. John's Episcopal
93   Stone Ridge School
94   Thornton Friends
     Middle
96   Thornton Friends
     School (MD)
98   Washington Episcopal
100   Washington Waldorf
102   Woods Academy

Prince George's County
32   Friends Community
47   Holy Trinity Episcopal
78   Queen Anne School

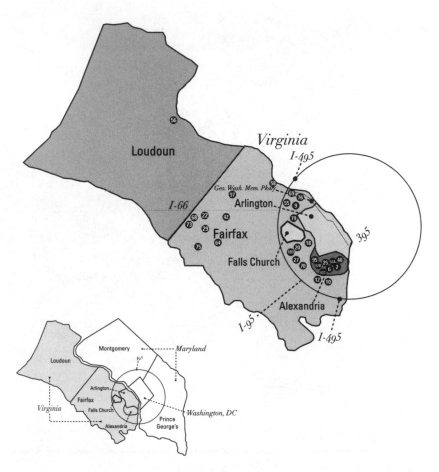

Virginia Independent Schools

Northern Virginia

2 Alexandria Country Day

6 Bishop Ireton High

9 Brooksfield School

10 Browne Academy

12 Burgunday Farm Country Day

18 Commonwealth

20 Congressional Schools

22 Edlin School

25 Episcopal High School

27 Fairfax Collegiate School

29 Flint Hill School

40 Grace Episcopal

42 Green Hedges

55 Langley School (The)

58 Madeira School (The)

64 New School

68 Nysmith School for the Gifted

69 Oakcrest School

70 Oakwood School

73 Paladin Academy

75 Paul VI

76 Potomac School

79 Rivendell

St. Stephen's & St. Agnes

92A Lower

92B Middle

92C Upper

95 Thornton Friends School (VA)

97 Town and Country

101 Westminster School

Loudoun County

56 Loudoun Country Day School

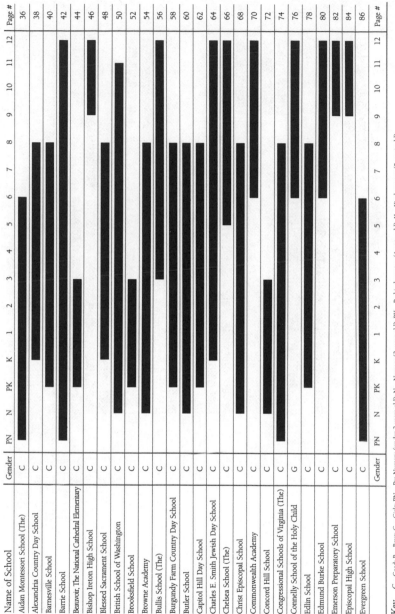

Name of School	Gender	PN	N	PK	K	1	2	3	4	5	6	7	8	9	10	11	12	Page #
Aidan Montessori School (The)	C	■	■	■	■	■	■	■	■	■	■							36
Alexandria Country Day School	C			■	■	■	■	■	■	■	■	■	■					38
Barnesville School	C			■	■	■	■	■	■	■	■	■	■					40
Barrie School	C	■	■	■	■	■	■	■	■	■	■	■	■	■	■	■	■	42
Beauvoir, The National Cathedral Elementary	C	■	■	■	■	■	■	■										44
Bishop Ireton High School	C													■	■	■	■	46
Blessed Sacrament School	C				■	■	■	■	■	■	■	■	■					48
British School of Washington	C				■	■	■	■	■	■	■	■	■	■	■	■		50
Brooksfield School	C		■	■	■	■	■	■										52
Browne Academy	C		■	■	■	■	■	■	■	■	■	■	■					54
Bullis School (The)	C							■	■	■	■	■	■	■	■	■	■	56
Burgundy Farm Country Day School	C		■	■	■	■	■	■	■	■	■	■	■					58
Butler School	C			■	■	■	■	■	■	■	■	■	■					60
Capitol Hill Day School	C			■	■	■	■	■	■	■	■	■	■					62
Charles E. Smith Jewish Day School	C				■	■	■	■	■	■	■	■	■	■	■	■	■	64
Chelsea School (The)	C									■	■	■	■	■	■	■	■	66
Christ Episcopal School	C		■	■	■	■	■	■	■	■	■	■	■					68
Commonwealth Academy	C		■	■	■	■	■	■	■	■	■	■	■	■	■	■	■	70
Concord Hill School	C		■	■	■	■	■	■										72
Congressional Schools of Virginia (The)	C	■	■	■	■	■	■	■	■	■	■	■	■					74
Connelly School of the Holy Child	G										■	■	■	■	■	■	■	76
Edlin School	C			■	■	■	■	■	■	■	■	■	■					78
Edmund Burke School	C										■	■	■	■	■	■	■	80
Emerson Preparatory School	C													■	■	■	■	82
Episcopal High School	C													■	■	■	■	84
Evergreen School	C		■	■	■	■	■	■	■	■	■							86
	Gender	PN	N	PK	K	1	2	3	4	5	6	7	8	9	10	11	12	Page #

Key C = Coed; B = Boys; G = Girls; PN = Pre Nursery (under 3 years old); N = Nursery (3 years old); PK = Prekindergarten (4 years old); K = Kindergarten (5 years old)

Name of School	Gender	PN	N	PK	K	1	2	3	4	5	6	7	8	9	10	11	12	Page #
Fairfax Collegiate School	C								X	X	X	X	X	X				88
Field School (The)	C											X	X	X	X	X	X	90
Flint Hill School	C				X	X	X	X	X	X	X	X	X	X	X	X	X	92
Fourth Presbyterian School	C									X	X	X	X	X	X	X	X	94
French International School (Lycée Rochambeau)	C		X	X	X	X	X	X	X	X	X	X	X	X	X	X	X	96
Friends Community School	C				X	X	X	X	X	X	X							98
Georgetown Day School	C			X	X	X	X	X	X	X	X	X	X	X	X	X	X	100
Georgetown Preparatory School	B													X	X	X	X	102
Georgetown Visitation Preparatory School	G													X	X	X	X	104
Gonzaga College High School	B													X	X	X	X	106
Good Counsel High School	C													X	X	X	X	108
Grace Episcopal Day School	C			X	X	X	X	X	X	X	X							110
Grace Episcopal School	C			X	X	X	X	X	X	X								112
Green Acres School	C			X	X	X	X	X	X	X	X	X	X					114
Green Hedges School	C			X	X	X	X	X	X	X	X	X	X					116
Harbor School (The)	C			X	X	X												118
Heights School (The)	B							X	X	X	X	X	X	X	X	X	X	120
Holton-Arms School	G							X	X	X	X	X	X	X	X	X	X	122
Holy Cross, Academy of the	G													X	X	X	X	124
Holy Trinity Episcopal Day School	C			X	X	X	X	X	X	X	X	X	X					126
Holy Trinity School	C			X	X	X	X	X	X	X	X	X	X					128
Ivymount School	C		X	X	X	X	X	X	X	X	X	X	X	X	X	X	X	130
Jewish Primary Day School of the Nation's Capital	C				X	X	X	X	X	X	X							132
	Gender	PN	N	PK	K	1	2	3	4	5	6	7	8	9	10	11	12	Page #

Key C = Coed; B = Boys; G = Girls; PN = Pre Nursery (under 3 years old); N = Nursery (3 years old); PK = Prekindergarten (4 years old); K = Kindergarten (5 years old)

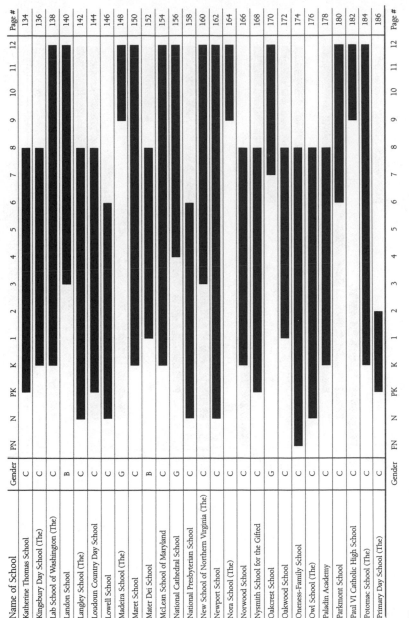

Name of School	Gender	PN	N	PK	K	1	2	3	4	5	6	7	8	9	10	11	12	Page #
Katherine Thomas School	C	■	■	■	■	■	■	■	■	■	■	■	■					134
Kingsbury Day School (The)	C				■	■	■	■	■	■	■	■	■					136
Lab School of Washington (The)	C				■	■	■	■	■	■	■	■	■	■	■	■	■	138
Landon School	B			■	■	■	■	■	■	■	■	■	■	■	■	■	■	140
Langley School (The)	C		■	■	■	■	■	■	■	■	■	■	■					142
Loudoun Country Day School	C		■	■	■	■	■	■	■	■	■	■	■					144
Lowell School	C		■	■	■	■	■	■										146
Madeira School (The)	G													■	■	■	■	148
Maret School	C				■	■	■	■	■	■	■	■	■	■	■	■	■	150
Mater Dei School	B				■	■	■	■	■	■	■	■	■					152
McLean School of Maryland	C				■	■	■	■	■	■	■	■	■	■	■	■	■	154
National Cathedral School	G								■	■	■	■	■	■	■	■	■	156
National Presbyterian School	C		■	■	■	■	■	■										158
New School of Northern Virginia (The)	C							■	■	■	■	■	■	■	■	■	■	160
Newport School	C			■	■	■	■	■	■	■	■	■	■	■	■	■	■	162
Nora School (The)	C												■	■	■	■	■	164
Norwood School	C			■	■	■	■	■	■	■	■	■	■					166
Nysmith School for the Gifted	C			■	■	■	■	■	■	■	■	■	■					168
Oakcrest School	G											■	■	■	■	■	■	170
Oakwood School	C				■	■	■	■	■	■	■	■	■					172
Oneness-Family School	C		■	■	■	■	■	■	■	■	■	■	■					174
Owl School (The)	C			■	■	■	■	■	■	■	■	■	■					176
Paladin Academy	C				■	■	■	■	■	■	■	■	■					178
Parkmont School	C											■	■	■	■	■	■	180
Paul VI Catholic High School	C													■	■	■	■	182
Potomac School (The)	C				■	■	■	■	■	■	■	■	■	■	■	■	■	184
Primary Day School (The)	C		■	■	■	■												186
	Gender	PN	N	PK	K	1	2	3	4	5	6	7	8	9	10	11	12	Page #

Key C = Coed; B = Boys; G = Girls; PN = Pre Nursery (under 3 years old); N = Nursery (3 years old); PK = Prekindergarten (4 years old); K = Kindergarten (5 years old)

Name of School	Gender	PN	N	PK	K	1	2	3	4	5	6	7	8	9	10	11	12	Page #
Queen Anne School	C										█	█	█	█	█	█	█	188
Rivendell	C			█	█	█	█	█	█	█	█	█	█					190
River School (The)	C	█	█	█	█	█	█	█										192
Rock Creek International School	C		█	█	█	█	█	█										194
Sandy Spring Friends School	C			█	█	█	█	█	█	█	█	█	█	█	█	█	█	196
Sheridan School	C			█	█	█	█	█	█	█	█	█	█					198
Sidwell Friends School	C			█	█	█	█	█	█	█	█	█	█	█	█	█	█	200
St. Albans School	B								█	█	█	█	█	█	█	█	█	202
St. Andrew's Episcopal School	C										█	█	█	█	█	█	█	204
St. Anselm's Abbey School	B										█	█	█	█	█	█	█	206
St. Francis Episcopal Day School	C	█	█	█	█	█	█	█	█	█								208
St. John's College High School	C													█	█	█	█	210
St. John's Episcopal School	C			█	█	█	█	█	█	█	█	█	█					212
St. Patrick's Episcopal Day School	C		█	█	█	█	█	█	█	█	█	█	█					214
St. Stephen's & St. Agnes School	C			█	█	█	█	█	█	█	█	█	█	█	█	█	█	216
Stone Ridge School of the Sacred Heart	G			█	█	█	█	█	█	█	█	█	█	█	█	█	█	218
Thornton Friends Upper School (MD)	C										█	█	█					220
Thornton Friends School (VA)	C		█	█	█	█	█	█	█	█	█	█	█					222
Thornton Friends Middle School (MD)	C													█	█	█	█	224
Town and Country School of Vienna	C		█	█	█	█	█	█										226
Washington Episcopal School	C		█	█	█	█	█	█	█	█	█	█	█					228
Washington International School	C		█	█	█	█	█	█	█	█	█	█	█	█	█	█	█	230
Washington Waldorf School	C			█	█	█	█	█	█	█	█	█	█	█	█	█	█	232
Westminster School	C		█	█	█	█	█	█	█	█	█	█	█					234
Woods Academy (The)	C		█	█	█	█	█	█	█	█	█	█	█					236
	Gender	PN	N	PK	K	1	2	3	4	5	6	7	8	9	10	11	12	Page #

Key   C = Coed; B = Boys; G = Girls; PN = Pre Nursery (under 3 years old); N = Nursery (3 years old); PK = Prekindergarten (4 years old); K = Kindergarten (5 years old)

Admission Worksheet

Name of School: _____ Telephone: _____

Location: _____ Contact Person: _____ Tuition: _____

Deadline for receipt of application: _____ Fee: _____

Date application and fee submitted: _____ Deadline for completion of file: _____

Date & time of appointment for open house/tour: _____ Student included: Yes _____ No _____

Parent interview required?: Yes _____ No _____ Date & time: _____

Student essay required?: Yes _____ No _____

Photo required?: Yes _____ No _____

Parent essay required?: Yes _____ No _____ Other: _____

Name of required test(s): _____ Date & time of test(s): _____

Test site: _____ Test fee: _____

Date transcript requested: _____

Recommendation forms: Date given _____ to _____ (Usually English)
                                                           Name of teacher

                         Date given _____ to _____ (Usually Math)
                                                           Name of teacher

                         Date given _____ to _____ (Optional)
                                                           Name

Date & time of play date, school visit, and/or interview: _____

Deadline for financial aid information: _____ Date completed, if appropriate: _____

Other requirements:

Date that schools notify of decision: _____ Date enrollment contract is due: _____

Notes, impressions or special concerns:

Public Schools

Many of the public schools in Metropolitan Washington are considered to be among the best in the nation. Numerous options exist for families in this area including schools in the District of Columbia, Prince George's and Montgomery Counties in Maryland, Fairfax, Arlington, and Loudoun Counties, and the cities of Alexandria and Falls Church in Virginia. This chapter includes general guidelines for evaluating public schools, general information about each of the school systems, and identifies individual schools with which I am familiar and/or those with the highest test scores within a school district.

WHAT TO LOOK FOR IN A PUBLIC SCHOOL

As a former public school teacher, I have great respect for the opportunities available in the eight public school districts in this guide. The educational resources and commitment of individual faculty and staff can be of the highest quality; however, not every school meets the needs of all children equally well. Quality varies. To take maximum advantage of public schools, you must be well-informed on current practices and diligent in pursuing the available opportunities.

Registration Process

Registering for a public school usually requires a proof of residency (rental contract or evidence of home ownership), the student's birth certificate, report cards, or transcript from the student's previous school, immunization records (including a TB test within the last twelve months), and a parent's social security number. Registration usually takes place at the student's neighborhood school. Students who are non-U.S. residents must be accompanied by a parent with proper identification and register at the central office of the local board of education.

Enrolling Outside of School Boundaries

If you wish to enroll your child in a school and do not live within that school's boundaries, inquire about procedures at the school in which you want to enroll. Policies and procedures change often.

Using Test Scores to Evaluate a School

There is no single criterion for assessing the merits of a school or evaluating its strengths and weaknesses. Test scores are by no means the only or even the best criteria for an evaluation, but they are a reasonable place to start. However, you must use caution when interpreting test scores. Scores may vary from year to year without a corresponding decline or improvement in the quality of the school. Percentages do not provide information about the number of students scoring at a high level or the number scoring at a low level. Scores for smaller schools may vary more from year to year than scores for larger schools, and each year's scores represent the results for an entirely different group of students.

Test scores are based on statewide assessments designed to evaluate schools. These assessment tools are controversial and are undergoing constant review.

The District of Columbia uses the Stanford Achievement Test, Ninth Edition (Stanford 9) which is given once a year to all students in grades one through eleven. Scores indicate the percent of students who achieved in the Advanced or Proficient range.

In Maryland and Virginia, the Maryland State Performance Assessment Program (MSPAP) and the Virginia Standards of Learning (SOL), respectively, assess the quality of schools but do not grade the abilities of individual students. A satisfactory level of achievement for a school indicates that 70% or more of the students scored in the satisfactory or above range. Generally, I have selected schools with the highest test scores at the fifth and eighth grades in each school district, but the specific standard for inclusion varies.

Inclusion of schools was based upon:

District of Columbia
Stanford 9 Scores   Schools with the highest test
                                       scores

Maryland
MSPAP
Montgomery County   Selected individual schools
                                       within four selected clusters

Prince George's County   Schools with the highest scores

Virginia
SOL
Alexandria City   70% or higher
Arlington County   70% or higher
Fairfax County   90% or higher
Falls Church City   All four schools in the school
                                       district

Loudoun County   80% or higher

All School Districts
Scholastic Assessment Test (SAT)   Scores for the highest achieving
                                       high schools, as reported by
                                       each school system

Note: 70% is required to be accredited.

LEARNING MORE ABOUT EACH SCHOOL

Public schools welcome parents who want to visit before enrolling their child. Before your visit, review the district website, talk to parents whose children attend the school, and make an appointment.

What to look for when you visit

In addition to researching test scores, when you visit, consider the facilities, the faculty, and the attitudes exhibited within the school.

Facilities

- A safe and hospitable climate in the halls and classrooms.
- Cheerful, interesting, and engaging classrooms.
- Equipment and supplies that are appropriate to the grade/age.
- Current textbooks and other teaching tools such as computers, books, and maps.
- Facilities for and evidence of school support and student participation in sports and the arts.
- Outdoor space that is well maintained, safe, and age-appropriate.
- Availability and use of technology.

Faculty

- A low student/teacher ratio.
- Evidence of a high level of proficiency in each subject area.
- Energy and engagement with the students.
- Understanding of classroom management and discipline.
- Use of multiple approaches and methodologies.
- Resource personnel including nurse, special education teachers, and counselors.

Attitudes

- Students' interests and involvement.
- Mutual respect of students toward each other and toward teachers.

- A sense of excitement and purposefulness about learning.
- Parental involvement.

Questions to Ask

During your visit and throughout your research, seek answers that will give you an understanding of what to expect if your child were enrolled in the school.

- What are the teachers' qualifications and years of tenure?
- What professional development is available for faculty?
- What is the average amount of homework?
- What services are available for gifted, special needs, and English as a Second Language or English for Speakers of Other Languages (ESL or ESOL) students?
- What are student and teacher attendance rates?
- What kind of access do parents and students have to teachers and administrators by telephone, email, or appointment?
- What does a parent do when something goes wrong?
- What opportunities are available for parental involvement, and what is the commitment of parents whose children are currently enrolled at the school?
- At what grade level do foreign languages become available and are required? Which foreign languages are available?
- For high schools:
  - What is the program of studies? Is a curriculum guide available?
  - What are the required courses, electives, and special programs?
  - Is there an International Baccalaureate program? How many Advanced Placement courses are available? What is the number of students scoring 3 or higher?
  - What is the graduation rate? What colleges do graduates attend?
- What would be on a teachers' wish list?
- What would be on the principal's wish list (in additional to a most justifiable wish for faculty salaries that better reflect the time, expertise, and grave responsibility of their work!)?

Public School Directory

FACTS AT A GLANCE

District of Columbia
825 N. Capitol Street, NE
Washington, DC 20002
202-442-4080
www.k12.dc.us

School system	Total enrollment:	
	Total number of schools:	About 150
	Total number of elementary schools:	104
	Total number of middle schools:	11
	Total number high schools:	19
	SAT 2001:	Verbal 402 Math 396
	Diversity within system:	
School system programs	Before or after school care:	Available free in all elementary schools from 3:30–6:30
	Pre-kindergarten programs:	3 or 4 years olds by December 31; Full day available in all schools
	Kindergarten:	5 years old by December 31; Full day available in all schools
	Foreign language programs:	Spanish immersion at Oyster and Hardy; large number of foreign languages are available at Wilson
	ESL/ESOL availability:	
	Accelerated programs:	IB program at Banneker Academic High, School Without Walls, AP Programs in 15 high schools
	LD/special needs:	Child Find & Testing for Individualized Educational Plan & assistance from specialists. Some students with severe documented disabilities are enrolled in independent schools, call 202-442-4800

Data Sources:
District of Columbia Public Schools website: www.k12.dc.us
Dr. Doney Olivieri, Department of Academic Services

SELECTED PUBLIC SCHOOLS

District of Columbia

High Schools

Bannecker
800 Euclid St., NW
Washington, DC 20001
202-673-7322
Grades: 9–12
Size: 432
Diversity:
Hours:
Average class size:
SAT 1999:
    Verbal 553 Math 522
    Total 1075

School Without Walls
2130 G St., NW
Washington, DC 20037
202-724-4889
Grades: 9–12
Size: 339
Diversity:
Hours:
Average class size:
SAT 1999:
    Verbal 542 Math 510
    Total 1052

Wilson
3950 Chesapeake St., NW
Washington, DC 20016
202-282-0120
Grades: 9–12
Size: 1,510
Diversity:
Hours:
Average class size:
SAT 1999:
    Verbal 478 Math 478
    Total 956

Junior High

Deal
3815 Fort Dr., NW
Washington, DC 20016
202-282-0100
Grades: 7–9
Size: 888
Diversity:
Hours:
Average class size:
Stanford 9 Spring 2001
    Reading: Advanced: 21%,
                    Proficient: 44%
    Math: Advanced: 17%,
                    Proficient: 36%

Middle School
Hardy
1819 35th St., NW
Washington, DC 20007
202-282-0057
Grades: 5–8
Size: 310
Diversity:
Hours:
Average class size:
Stanford 9 Spring 2001
   Reading: Advanced: 13%,
              Proficient: 53%
   Math: Advanced: 12%,
              Proficient: 28%

Elementary Schools

Eaton
3301 Lowell St., NW
Washington, DC 20008
202-282-0103
Grades: PK–6
Size: 409
Diversity:
Hours:
Average class size:
Stanford 9 Spring 2001
   Reading: Advanced: 27%,
            Proficient: 42%
   Math: Advanced: 28%,
            Proficient: 45%

Hyde
3219 O St., NW
Washington, DC 20007
202-282-0170
Grades: PK–5
Size: 185
Diversity:
Hours:
Average class size:
Stanford 9 Spring 2001
   Reading: Advanced: 27%,
            Proficient: 53%
   Math: Advanced: 40%,
            Proficient: 47%

Key
5001 Dana Pl., NW
Washington, DC 20016
202-282-0113
Grades: PK–5
Size: 199
Diversity:
Hours:
Average class size:
Stanford 9 Spring 2001
   Reading: Advanced: 43%,
            Proficient: 43%
   Math: Advanced: 43%
            Proficient: 44%

Hearst
3950 37th St., NW
Washington, DC 20008
202-282-0106
Grades: PK–3
Size: 170
Diversity:
Hours:
Average class size:
Stanford 9 Spring 2001
   Reading: Advanced: 40%,
            Proficient: 34%
   Math: Advanced: 34%,
            Proficient: 37%

Janney
4130 Albemarle St., NW
Washington, DC 20016
202-282-0110
Grades: PK–6
Size: 444
Diversity:
Hours:
Average class size:
Stanford 9 Spring 2001
   Reading: Advanced: 50%,
            Proficient: 36%
   Math: Advanced: 44%,
            Proficient: 40%

Lafayette
5701 Broad Branch Rd., NW
Washington, DC 20015
202-282-0116
Grades: PK–6
Size: 488
Diversity:
Hours:
Average class size:
Stanford 9 Spring 2001
   Reading: Advanced: 49%,
            Proficient: 42%
   Math: Advanced: 42%,
            Proficient: 44%

Elementary Schools

Mann
4430 Newark St., NW
Washington, DC 20016
202-282-0126
Grades: PK–6
Size: 211
Diversity:
Hours:
Average class size:
Stanford 9 Spring 2001
  Reading: Advanced: 59%,
       Proficient: 28%
  Math: Advanced: 71%,
       Proficient: 25%

Oyster
2801 Calvert Street., NW
Washington, DC 20008
202-671-0081
Grades: PK–6
Size: 325
Diversity:
Hours:
Average class size:
Stanford 9 Spring 2001
  Reading: Advanced: 31%,
       Proficient: 47%
  Math: Advanced: 42%,
       Proficient: 36%

Murch
4810 36th St., NW
Washington, DC 20008
202-282-0130
Grades: PK–6
sizes: 467
Diversity:
Hours:
Average class size:
Stanford 9 Spring 2001
  Reading: Advanced: 41%,
       Proficient: 41%
  Math: Advanced: 39%,
       Proficient: 43%

Stoddert
4001 Calvert St., NW
Washington, DC 20007
202-282-0143
Grades: PK–5
Size: 223
Diversity:
Hours:
Average class size:
Stanford 9 Spring 2001
  Reading: Advanced: 40%,
       Proficient: 47%
  Math: Advanced: 44%,
       Proficient: 43%

Data Source:
All data was found on the District of Columbia Public School Web Site: www.k12.dc.us/dcps/data

Includes:
2001 Stanford Achievement Test Scores
1999 SAT Test Scores.

FACTS AT A GLANCE

Montgomery County
850 Hungerford Drive, Room 112
Rockville, MD 20850
301-279-3391
www.mcps.k12.md.us

School system	Total enrollment:	136,832
	Total number of schools:	190
	Total number of elementary: Schools:	125
	Total number of middle schools:	35
	Total number high schools:	23
	Total number of special centers:	7
	SAT 2001:	Verbal 536 Math 556 Total 1092 79% of students tested
	Diversity within system:	52.5%
School system programs	Before or after school care:	
	Pre-kindergarten programs:	Limited, call 301-431-7636
	Kindergarten:	5 years old by December 31, most schools have half-day programs, call 301-320-0691
	Foreign language programs:	Full immersion French at Maryvale Elementary and Sligo Creek Elementary and Spanish at Rock Creek Forest Elementary and Rolling Terrace Elementary; partial immersion Chinese at Potomac Elementary

ESL/ESOL availability:	Most schools have a program, call ESOL/ Bilingual Programs at 301-230-0670
Accelerated programs:	Third grade GT programs in school or cluster, honors, AP & IB, call Accelerated & Enriched Instruction at 301-279-3163, magnet programs: Montgomery Blair and Richard Montgomery, other signature programs
LD/Special Needs:	Mainstreamed, call Department of Special Education at 301-279-3135; Child Find for young children, call 301-929-2224

Data Sources:
Montgomery County public schools website, www.mcps.k12.md.us
Maryland State Performance website, www.msp.msde.state.md.us
SAT Scores: Washington Post SAT scores are for public and independent combined.
Montgomery County Department of Communications

SELECTED PUBLIC SCHOOLS

Montgomery County

High Schools

Bethesda-Chevy Chase
4301 East-West Hwy.
Bethesda, MD 20814
240-497-6300
Grades: 9–12
Size: 1,338
Hours: 7:35–2:20
Diversity: 37.2%
Average class size:
SAT 2001:
   Verbal 564 Math 575
   Total 1139

Walter Johnson
6400 Rock Spring Dr.
Bethesda, MD 20814
301-571-6900
Grades: 9–12
Size: 1,797
Hours: 7:25–2:10
Diversity: 32.3%
Average class size:
SAT 2001:
   Verbal 560 Math 591
   Total 1151

Winston Churchill
11300 Gainsboro Rd.
Potomac, MD 20854
301-469-1200
Grades: 9–12
Size: 1,884
Hours: 7:25–2:10
Diversity: 32.6%
Average class size:
SAT 2001:
   Verbal: 590 Math: 621
   Total: 1211

Walt Whitman
7100 Whittier Blvd.
Bethesda, MD 20817
301-320-6600
Grades: 9–12
Size: 1,818
Hours: 7:25–2:10
Diversity: 22.2%
Average class size:
SAT 2001:
   Verbal 601 Math 622
   Total 1223

Middle Schools

Cabin John
10701 Gainsboro Rd.
Potomac, MD 20854
301-469-1160
Grades: 6–8

North Bethesda
8935 Bradmoor Dr.
Bethesda, MD 20817
301-571-3883
Grades: 6–8

Tilden
11211 Old Georgetown Rd.
Rockville, MD 20852
301-230-5930
Grades: 6–8

Cabin John (cont.)
Size: 993
Hours: 7:55–2:40
Diversity: 40.4%
Average class size:
MSPAP 2000 8th
Satisfactory
    Reading: 54%
    Math: 84%

Herbert Hoover
8810 Postoak Rd.
Rockville, MD 20854
301-469-1010
Grades: 6–8
Size: 1,071
Hours: 7:55–2:40
Diversity: 32.7%
Average class size:
MSPAP 2000 8th
Satisfactory
    Reading: 60%
    Math: 84%

Elementary Schools
Ashburton
6314 Lone Oak Dr.
Bethesda, MD 20817
301-571-6959
Grades: K–5
Size: 537
Hours: 8:50–3:05
Diversity: 43.3%
Average class size:
MSPAP 2000 5th
Satisfactory
    Reading: 57%
    Math: 75%

North Bethesda (cont.)
Size: 676
Hours: 7:55–2:40
Diversity: 28.6%
Average class size:
MSPAP 2000 8th
Satisfactory
Not Available

Thomas W. Pyle
6311 Wilson Ln.
Bethesda, MD 20817
301-320-6540
Grades: 6–8
Size: 1,275
Hours: 7:55–2:40
Diversity: 18.1%
Average class size:
MSPAP 2000 8th
Satisfactory
    Reading: 50%
    Math: 87%

Bradley Hills
8701 Hartsdale Ave.
Bethesda, MD 20817
301-571-6966
Grades: K–5
Size: 400
Hours: 8:50–3:05
Diversity: 20.8%
Average class size:
MSPAP 2000 5th
Satisfactory
    Reading: 52%
    Math: 79%

Tilden (cont.)
Size: 724
Hours: 7:55–2:40
Diversity: 33.6%
Average class size:
MSPAP 2000 8th
Satisfactory
    Reading: 42%
    Math: 79%

Westland
5511 Massachusetts Ave.
Bethesda, MD 20816
301-320-6515
Grades: 6–8
Size: 1,029
Hours: 7:55–2:40
Diversity:38.2%
Average class size:
MSPAP 2000 8th
Satisfactory
    Reading: 42%
    Math: 79%

Garrett Park
4810 Oxford St.
Garrett Park, MD 20895
301-929-2170
Grades: K–5
Size: 484
Hours: 8:50–3:05
Diversity: 45.9%
Average class size:
MSPAP 2000 5th
Satisfactory
    Reading: 77%
    Math: 83%

Bannockburn
6520 Dalroy Lane
Bethesda, MD 20817
301-320-6555
Grades: K–5
Size: 427
Hours: 9:15–3:30
Diversity: 14%
Average class size:
MSPAP 2000 5th
Satisfactory
    Reading: 65%
    Math: 85%

Bells Mill
8225 Bells Mill Rd.
Potomac, MD 20874
301-469-1046
Grades: PK–5
Size: 526
Hours: 8:50–3:05
Diversity: 83.7%
Average class size:
MSPAP 2000 5th
Satisfactory
    Reading: 76%
    Math: 76%

Bethesda
7600 Arlington Rd.
Bethesda, MD 20814
301-657-4979
Grades: K–5
Size: 416
Hours: 8:50–3:05
Diversity: 36.1%
Average class size:
MSPAP 2000 5th
Satisfactory
    Reading: 58%
    Math: 79%

Burning Tree
7900 Beech Tree Rd.
Bethesda, MD 20817
301-320-6510
Grades: K–5
Size: 493
Hours: 9:15–3:30
Diversity: 25.5%
Average class size:
MSPAP 2000 5th
Satisfactory
    Reading: 69%
    Math: 92%

Carderock Springs
7401 Persimmon Tree Rd.
Bethesda, MD 20817
301-469-1034
Grades: K–5
Size: 310
Hours: 8:50–3:05
Diversity: 21.3%
Average class size:
MSPAP 2000 5th
Satisfactory
    Reading: 75%
    Math: 95%

Chevy Chase
4015 Rosemary St.
Chevy Chase, MD 20815
301-657-4994
Grades: 3–6
Size: 374
Hours: 8:50–3:05
Diversity: 35.3%
Average class size:
MSPAP 2000 5th
Satisfactory
    Reading: 59%
    Math: 74%

Kensington Parkwood
4710 Saul Rd.
Kensington, MD 20895
301-571-6949
Grades: K–5
Size: 404
Hours: 8:50–3:05
Diversity: 26.7%
Average class size:
MSPAP 2000 5th
Satisfactory
    Reading: 69%
    Math: 80%

Luxmanor
6201 Tilden Lane
Rockville, MD 20852
301-230-5914
Grades: K–5
Size: 281
Hours: 8:50–3:05
Diversity: 32.3%
Average class size:
MSPAP 2000 5th
Satisfactory
    Reading: 62%
    Math: 65%

North Chevy Chase
3700 Jones Bridge Rd.
Chevy Chase, MD 20815
301-657-4950
Grades: 3–6
Size: 332
Hours: 9:15–3:30
Diversity: 30.4%
Average class size:
MSPAP 2000 5th
Satisfactory
    Reading: 63%
    Math: 73%

Public Schools **265**

Beverly Farms
8501 Postoak Rd.
Potomac, MD 20854
301-469-1050
Grades: K–5
Size: 544
Hours: 8:50–3:05
Diversity: 34%
Average class size:
MSPAP 2000 5th
Satisfactory
    Reading: 66%
    Math 79%

Rock Creek Forest
8330 Grubb Rd.
Chevy Chase, MD 20815
301-650-6410
Grades: PK–5
Size: 518
Hours: 9:15–3:30
Diversity: 57.2%
Average class size:
MSPAP 2000 5th
Satisfactory
    Reading: 53%
    Math: 66%

Rosemary Hills
2111 Porter Rd.
Silver Spring, MD 20910
301-650-6400
Grades: PK–2
Size: 516
Hours: 9:15–3:30
Diversity: 35.7%
Average class size:
scores not applicable

Farmland
7000 Old Gate Rd.
Rockville, MD 20852
301-230-5919
Grades: K–5
Size: 603
Hours: 9:15–3:30
Diversity: 43.3%
Average class size:
MSPAP 2000 5th
Satisfactory
    Reading: 74%
    Math: 90%

Wayside
10011 Glen Rd.
Potomac, MD 20854
301-279-8484
Grades: K–5
Size: 633
Hours: 9:15–3:30
Diversity:42.5%
Average class size:
MSPAP 2000 5th
Satisfactory
    Reading: 75%
    Math: 96%

Westbrook
5110 Allan Terr.
Bethesda, MD 20816
301-320-6506
Grades: K–5
Size: 300
Hours: 8:50–3:05
Diversity: 14.2%
Average class size:
MSPAP 2000 5th Satisfactory
    Reading: 75%
    Math: 83%

Potomac
10311 River Rd.
Potomac, MD 20854
301-469-1042
Grades: K–5
Size: 648
Hours: 9:15–3:30
Diversity: 23.7%
Average class size:
no testing available

Seven Locks
9500 Seven Locks Rd.
Bethesda, MD 20817
301-469-1038
Grades: K–5
Size: 261
Hours: 8:50–3:05
Diversity: 20.0%
Average class size:
MSPAP 2000 5th
Satisfactory
   Reading: 49%
   Math: 82%

Somerset
5811 Warwick Pl.
Chevy Chase, MD 20815
301-657-4985
Grades: K–5
Size: 442
Hours: 8:50–3:05
Diversity: 21.0%
Average class size:
MSPAP 2000 5th
Satisfactory
   Reading: 72%
   Math: 91%

Wood Acres
5800 Cromwell Dr.
Bethesda, MD 20816
301-320-6502
Grades: K–5
Size: 518
Hours: 8:50–3:05
Diversity: 12.1%
Average class size:
MSPAP 2000 5th
Satisfactory
   Reading: 76%
   Math: 96%

Wyngate
9300 Wadsworth Dr.
Bethesda, MD 20817
301-571-6979
Grades: K–5
Size: 502
Hours: 8:50–3:05
Diversity: 21.2%
Average class size:
MSPAP 2000 5th
Satisfactory
   Reading: 78%
   Math: 87%

Notes:
State satisfactory standard is 70%.

Source:
www.msp.msde.state.md.us
www.mcps.k12.md.us
Montgomery County Department of Communications

FACTS AT A GLANCE

Prince George's County
14201 School Lane
Upper Marlboro, MD 20772
301-952-6001
www.pgps.pg.k12.md.us

School system	**Total enrollment:**	134,548
	Total number of schools:	188
	Total number of elementary Schools:	127
	Total number of middle schools:	27
	Total number high schools:	23
	Total number of special centers:	11
	SAT 2001:	Verbal 448 Math 438 Total 886 % of students taking exam not available
	Diversity within system:	77%
School system programs	**Before or after school care:**	Call 301-636-8090
	Pre-kindergarten programs:	Head Start for 3 and 4 year olds in Community Centers, Montessori beginning with 3 year olds, call 301-408-7100
	Kindergarten:	5 years old by Dec. 31, full day
	Foreign language programs:	Foreign language programs: French immersion K–12, Latin at Beltsville Elem. & M. L. King Jr. Middle, Spanish at Phyllis Williams, French, Spanish, German, Japanese in selected high schools, call 301-808-8265

ESL/ESOL Availability:	Call 301-445-8450
Accelerated Programs:	Submit application, lottery system; Academic Center Programs, IB in selected schools
LD/Special Needs:	Call 301-952-6336

Data Sources:
Prince George's County Public Schools website: www.pgps.pg.k12.md.us
Maryland School Performance website: www.msp.msde.state.md.us
SAT Scores: Washington Post SAT scores are for public and independent combined.
Dorothy D. Harrison, Ed.D., Community Relations Specialist

SELECTED PUBLIC SCHOOLS

Prince George's County

High School
Eleanor Roosevelt
7601 Hanover Pkwy.
Greenbelt, MD 20770
301-513-5400
Grades: 9–12
Size: 2,914
Diversity:
Hours: 9:25–4:05
Average class size: varies
SAT 2000:
    Verbal 530 Math 541
    Total 1071

Middle School
Walker Mill
800 Karen Blvd.
Capitol Heights, MD 20743
301-808-4055
Grades: 7–8
Size: 727
Diversity:
Hours: 9:30–4:10
Average class size: varies
MSPAP 2000 8th Satisfactory
    Reading: 47%
    Math: 50%

Elementary Schools

Bond Mill
16001 Sherwood Ave.
Laurel, MD 20702
301-497-3600
Grades: K–6
Size: 517
Diversity:
Hours: 8:00–2:10
Average class size: varies
MSPAP 2000 5th
Satisfactory
    Reading: 58%
    Math: 73%

Montpelier
9200 Muirkirk Rd.
Laurel, MD 20708
301-497-3670
Grades: K–6
Size: 632
Diversity:
Hours: 9:00–3:10
Average class size: varies
MSPAP 2000 5th
Satisfactory
    Reading: 55%
    Math: 55%

University Park
4315 Underwood St.
Hyattsville, MD 20782
301-985-1898
Grades: K–6
Size: 658
Diversity:
Hours: 9:10–3:20
Average class size: varies
MSPAP 2000 5th
Satisfactory
    Reading: 51%
    Math: 56%

Fort Foote
8300 Oxon Hill Rd.
Fort Washington, MD 20744
301-749-4230
Grades: K–6
Size: 484

Oaklands
13710 Laurel-Bowie Rd.
Laurel, MD 20708
301-497-3110
Grades: K–6
Size: 518

Yorktown
7301 Race Track Rd.
Bowie, MD 20715
301-805-6610
Grades: K–6
Size: 591

Fort Foote (cont.)
Diversity:
Hours: 9:00–3:10
Average class size: varies
MSPAP 2000 5th
Satisfactory
   Reading: 52%
   Math: 66%

Oaklands (cont.)
Diversity:
Hours: 9:00–3:10
Average class size: varies
MSPAP 2000 5th
Satisfactory
   Reading: 60%
   Math: 75%

Yorktown (cont.)
Diversity:
Hours: 9:00–3:10
Average class size: varies
MSPAP 2000 5th
Satisfactory
   Reading: 56%
   Math: 87%

Kenilworth
12520 Kembridge Dr.
Bowie, MD 20715
301-805-6600
Grades: K–6
Size: 697
Diversity:
Hours: 9:00–3:10
Average class size: varies
MSPAP 2000 5th
Satisfactory
   Reading: 72%
   Math: 78%

Tulip Grove
2909 Trainor Rd.
Bowie, MD 20715
301-805-2680
Grades: K–6
Size: 580
Diversity:
Hours: 8:50–3:00
Average class size: varies
MSPAP 2000 5th
Satisfactory
   Reading: 52%
   Math: 53%

Notes:
State satisfactory standard is 70%.

Source:
www.msp.msde.state.md.us
www.pgps.pg.k12.md.us

FACTS AT A GLANCE

Alexandria City
2000 North Beauregard Street
Alexandria, VA 22311
703-824-6600
www.acps.k12.va.us

School system

Total enrollment:	Over 11,000
Total number of schools:	18
Total number of elementary schools:	13
Total number of middle schools:	2
Total number high schools:	1 (9th only), 1 (10th–12th grades)
SAT 2001:	Verbal 478 Math 485 Total 963 73% of students tested
Diversity within system:	79%

School system programs

Before or after school care:	7:00–6:00 in elementary schools, after school programs in middle and high schools
Pre-kindergarten programs:	Limited, call 703-824-6655
Kindergarten:	5 years old by September 30; full day program, call 703-824-6680
Foreign language programs:	Offered in two elementary schools, Mount Vernon and John Adams, apply by April 1, provide own transportation; Spanish, French, Latin, German in middle and high schools

ESL/ESOL availability:	At all grade levels for 45 languages, call 703-465-6550
Accelerated programs:	Talented and gifted grades K–12 in all schools; Cora Kelly Magnet school and focus programs enroll through lottery or boundary; call 703-824-6680
LD/special needs:	Call 703-824-6650

Data Sources:
Alexandria Public Schools website: www.acps.k12.va.us
Virginia Department of Education website: www.pen.k12.va.us
SAT Scores: Washington Post SAT scores are for public and independent combined.
Barbara M. Hunter, Director Communications

SELECTED PUBLIC SCHOOLS

Alexandria City

High School
Minnie Howard
3801 W. Braddock Rd.
Alexandria, VA 22302
703-824-6750
Grade: 9
Size: 714
Diversity: 75%
Hours: 8:40–3:10
Average class size: 20
SOL 2001 9th passing
Math: 75%

Elementary Schools

Charles Barrett
1115 Martha Custis Dr.
Alexandria, VA 22302
703-824-6960
Grades: K–5
Size: 253
Diversity 55%
Hours: 8:35–2:45
Average class size: 20
SOL 2001 5th passing
   English: 86%
   Math: 78%

George Mason
2601 Cameron Mills Rd.
Alexandria, VA 22302
703-706-4470
Grades: K–5
Size: 304
Diversity: 51%
Hours: 8:35–2:45
Average class size: 20
SOL 2001 5th passing
   English: 80%
   Math: 85%

Douglas MacArthur
1101 Janneys Ln.
Alexandria, VA 22302
703-461-4190
Grades: K–5
Size: 535
Diversity: 52%

Samuel Tucker
435 Ferdinand Day Dr.
Alexandria, VA 22304
703-933-6300
Grades: K–5
Size: 608
Diversity: 83%

Douglas MacArthur (cont.)
Hours: 8:35–2:45
Average class size: 22
SOL 2001 5th passing
   English: 93%
   Math: 96%

Samuel Tucker (cont.)
Hours: 8:00–2:10
Average class size: 22
SOL 2001 5th passing
   English: 93%
   Math: 93%

Notes:
State passing standard is 70%

Data Sources:
www.acps.k12.va.us
www.pen.k12.va.us
SOL Spring 2001 Test Scores: Alexandria City News Release, September, 2001

FACTS AT A GLANCE

Arlington County
1425 North Quincy Street
Arlington, VA 22207
703-228-7660
www.arlington.k12.va.us

School system	Total enrollment:	19,130
	Total number of schools:	30
	Total number of elementary schools:	21
	Total number of middle schools:	5
	Total number high schools:	4
	SAT 2001:	Verbal 518 Math 523 Total 1041 75% of students tested
	Diversity within system:	60%
School system programs	Before or after school care:	7:00–6:00 in elementary, "check in" programs for middle school
	Pre-kindergarten programs:	Limited
	Kindergarten:	5 years old by Sept. 30, full day program
	Foreign language programs:	Spanish partial immersion at Key, Abingdon, & Oakridge Elementary Schools, & Gunston Middle, and Wakefield High; Japanese and German taught through Distance Learning, 4 years of German and Latin, 5 years of French and Spanish

ESL/ESOL availability:	Serves over 4,600 students speaking over 82 languages; ESOL for 1st–5th, HILT (High Intensity Language Training) for 1st–12th
Accelerated programs:	Accelerated programs: countywide gifted programs, Arlington Traditional and Drew Model School countywide lottery process, AP Courses, IB Program at Washington-Lee
LD/special needs:	Available in Pre-kindergarten–12th grades, Child Find identifies young children with special needs and plans early intervention

Data Sources:
Arlington County Public Schools website: www.arlington.k12.va.us
Virginia Department of Education website: www.pen.k12.va.us
SAT Scores: Washington Post SAT scores are for public and independent combined.
Linda M. Erdos, Director of School and Community Relations

SELECTED PUBLIC SCHOOLS

Arlington County

High School

Yorktown
5201 N. 28th St.
Arlington, VA 22207
703-228-5400
Grades: 9–12
Size: 1,557
Diversity: 34%
Hours: 8:15–2:55
Average class size: See Notes
SAT 2001:
  Verbal 563 Math 564
  Total 1127

Middle Schools

Swanson
5800 Washington Blvd.
Arlington, VA 22205
703-228-5500
Grades: 6–8
Size: 752
Diversity: 36%
Hours: 7:50–2:20
Average class size: See Notes
SOL 2001 8th passing
  English: 83% Math: 87%

Williamsburg
3600 N. Harrison St.
Arlington, VA 22207
703-228-5450
Grades: 6–8
Size: 898
Diversity:
Hours: 7:50–2:20
Average class size: See Notes
SOL 2001 8th passing
  English: 80% Math: 84%

Elementary Schools

Arlington Science Focus
1501 N. Lincoln. St.
Arlington, VA 22201
703-228-7670
Grades: K–5
Size: 410
Diversity:
Hours: 9:00–3:35
Average class size:
See Notes
SOL 2001 5th passing
   English: 93%
   Math: 91%

Arlington Traditional
855 N. Edison St.
Arlington, VA 22205
703-228-6290
Grades: K–5
Size: 410
Diversity:
Hours: 8:25–3:00
Average class size:
See Notes
SOL 2001 5th passing
   English: 100%
   Math: 100%

Ashlawn
5950 N. Edison St.
Arlington, VA 22205
703-228-5270
Grades: K–5
Size: 368
Diversity:
Hours: 9:00–3:35
Average class size:
See Notes
SOL 2001 5th passing
   English: 88%
   Math: 88%

Glebe
1770 N. Glebe Rd.
Arlington, VA 22207
703-228-6280
Grades: K–5
Size: 282
Diversity:
Hours: 9:00–3:35
Average class size:
See Notes
SOL 2001 5th passing
   English: 90%
   Math: 92%

Henry
702 S. Highland St.
Arlington, VA 22201
703-228-5820
Grades: K–5
Size: 442
Diversity:
Hours: 9:00–3:35
Average class size:
See Notes
SOL 2001 5th passing
   English: 86%
   Math: 77%

Jamestown
3700 N. Delaware St.
Arlington, VA 22207
703-228-5275
Grades: K–5
Size: 582
Diversity:
Hours: 9:00–3:35
Average class size:
See Notes
SOL 2001 5th passing
   English: 95%
   Math: 97%

McKinley
1030 N. McKinley Rd.
Arlington, VA 22205
703-228-5280
Grades: K–5
Size: 406
Diversity:
Hours: 9:00–3:35
Average class size:
See Notes
SOL 2001 5th passing
   English: 95%
   Math: 89%

Nottingham
5900 Little Falls Rd.
Arlington, VA 22207
703-228-5290
Grades: K–5
Size: 404
Diversity:
Hours: 9:00–3:35
Average class size:
See Notes
SOL 2000: 5th grade
   English: 86%
   Math: 84%

Taylor
2600 N. Stuart St.
Arlington, VA 22207
703-228-6275
Grades: K–5
Size: 552
Diversity:
Hours: 9:00–3:35
Average class size:
See Notes
SOL 2001 5th passing
   English: 85%
   Math: 81%

Barcroft
625 S. Wakefield St.
Arlington, VA 22204
703-228-5838
Grades: K–5
Size: 554
Diversity:
Hours: 9:00–3:35
Average class size:
See Notes
SOL 2001 5th passing
  English: 81%
  Math: 91%

Long Branch
33 N. Fillmore St.
Arlington, VA 22201
703-228-4220
Grades: K–5
Size: 460
Diversity:
Hours: 8:25–3:00
Average class size:
See Notes
SOL 2001 5th passing
  English: 82%
  Math: 77%

Tuckahoe
6550 N. 26th St.
· Arlington, VA 22213
703-228-5288
Grades: K–5
Size: 446
Diversity:
Hours: 9:00–3:35
Average class size:
See Notes
SOL 2001 5th passing
  English: 91%
  Math: 93%

Notes:
Average class size system-wide: Kindergarten: 25, 1st: 20, 2nd–3rd: 22, 4th–5th: 26, middle and high schools: 23.4
State passing standard is 70%

Data Sources:
www.arlington.k12.va.us
www.pen.k12.va.us

FACTS AT A GLANCE

Fairfax County
10700 Page Ave.
Fairfax, VA 22030
703-246-2991
www.fcps.edu

School system	Total enrollment:	165,016; expected to increase 4,000 per year
	Total number of schools:	238
	Total number of elementary Schools:	132
	Total number of middle schools:	21 (3 are 6th–8th, 18 are 7th–8th)
	Total number high schools:	24 (3 are 7th–12th, 21 are 9th–12th)
	SAT 2001:	Verbal 540 Math 553 Total 1093 74% of students tested (PSAT exams funded by county)
	Diversity within system:	42.4%
School System Programs	Before or after school care:	SACC (School-Age Children Care), call 703-449-8989
	Pre-kindergarten programs:	None
	Kindergarten:	5 years old by September 30, most are 1/2 day, call 703-246-7763
	Foreign language programs:	Partial immersion in French, German, Japanese, Spanish in selected elementary schools, call 703-208-7724

ESL/ESOL availability:	16,000 students, over 100 languages. Extensive program for all grade levels, call 703-846-8632
Accelerated programs:	3rd–6th full-time, center-based; 7th–8th school-based honors program; 9th–12th Thomas Jefferson for Science & Technology or IB or AP Diploma Programs in all high schools; AP and IB exams funded by county, call 703-876-5272
LD/special needs:	For learning disabilities, autism, hearing, visual, speech, language impaired, emotional difficulties, call 703-846-8677

Data Sources:
Fairfax County Public Schools website: www.fcps.edu
Virginia Department of Education website: www.pen.k12.va.us
SAT Scores: Washington Post SAT scores are for public and independent combined.
Paul Regnier, Community Relations Officer

SELECTED PUBLIC SCHOOLS

Fairfax County

High Schools

Lake Braddock Secondary
9200 Burke Lake Rd.
Burke, VA 22015
703-426-1000
Grades: 7–12
Size: 3,905
Diversity: 33.7%
Hours: 7:30–2:15
Average class size: 28
SOL 2001 8th passing
  English: 89%
  Math: 92%
SAT 2001:
  Verbal 560 Math 577
  Total 1137

Oakton
2900 Sutton Rd.
Vienna, VA 22181
703-319-2700
Grades: 9–12
Size: 2,380
Diversity: 29.1%
Hours: 7:20–2:05
Average class size: 28
SAT 2001:
  Verbal 556 Math 569
  Total 1125

West Springfield
6100 Rolling Rd.
Springfield, VA 22152
703-913-3800
Grades: 9–12
Size: 2,184
Diversity: 30.2%
Hours: 7:30–2:15
Average class size: 28
SAT 2001:
  Verbal 562 Math 579
  Total 1141

Langley
6520 Georgetown Pike
McLean, VA 22101
703-287-2700
Grades: 9–12
Size: 1,829
Diversity: 19.7%
Hours: 7:20–2:10
Average class size: 28
SAT 2001:
  Verbal 595 Math 616
  Total 1211

Robinson Secondary
5035 Sideburn Rd.
Fairfax, VA 22032
703-426-2100
Grades: 7–12
Size: 4,084
Diversity: 26.5%
Hours: 7:20–2:10
Average class size: 28
SAT 2001:
  Verbal 554 Math 566
  Total 1120

Woodson
9525 Main St.
Fairfax, VA 22031
703-503-4600
Grades: 9–12
Size: 1,833
Diversity: 24.3%
Hours: 7:20–2:05
Average class size: 28
SAT 2001:
  Verbal 579 Math 589
  Total 1168

Madison
2500 James Madison Dr.
Vienna, VA 22181
703-319-2300

South Lakes
11400 S. Lakes Drive
Reston, VA 20191
703-715-4500

Madison (cont.)
Grades: 9–12
Size: 1,565
Diversity: 19.9%
Hours: 7:20–2:10
Average class size: 28
SAT 2001:
   Verbal 573 Math 585
   Total 1158

McLean
1633 Davidson Rd.
McLean, VA 22101
703-714-5700
Grades: 9–12
Size: 1,503
Diversity: 31.8%
Hours: 7:15–2:10
Average class size: 28
SAT 2001:
   Verbal 572 Math 590
   Total 1162

South Lakes (cont.)
Grades: 9–12
Size: 1,646
Diversity: 44.7%
Hours: 7:20–2:10
Average class size: 28
SAT 2001:
   Verbal 559 Math 555
   Total 1114

Thomas Jefferson for Science and Technology Magnet
6560 Braddock Rd.
Alexandria, VA 22312
703-750-8300
Grades: 9–12
Size: 1,635
Diversity: 30.1%
Hours: 8:30–3:50
Average class size: 28
SAT 2001:
   Verbal 725 Math 745
   Total 1470

Middle Schools

Carson
13618 McLearen Rd.
Herndon, VA 20171
703-925-3600
Grades: 7–8
Size: 976
Diversity: 26.3%
Hours: 8:05–2:50
Average class size: 28
SOL 2001 8th passing
   English: 92%
   Math: 92%

Franklin
3300 Lees Corner Rd.
Chantilly, VA 20151
703-904-5100
Grades: 6–8
Size: 886
Diversity: 22.0%
Hours: 7:20–2:10
Average class size: 28
SOL 2001 8th passing
   English: 96%
   Math: 95%

Longfellow
2000 Westmoreland St.
Falls Church, VA 22043
703-533-2600
Grades: 7–8
Size: 901
Diversity: 27.9%
Hours: 7:30–2:30
Average class size: 28
SOL 2001 8th passing
   English: 93%
   Math: 93%

Cooper
977 Balls Hill Rd.
McLean, VA 22101
703-442-5800
Grades: 7–8
Size: 875
Diversity: 20.5%
Hours: 7:30–2:20
Average class size: 28
SOL 2001 8th passing
    English: 94%
    Math: 96%

Frost
4101 Pickett Rd.
Fairfax, VA 22032
703-503-2600
Grades: 7–8
Size: 1,020
Diversity: 25.2%
Hours: 7:25–2:20
Average class size: 28
SOL 2001 8th passing
    English: 88%
    Math: 92%

Thoreau
2505 Cedar Ln.
Vienna, VA 22180
703-846-8000
Grades: 7–8
Size: 749
Diversity: 25.8%
Hours: 7:30–2:30
Average class size: 28
SOL 2001 8th passing
    English: 87%
    Math: 90%

Elementary Schools

Louise Archer
324 Nutley Street, NW
Vienna, VA 22180
703-937-6200
Grades: K–6
Size: 610
Diversity: 28.9%
Hours: 9:15–3:45
Average class size: 22–27
SOL 2001 5th passing
    English: 94%
    Math: 93%

Churchill Road
7100 Churchill Rd.
McLean, VA 22101
703-288-8400
Grades: K–6
Size: 613
Diversity: 25.0%
Hours: 8:35–3:10
Average class size: 22–27
SOL 2001 5th passing
    English: 96%
    Math: 96%

Fairhill
3001 Chichester Ln.
Fairfax, VA 22031
703-208-8100
Grades: K–6
Size: 448
Diversity: 52.5%
Hours: 9:05–3:35
Average class size: 22–27
SOL 2001 5th passing
    English: 95%
    Math: 98%

Canterbury Woods
4910 Willet Dr.
Annandale, VA 22003
703-764-5600
Grades: K–6
Size: 578
Diversity: 22.4%
Hours: 9:00–3:35
Average class size: 22–27
SOL 2001 5th passing
    English: 95%
    Math: 88%

Cub Run
5301 Sully Station Dr.
Centreville, VA 20120
703-830-4000
Grades: K–6
Size: 736
Diversity: 22.9%
Hours: 8:25–3:00
Average class size: 22–27
SOL 2001 5th passing
    English: 92%
    Math: 85%

Flint Hill
2444 Flint Hill Rd.
Vienna, VA 22181
703-242-6100
Grades: K–6
Aize: 753
Diversity: 14.8%
Hours: 8:30–3:10
Average class size: 22–27
SOL 2001 5th passing
    English: 94%
    Math: 90%

Chesterbrook
1753 Kirby Rd.
McLean, VA 22101
703-714-8200
Grades: K–6
Size: 523
Diversity: 20.2%
Hours: 8:35–3:10
Average class size: 22–27
SOL 2001 5th passing
   English: 92%
   Math: 89%

Fairfax Villa
10900 Santa Clara Dr.
Fairfax, VA 22030
703-267-2800
Grades: K–6
Size: 448
Diversity: 42.8%
Hours: 9:00–3:30
Average class size: 22–27
SOL 2001 5th passing
   English: 94%
   Math: 63%

Forestville
1085 Utterback Store Rd.
Great Falls, VA 22066
703-404-6000
Grades: PK–6
Size: 988
Diversity: 17.2%
Hours: 9:10–3:45
Average class size: 22–27
SOL 2001 5th passing
   English: 94%
   Math: 93%

Elementary Schools

Fox Mill
2601 Viking Dr.
Herndon, VA 20171
703-860-1800
Grades: K–6
Size: 643
Diversity: 23.9%
Hours: 8:05–2:40
Average class size: 22–27
SOL 2001 5th passing
   English: 87%
   Math: 93%

Mantua
9107 Horner Ct.
Fairfax, VA 22031
703-645-6300
Grades: PK–6
Size: 799
Diversity: 32.7%
Hours: 9:05–3:35
Average class size: 22–27
SOL 2001 5th passing
   English: 93%
   Math: 88%

Union Mill
13611 Springstone Dr.
Clifton, VA 20124
703-322-8500
Grades: K–6
Size: 735
Diversity: 11.7%
Hours: 8:30–3:05
Average class size: 22–27
SOL 2001 5th passing
   English: 88%
   Math: 92%

Great Falls
701 Walker Rd.
Great Falls, VA 22066
703-757-2100
Grades: K–6
Size: 790
Diversity: 17.1%
Hours: 8:40–3:15
Average class size: 22–27
SOL 2001 5th passing
   English: 92%
   Math: 86%

Navy
3500 West Ox Rd.
Fairfax, VA 22033
703-262-7100
Grades: K–6
Size: 777
Diversity: 19.7%
Hours: 8:45–3:20
Average class size: 22–27
SOL 2001 5th passing
   English: 97%
   Math: 96%

Waples Mill
11509 Waples Mill Rd.
Oakton, VA 22124
703-390-7700
Grades: K–6
Size: 785
Diversity: 18.5%
Hours: 9:10–3:50
Average class size: 22–27
SOL 2001 5th passing
   English: 90%
   Math: 86%

Haycock
6616 Haycock Rd.
Falls Church, VA 22043
703-531-4000
Grades: K–6
Size: 551
Diversity: 24.5%
Hours: 9:10–3:45
Average class size: 22–27
SOL 2001 5th passing
English: 92%
Math: 92%

Keene Mill
6310 Bardu Ave.
Springfield, VA 22152
703-644-4700
Grades: PK–6
Size: 596
Diversity: 37.2%
Hours: 9:05–3:35
Average class size: 22–27
SOL 2001 5th passing
English: 95%
Math: 94%

Kent Gardens
1717 Melbourne Dr.
McLean, VA 22101
703-394-5600
Grades: K–6
Size: 828
Diversity: 27.5%
Hours: 8:35–3:10
Average class size: 22–27
SOL 2001 5th passing
English: 94%
Math: 91%

Oak Hill
3210 Kinross Cir.
Herndon, VA 22071
703-467-3500
Grades: K–6
Size: 794
Diversity: 20.6%
Hours: 8:20–2:55
Average class size: 22–27
SOL 2001 5th passing
English: 92%
Math: 86%

Ravensworth
5411 Nutting Dr.
Springfield, VA 22151
703-426-5380
Grades: K–6
Size: 527
Diversity: 32.1%
Hours: 8:35–3:10
Average class size: 22–27
SOL 2001 5th passing
English: 93%
Math: 95%

Spring Hill
8201 Lewinsville Rd.
McLean, VA 22102
703-506-3400
Grades: K–6
Size: 1,042
Diversity: 22.3%
Hours: 8:40–3:15
Average class size: 22–27
SOL 2001 5th passing
English: 91%
Math: 91%

West Springfield
6802 Deland Dr.
Springfield, VA 22152
703-912-4400
Grades: K–6
Size: 357
Diversity: 26.8%
Hours: 9:00–3:30
Average class size: 22–27
SOL 2001 5th passing
English: 92%
Math: 90%

Westbriar
1741 Pine Valley Dr.
Vienna, VA 22182
703-937-1700
Grades: K–6
Size: 384
Diversity: 25.0%
Hours: 9:05–3:40
Average class size: 22–27
SOL 2001 5th passing
English: 92%
Math: 92%

Notes:
State passing standard
is 70%
High schools included
have SAT scores
above 500
Schools listed have
English/Reading or
Math scores 90%
and higher
Data Sources:
www.fcps.edu
www.pen.k12.va.us

FACTS AT A GLANCE

Falls Church City
803 West Broad Street, Suite 300
Falls Church, VA 22046
703-248-5600
www.fccps.k12.va.us

School system

Total enrollment:	1,722
Total number of schools:	4
Total number of elementary schools:	2
Total number of middle schools:	1
Total number high schools:	1
SAT 2001:	Verbal 589 Math 570 Total 1159 85% of students tested
Diversity within system:	21.3%

School system programs

Before or after school care:	Extended day care for K–5th; after school for 6th–8th, call 703-248-5682
Pre-kindergarten programs:	Limited, call 703-248-5653
Kindergarten:	5 years old by September 30, full day program
Foreign language programs:	FLES: 2nd–5th; Spanish required; 6th exploratory; 7th–8th: Spanish or French required; 9th–12th: French, Latin or Spanish offered

ESL/ESOL availability:	Beginning, intermediate, and advanced levels in each of the four schools
Accelerated programs:	TAAP (The Academically Advanced Program) for students identified in 4th grade, call 703-248-5620; IB in 9th–12th, call 703-248-5590
LD/special needs:	Available at all grade levels; 9th–12th tutoring and study skills, call 703-248-5635

Data Sources:
Falls Church City Public Schools website: www.fccps.k12.va.us
Virginia Department of Education website: www.pen.k12.va.us
SAT Scores: Washington Post SAT scores are for public and independent combined.
Mary Ellen Shaw, Division Superintendent

SELECTED PUBLIC SCHOOLS

Falls Church City

High School

George Mason HS
7124 Leesburg Pike
Falls Church, VA 22043
703-248-5500
Grades: 9–12
Size: 569
Diversity:
Hours: 7:45–2:45
Average class: 20
SAT 2001:
   Verbal 589 Math 570
   Total 1159

Middle School

George Mason MS
7124 Leesburg Pike
Falls Church, VA 22043
703-248-5550
Grades: 6–8
Size: 401
Diversity:
Hours: 7:45–2:45
Average class size: 21
SOL 2001 8th passing
   English: 93%
   Math: 93%

Elementary Schools

Thomas Jefferson
601 S. Oak St.
Falls Church, VA 22046
703-248-5660
Grades: 2–5
Size: 515
Diversity:
Hours: 8:30–3:15
Average class size: 23
SOL 2001 5th passing
   English: 89%
   Math: 85%

Mount Daniel
2328 N. Oak St.
Falls Church, VA 22046
703-248-5640
Grades: K–1
Size: 237
Diversity:
Hours: 8:30–3:05
Average class size:
K: 17.5, 1st: 22.5
Scores not applicable

Notes:
State passing standard is 70%

Data Sources:
www.fccps.k12.va.us
www.pen.k12.va.us
Mary Ellen Shaw, Division Superintendent

FACTS AT A GLANCE

Loudoun County
102 North Street NW
Leesburg, VA 20176
703-771-6440
www.loudoun.k12.va.us

School system	**Total enrollment:**	34,589; expected to increase 3,000 per year
	Total number of schools:	51; 20 new schools in the next 5 years
	Total number of elementary schools:	36
	Total number of middle schools:	6
	Total number high schools:	6
	SAT 2001:	Verbal 521 Math 515 Total 1036 73% of students tested
	Diversity within system:	22%
School system programs	**Before or after school care:**	Limited, call 703-777-0343
	Pre-kindergarten programs:	Limited, call 703-779-8885
	Kindergarten:	5 years old by September 30, ½ day sessions
	Foreign language programs:	Foreign Language in Elementary Schools (FLES) offers Spanish in 10 schools, French, German, Latin, Spanish offered in middle/high schools
	ESL/ESOL availability:	Eight instructional centers, call 703-771-6435

Accelerated programs:	Gifted programs available in all grades at all schools; honors and AP classes offered, students can qualify for Thomas Jefferson program
LD/special needs:	Integrated into regular classrooms, call 703-771-6430; Parent Resource Center, call 703-771-6765

Data Sources:
Loudoun County Public Schools website: www.loudoun.k12.va.us
Virginia Department of Education website: www.pen.k12.va.us
SAT Scores: Washington Post SAT scores are for public and independent combined.
Wayde B. Byard, Information Officer

SELECTED PUBLIC SCHOOLS

Loudoun County

High School
Loudoun Valley
340 N. Maple Ave.
Purcellville, VA 20132
540-338-6800
Grades: 9–12
Size: 1,503
Diversity: 4%
Hours: 8:40–3:20
Average class size: 26.6
SAT 2001
   Verbal 544 Math 533
   Total 1077

Middle School
Blue Ridge
551 East A St.
Purcellville, VA 20132
540-338-6820
Grades: 6–8
Size: 1,212
Diversity: 5%
Hours: 8:40–3:25
Average class size: 21.6
SOL 2001 8th passing
   English: 87%
   Math: 91%

Elementary Schools

Aldie
23269 Meetinghouse Ln.
Aldie, VA 20105
703-444-7400
Grades: K–5
Size: 94
Diversity: 17%
Hours: 8:00–2:25
Average class size: 22
SOL 2001 5th passing
   English: 86% Math: 84%

Cedar Lane
43700 Tolamac Dr.
Ashburn, VA 20147
703-771-6515
Grades: K–5
Size: 860
Diversity: 20%
Hours: 8:00–2:25
Average class size: 22
SOL 2001 5th passing
   English: 85% Math: 85%

Evergreen Mill
491 Evergreen Mill Rd., SE
Leesburg, VA 20175
703-779-8834
Grades: K–5
Size: 790
Diversity: 15%
Hours: 8:00–2:25
Average class size: 22
SOL 2001 5th passing
   English: 88% Math: 88%

Ashburn
44062 Fincastle Dr.
Ashburn, VA 20147
703-771-6790
Grades: K–5
Size: 622
Diversity: 18%
Hours: 8:00–2:25
Average class size: 22
SOL 2001 5th passing
   English: 81% Math: 86%

Dominion Trail
44045 Bruceton Mills Cir.
Ashburn, VA 20147
703-779-8812
Grades: K–5
Size: 716
Diversity: 23%
Hours: 8:00–2:25
Average class size: 22
SOL 2001 5th passing
   English: 88% Math: 91%

Hillsboro
37110 Charles Town Pike
Purcellville, VA 20132
703-771-6730
Grades: K–5
Size: 145
Diversity: 5%
Hours: 8:00–2:25
Average class size: 22
SOL 2001 5th passing
   English: 86% Math: 85%

Catoctin
311 Catoctin Cir., SW
Leesburg, VA 20175
703-771-6770
Grades: K–5
Size: 550
Diversity: 19%
Hours: 8:00–2:25
Average class size: 22
SOL 2001 5th passing
    English: 84% Math: 84%

Emerick
440 S. Nursery Ave.
Purcellville, VA 20132
540-338-6870
Grades: K–5
Size: 501
Diversity: 10%
Hours: 8:50–3:15
Average class size: 22
SOL 2001 5th passing
    English: 91% Math: 90%

Hillside
43000 Ellzey Dr.
Ashburn, VA 20148
703-779-8847
Grades: K–5
Size: 693
Diversity: 12%
Hours: 8:00–2:25
Average class size: 22
SOL 2001 5th passing
    English: 84% Math: 88%

Elementary Schools

Horizon
46665 Broadmore Dr.
Sterling, VA 20165
703-444-7402
Grades: K–5
Size: 905
Diversity: 19%
Hours: 8:00–2:25
Average class size: 22
SOL 2001 5th passing
    English: 89% Math: 88%

Lowes Island
20755 Whitewater Dr.
Sterling, VA 20165
703-444-7532
Grades: K–5
Size: 770
Diversity: 16%
Hours: 8:00–2:25
Average class size: 22
SOL 2001 5th passing
    English: 91% Math: 93%

Waterford
15513 Loyalty Rd.
Waterford, VA 20194
703-771-6660
Grades: K–5
Size: 164
Diversity: 4%
Hours: 8:00–2:25
Average class size: 22
SOL 2001 5th passing
    English: 97% Math: 93%

Leesburg
323 Plaza St., NE
Leesburg, VA 20176
703-771-6720
Grades: K–5
Size: 593
Diversity: 16%
Hours: 8:00–2:25
Average class size: 22
SOL 2001 5th passing
    English: 82% Math: 87%

Lucketts
14550 James Monroe Hwy.
Leesburg, VA 20716
703-444-7430
Grades: K–5
Size: 184
Diversity: 7%
Hours: 8:45–3:10
Average class size: 22
SOL 2001 5th passing
    English: 80% Math: 82%

Lincoln
18048 Lincoln Rd.
Purcellville, VA 20132
504-338-6860
Grades: K–5
Size: 117
Diversity: 6%
Hours: 8:00–2:25
Average class size: 22
SOL 2001 5th passing
    English: 87% Math: 86%

Sanders Corner
43100 Ashburn Farm Pkwy.
Ashburn, VA 20147
703-771-6610
Grades: K–5
Size: 756
Diversity: 11%
Hours: 8:00–2:25
Average class size: 22
SOL 2001 5th passing
    English: 87% Math: 83%

Notes:
State passing standard is 70%
Average class size available for county, not individual schools
Schools listed have both English/Reading and Math scores of 80% or higher

Data Sources:
www.loudounk12.va.us
www.pen.k12.va.us

Public School Maps

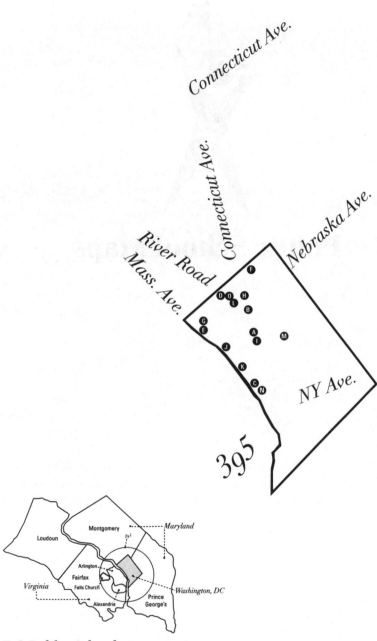

DC Public Schools

A Eaton	F Lafayette	K Hardy
B Hearst	G Mann	L Deal
C Hyde	H Murch	M Bannecker
D Janney	I Oyster	N School Without Walls
E Key	J Stoddert	O Wilson

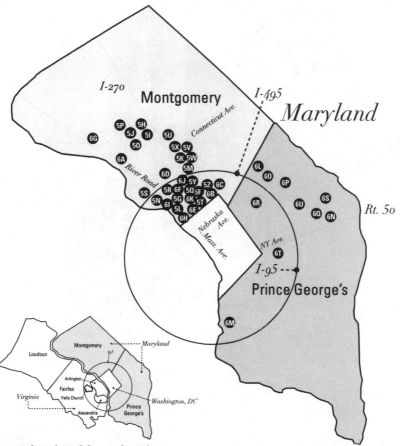

Maryland Public Schools

Montgomery County

5F	Bethesda-Chevy Chase
5G	Walt Whitman
5H	Winston Churchill
5I	Cabin John
5J	Herbert Hoover
5K	Tilden
5L	Westland
5M	Ashburton
5N	Bannockburn
5O	Bells Mill
5P	Beverly Farms
5Q	Bradley Hills
5R	Burning Tree
5S	Carderock Springs

5T	Chevy Chase
5U	Farmland
5V	Garrett Park
5W	Kensington Parkwood
5X	Luxmanor
5Y	North Bethesda
5Z	North Chevy Chase
6A	Potomac
6B	Rock Creek Forest
6C	Rosemary Hills
6D	Seven Locks
6E	Somerset
6F	Thomas Pyle
6G	Wayside
6H	Westbrook

6I	Wood Acres
6J	Wyngate
6K	Bethesda

Prince George's County

6L	Bond Mill
6M	Fort Foote
6N	Kenilworth
6O	Montpelier
6P	Oaklands
6Q	Tulip Grove
6R	University Park
6S	Yorktown
6T	Walker Mill
6U	Eleanor Roosevelt

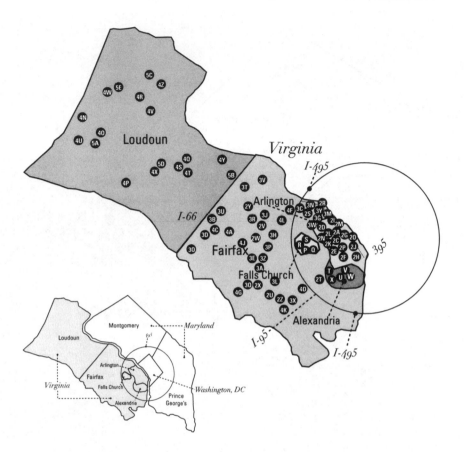

Virginia Public Schools

Falls Church
P   George Mason High
Q   George Mason Middle
R   Thomas Jefferson
    Elementary
S   Mount Daniel

Alexandria City
T   Minnie Howard
U   Douglas MacArthur
V   Charles Barrett
W   George Mason
X   Samuel Tucker

Arlington
2A   Yorktown
2C   Swanson
2D   Williamsburg
2E   Ashlawn
2F   Barcroft
2G   Glebe
2H   Henry
2I   Jamestown
2J   Long Branch
2K   McKinley
2L   Nottingham
2M   Taylor

2N   Tuckahoe
2O   Arlington Science
     Focus
2P   Arlington Traditional

Fairfax
2R   Langley
2S   McLean High
2T   Thomas Jefferson
2U   Lake Braddock
2V   Madison
2W   Oakton
2X   Robinson
2Y   South Lakes

Virginia Public Schools

2Z	West Springfield High	3V	Great Falls	4P	Aldie
3A	Woodson	3W	Haycock	4Q	Ashburn
3B	Carson	3X	Keene Mill	4R	Catoctin
3C	Cooper	3Y	Kent Gardens	4S	Cedar Lane
3D	Franklin	3Z	Mantua	4T	Dominion Trail
3E	Frost	4A	Navy	4U	Emerick
3G	Longfellow	4C	Oak Hill	4V	Evergreen Mill
3H	Thoreau	4D	Ravensworth	4W	Hillsboro
3J	Louise Archer	4F	Spring Hill	4X	Hillside
3L	Canterbury Woods	4G	Union Mill	4Y	Horizon
3M	Chesterbrook	4J	Waples Mill	4Z	Leesburg
3N	Churchill Road	4K	West Springfield	5A	Lincoln
3O	Cub Run		Elementary	5B	Lowes Island
3P	Fairhill	4L	West Briar	5C	Lucketts
3Q	Fairfax Village			5D	Sanders Corner
3R	Flint Hill			5E	Waterford
3T	Forestville				
3U	Fox Mill				

Loudoun County

4N	Loudoun Valley
4O	Blue Ridge

A Conversation with Georgia Irvin

There are no formulas or easy answers to the questions that I am asked every day. What works in one family may not work in another. The approaches to parenting and decision making that follow have helped many of the parents and children with whom I have worked. Please use what I have learned to help determine what is best for your child and family, understanding that each child has his or her own specific needs.

KINDERGARTEN READINESS AND "TAKING AN EXTRA YEAR"

Is my child ready for kindergarten?

Being bright or "smart" has little to do with a child's readiness for kindergarten. Social and emotional development are more important than intellectual development because children need the tools to be able to function in a group and to learn collaboratively. Pushing a child ahead can impede this vital part of development, best acquired in the early years and important to both future success in school and long-term emotional health. Children with the same chronological age may develop at different paces. In determining kindergarten readiness, educators look for progress in the following areas, which, under normal circumstances, increase with age:

1. Memory—Ability to repeat nursery rhymes, sing songs, follow directions with three or more steps, recall three or more digits.

2. Attention span, impulse control, and concentration—Ability to listen attentively, follow a story line, persevere through an interest or activity without distraction.

3. Multi-tasking skills—Ability to perform two or more tasks simultaneously, such as talking and putting on mittens, moving from one activity to another with minimal frustration.

4. Social skills—Ability to cooperate, accept correction, share objects and attention, take turns, be a friend, work in a group, and modify rough play.

5. Speaking skills or language development—Ability to be understood by those other than parents, speak in complete sentences, listen to others, ask questions, make needs known, know his or her name and birth date, modulate voice.

6. Interest in reading—Ability to follow and enjoy a story, predict what is going to happen, ask the meaning of words or ideas, supply an omitted word.

7. Visual acuity—Ability to throw and catch a ball (hand-eye coordination), discern difference in symbols such as letters ("B" and "P", "E" and "F") and numbers ("6" and "9").

8. Small motor—Ability to use crayons, markers, pencils, scissors.

9. Gross motor—Ability to climb, hop, skip, ride a tricycle, throw and catch a ball.

10. Independence—Ability to separate from parents, try new things, communicate with other adults, enjoy play dates.

Most children enter and are successful in kindergarten before reaching all of these developmental milestones, but it is important that you are aware of your child's level of development and remain vigilant and supportive to assure that these basic skills are acquired in a timely manner.

Children born with low birth weight may take up to five years to catch up with their peers. Prolonged illness, medical trauma, persistent ear infections, and other health-related problems may lead to excessive separation anxiety or delayed development of speech and language. All families experience change, but some events can be more traumatic than others. The birth of siblings, death, moving, serious illness in the immediate family, divorce, remarriage, and new step-siblings may contribute to delayed development. We also know that the neurological and psychological development of boys is often slower than that of girls.

Public schools in this area adhere to chronological readiness for kindergarten and require a child to be five years old by December 31 in Maryland* and in the District of Columbia, and by September 30 in Virginia. A few school principals will consider exceptions but the school-wide policy is usually inflexible. Some parents who believe their child is not ready for kindergarten let him or her remain in nursery school for another year before entering kindergarten. This is often wise because a child's first school experience should be a happy and successful one.

Should I hold my child back a grade?

When considering grade placement for a student, be careful not to use the words "hold back" or "repeat." I prefer, "take an extra year." It is important to approach this issue with confidence and to frame discussions positively. Deciding whether your child needs to take an extra year can be difficult. Make this decision only after talking with your child's current teachers, pediatrician, and other professionals who know how children learn and mature. Have sound reasons to believe it will help your child and realistic expectations about what can be achieved. It is wise to consider educational diagnostic tests, which can often help confirm or identify what is best for the child.

*Subject to change

An extra year will not help a child with average ability sustain a higher performance over the years; however, a child who has superior ability and is not performing at a superior level can experience success with the "gift of time," as noted child psychologist David Elkin discusses in his book, *The Hurried Child*. Children develop at different rates, and some need more time to gain the ability required to master basic skills such as reading and writing. Keep in mind that delayed development in these areas may have more to do with physical maturity or genes than intellectual ability. Parents often say, "I have never liked to read, and my child is just like me." If either parent experienced difficulty acquiring basic skills, it may indicate that your child may be better served by taking an extra year.

Never threaten a child by saying, "Unless you do better or work harder, you will have to repeat." If you decide to have your child take another year, if possible, have someone else (an educational consultant, the director of admissions of the new school, a friend or relative who took an extra year) also talk to your child. Most children realize when school is not going well for them and can be led to understand the reasons for making this change; however, no matter how you frame it, this news hurts, even young children. Try not to be the sole perpetrator of the pain because that deprives your child of a loving shoulder to cry on.

If you decide to give your child an extra year, it is always best if he or she can move to another school. This helps avoid the social implications of perceived failure. Among other benefits of being one of the oldest instead of among the youngest is the ego boost of being one of the first in the class to get a driver's license. Also keep in mind that taking an extra year does not mean that your child has to change the grade level in scouts, sports leagues, or religious activities.

HELPING YOUR CHILD BE SUCCESSFUL IN SCHOOL

Should I have my child tutored?

I think of tutoring as a short-term, supplemental educational service designed ultimately to enable a child to work independently. It is not a cure-all. Tutoring is most effective when your child recognizes his or her need for it, and the extra work does not interfere with activities that boost self-esteem. Like taking an extra year, tutoring does not enable a student with average ability to sustain a superior level of achievement. However, for the child who is frustrated or failing, tutoring can build the self-confidence that he or she needs.

You may seek tutoring in one subject or in skills applicable across subjects, such as organizational skills. Select a tutor qualified to provide the help your child needs and someone whom your child likes. You, your child, and the tutor should agree on specific, realistic goals. When the goals are reached, the tutoring should end. Otherwise, a child can become dependent upon tutoring, will not take risks nor do the work on his or her own, and can become more discouraged and less confident. Too much "support" can make a child feel "broken" and in need of being "fixed." One boy told me that he felt his parents were dissatisfied with him because they were always trying to "fix" something.

If your child is not progressing toward the tutoring goals, consult a physician about possible medical issues. You might also consider other alternatives such as changing schools or taking an extra year.

What should I do about the homework struggle?

Most children want their parents to know and care about their homework; however, no parent should become the homework police officer who is dreaded, even feared as the "homework laws" are enforced. Beware of implying that, "You need me because I don't think you can do it alone." This only makes a child feel inadequate, inferior, and, invariably, angry. You can be most helpful by saying, "If I can help you, let me know," or "Can I help?" Dignify the work, and reward the effort more than the finished product. Children may become resistant to help with their homework if they want and need reassurance and support and, instead, receive a harsh judgment.

How can you be helpful? Recognize and show respect for your child's needs. Some children are disorganized and forgetful and need help developing a checklist that parents can review. The best help you as a parent can give your child is to enable him or her to work independently.

Be careful not to start every conversation with, "Have you done your homework?" or "What grade did you get on the test?" Many children believe that the only thing their parents care about is grades. They get the impression that their own value as a human being is based upon the marks they receive in school. An "A" grade means you are an "A" person; a "C" implies you are not a really good person; an "F" means you are worthless. If you make good grades, you are loved; if the grades are poor, you are unloved. Some will cheat to make an "A" in order to please their parents, while others who make an honest "C" may feel they have failed. I never want a child to fail, but grades are not my standard of personal worth, and I trust they are not yours.

Fear of failure and perfectionism haunt many children. Some students allow themselves to fail, with the subconscious belief that if they had tried, success would have been possible. These same children usually make sincere promises to "do better," but get trapped in their subconscious, self-defeating method of managing fear of failure by failing. Their parents respond with a sincere, "All I want you to do is try," but to try hard and receive a poor grade is not tolerable to the child. Children who suffer from perfectionism are intolerant of their own mistakes and become easily upset if an assignment is difficult. They are inefficient and procrastinate because they may fear the inability to meet their own high standards. Often these children are highly verbal and have been told many times and in many ways how bright they are. Because they have often been the first to succeed at many of the linguistic tasks, they seem to feel they should already know what is being taught.

Being first to finish can be viewed as being the smartest, but it can be an avoidance technique. Perhaps the child reads well, but has a difficult time with math. Perfectionistic students cannot understand why, if they are so bright, they cannot accomplish the work in every subject area with equal ease. Self-doubt begins to erode the will to try, or fosters rushing through work as an attempt to minimize the fear of failure.

How do parents help these children? Gently reassure them that it is all right not to know in advance what the teacher is teaching. Remind them that if they already knew it all, they would not have to go to school. Surprisingly, this appears to be a new idea to some children, who seem relieved at the thought. Parents can contribute to the problem of perfectionism by being intolerant of their own mistakes or the mistakes of others. Children observe how their parents react to errors. Let your child know that you make mistakes, but you also learn from them. Show respect for those who try hard. Make sure your children are aware that you understand what it means to be wrong: it can be disappointing, but it is no reason to give up. It takes time to help children realize that they will be respected if they do not perform perfectly, but it can be done.

Sometimes professionals are needed to identify and clarify the parents' concerns and expectations and the child's perceptions and needs.

How can I help my children to do their best?

I am concerned about sleep deprivation and the constant fatigue I observe in many children. I am also concerned about the absence of opportunities for families to listen to and to help resolve the anxieties that keep some children awake at night.

Children should go to sleep early enough to enable them to get up with ease. Try to set a good example, then set firm boundaries about how the evening hours are used. There should be no overstimulation from TV or the Internet. The ideal is to have quiet family time in the evening as often as possible. Only when the environment is conducive will your child reveal worries to you.

The goal is to help your child identify ways to solve his or her own problems. From the moment of a child's birth, parents are conditioned to solve his or her problems and to make life as happy and comfortable as possible. Children learn and gain confidence in their own abilities when we listen and let them devise an acceptable solution. Just as we learn from our mistakes as adults, as parents we must allow children to experience some trial and error. Children are empowered and comforted when parents are good listeners. Allow them to find their own ways to respond to situations, and show respect for their capacity to solve the problems themselves.

It has been said that the greatest gift we give our children is the gift of *our* time. It is important to find time every day to play with the children. If you have young children, get down on the floor and play their games at their level. For older ones, find time to share an interest or hobby—not just homework.

I am adamant about the importance of eating breakfast. While breakfast does not have to be a sit-down meal, every child needs to eat something (preferably not too sweet) before going to school. Eating breakfast is like putting gas in the car; it provides children the energy to keep going. Studies have shown that good nutrition plays a role in children's performance in school by improving energy and concentration. Set a good example and eat a nutritious diet, including breakfast. All of this is easier said than done, I know, but your efforts will pay off.

Being successful in school is hard work that consumes a great deal of time and energy. On occasion, children take on more activities than they can accommodate without feeling stress and exhaustion. You may need to help your child define and limit his or her involvement. Children with many interests often require a great deal of parental support, such as driving to and from activities, having meals at special times, and being exempt from some household chores.

How much should I be involved in my child's school?

Schools depend on the interest, time, and financial resources that parents contribute. Studies indicate a positive correlation between parental involvement in the school and the motivation and achievement of their children. Being involved, even if your time is limited, is a meaningful way to show a child that his or her education is important. It also gives you more opportunities to meet classmates and other parents, to get to know the teachers, and to observe the social and academic climate of the school. Fathers who volunteer are especially welcome as role models for boys because the faculty of many schools is predominately female. At a minimum, attend school meetings. Your involvement is an investment in your child, not just in the school, and reduces the likelihood of problems arising. Often parents who complain about a teacher or situation have not made a sustained effort to communicate with faculty or school administrators. Most teachers appreciate thoughtful parents who participate in an honest and respectful dialogue. Many communicate through email to parents and older students. Parent Teacher Associations in public schools and parent organizations in independent schools contribute to the health of a school in many ways.

The years in which children rejoice in their parents' presence in school are limited. Little ones love having Mom or Dad come to class, but at about sixth grade, a parent's presence becomes more awkward for the child, and in high school, parents are generally persona non grata. Seize the moment and enjoy those years when parents who visit or work with the school are heroes to their children.

ATTENTION DEFICIT DISORDER
AND LEARNING DIFFERENCES

What is ADD?

Attention Deficit Disorder (ADD) is not uncommon and takes different forms. We think of children with attention issues as being fidgety and impatient, but the child who daydreams excessively and cannot concentrate or complete work in a timely fashion also has issues with attention. Among other characteristics of Attention Deficit Hyperactive Disorder (ADHD) is behavior that is inconsistent with the child's age for a period of more than six months. This includes being agitated, easily distracted, impulsive, and in constant motion. If you notice your child exhibiting these behaviors, try to determine what might be a contributing cause. Might these behaviors indicate depression, anxiety, or evidence of stress? Could they be triggered by diet, environmental factors, or overstimulation at home or at school? Consult your pediatrician, who may refer you to a psychologist or psychiatrist for a diagnosis. Work with professionals who will design and implement a plan to address the problems. Whenever feasible, I encourage alternatives to medication such as exercise, yoga, changes in diet, and an examination of stress in the family, but there are medications that provide hope and relief to children in need. The options in drugs are increasing, and if one medication does not work, be aware that others may be available.

What is a learning disability? Will my child be stigmatized if he or she goes to a special program or school? What does a learning disability mean for my child's future?

The term "learning disabled" describes a child with average or above average intelligence who shows a significant discrepancy between academic achievement and intellectual potential in class work and on standardized tests. The consequences are a mild to severe difficulty in learning how to read, understanding math, or expressing himself or herself orally or in writing. Some students instinctively learn how to compensate for their inadequacies, and may use a good memory and strong verbal skills to camouflage their problems until the work becomes more difficult or exacting. Significant progress has been made in helping children overcome or compensate for disabilities. Research in the field confirms that intelligence is not the issue; many of the world's most brilliant people are learning disabled. A child with a learning disability in math may write magnificently. Every child needs to feel competent, and learning disabled children need to be encouraged in their areas of strength, which often include the arts or athletics.

The most severely affected children need *remediation*, which is best provided by specially trained teachers. Usually, a wide range of materials and techniques are used. The teacher/student ratio must be very low, even one on one. A child with a severe learning disability needs special education daily, and sometimes social skills classes and occupational, speech and language, and physical therapy as well. Special education is expensive because children receive intense personal attention.

A second approach is *accommodation*. Here the student is taught like all others in the class. The teacher or teachers may not have had the additional training to provide specific expertise. In this environment, special exceptions may be made. Students might be given additional time on tests, use of calculators or computers in class, abbreviated homework assignments, and/or a waiver of the foreign language requirement. A specialist may work with the student for a class period each day. It can be emotionally more difficult for a child to be barely surviving in a school providing accommodation than to be in a special needs program with remediation; however, if a placement can be obtained where the disability can be managed effectively and the student's self-esteem, emotional well-being, and academic success are not compromised, accommodation is an appropriate choice.

Being learning disabled is neither a character fault nor a sign of mental incompetence; to the contrary, it may be a sign of greater creativity and sensitivity. To fail to use a special needs program or school when it is appropriate for fear of being stigmatized is like failing to put a cast on a broken leg. If the cast is never applied, the child may limp forever.

Some children with learning disabilities do not want to acknowledge their own condition. Often they have been teased or taunted and are afraid of further humiliation. You cannot let these fears prevent your child from getting help. I am gratified when parents tell me that, contrary to their expectations, their child found relief and comfort in a place where he or she was able to progress and relate to others with similar challenges. What a cause for celebration when a child who has never enjoyed success becomes one of the best in the class! Being ahead instead of behind is a welcome respite and often is necessary if the child is to gain energy and confidence for future challenges.

What does a learning disability portend for the future? To be honest, it means that high school may be stressful. College bound students must take all the required courses, even if their disability makes foreign languages, math, or the humanities difficult. Once in college, however, students may select courses at which they can succeed and avoid the classes in which their disability will preclude success. Children who have grappled with learning disabilities often have better study skills than others and can often excel. Graduate school can be even more rewarding. Future success is far more likely if the child receives academic help and if parents keep fragile egos intact during difficult times.

USE OF TIME

What should I do when all he wants to do is play on the computer?

In this era of technological toys, it is hard to find the balance between the positive and harmful use of computers, videos games, and television. They are often used as an escape from distress and can become addictive. You should not apologize for setting limits on how much time your children spend on these activities. Try to involve your child in defining a reasonable amount of computer or TV time, but the final decision is yours. At the time of day when your child is most apt to be on the computer or watching television, provide an option, an activity that you do together. Begin by sharing an activity that you hope he or she will continue independently of your participation. Shoot baskets or walk the dog. In the evening, if you can, watch a TV program together. Read aloud to one another. Parents tell me they read or reread their children's assigned books so they can discuss them. I like to see fathers and sons read the same novels or biographies. Book clubs for parents and children are thriving. Your best defense against abuse of technology is setting clear limits, sticking to them, and establishing acceptable alternatives.

Ideally, your child's passion requires engagement with peers and adults, hard work, and stretching himself or herself physically and mentally. Some activities are more solitary and these need to be respected. You need to worry if your child does not relate well to peers, seems more lonely and isolated than rewarded by an activity, or exhibits characteristics that signal an angry, addictive, or self-destructive personality. In these instances, consult professionals.

What activities should I arrange for the summer?

There is a summer camp or summer program that addresses almost any conceivable interest. I urge parents to insist that their children engage in activities that introduce new ideas or cultivate abilities. For children about nine years and older, a residential (sleep away) summer camp can be a wholesome adventure that teaches independence and self-reliance and enhances self-esteem and confidence. At camp, other adults reinforce the importance of participating and being responsible, without any of the judgments that are common in a parent/child or teacher/student relationship. Children can learn they are capable of being successful away from family. They make new friends, take safe risks, learn new skills, and explore their own possibilities under the watchful eye of caring adults and young counselors who often become role models. They return home with glorious memories and a vigor and self-confidence that can carry over into the classroom.

I am not as enthusiastic about remedial academic summer schools. I prefer to see students experience success in a nonacademic arena that energizes them. Some boarding schools have remedial and enrichment academic programs combined with organized sports and other activities in which students can have fun and be rejuvenated.

For older children, too much leisure in the summer is not advisable. "Hanging out" in the city or at the beach can be an accident waiting to happen. Older kids need constructive programs that enhance their physical skills as well as develop other interests. Most summer jobs do not require a sufficient number of hours at work to keep older children fully occupied. Ideally, a child with a summer job is also involved with sports or other organized activities with others whom their parents know and trust.

Colleges are interested in how students use their leisure time, especially in the summer. Challenging activities are considered evidence of curiosity, discipline, motivation, initiative, and independence.

TEEN ISSUES

When do I need to worry about depression or substance use?

All children, especially adolescents, undergo stress. They are often moody and disagreeable; however, for some, their emotions are overwhelming. Serious distress may occur after a trouble-free childhood. Adolescents may suffer from anxiety, depression, post-traumatic stress, low self-esteem, grief, drug and alcohol dependence, as well as various neurological disorders affecting behavior. When moods and attitudes interfere with your child's ability to function, seek medical advice. Do not ignore the signals even if the child protests that he or she is "fine." You cannot wish away depression, substance use, or other serious problems, which are manifested in different ways at different ages. Any one of the following behaviors should be carefully monitored and, if persistent, treated by competent professionals.

Young children who are depressed may cry excessively, be overly fearful, angry or violent, engage in shoplifting or other anti-social behaviors, complain of physical ailments, become withdrawn and prefer to be alone, exhibit less interest in school.

In older children, look for evidence of the above behaviors as well as defiance, rebelliousness, lying, cheating, excessive fatigue, excessive passivity, loss of interest in activities, negative thoughts, eating disorders, self-mutilation, addiction to the Internet or computers, sexual promiscuity, and self-medication by use of drugs and alcohol. These behaviors seriously disrupt the life of the child and of family members and must be addressed.

What can I do when I see my child going down the wrong road?

Until recent years, students who were experiencing severe emotional and behavioral difficulties had limited options if conventional psychotherapy was not effective. Today, there are options or a combination of options that are significantly different from anything that existed even ten years ago. Many fine therapeutic programs address serious depression and self-destructive behaviors by children from eleven to eighteen years old.

There are hundreds of these programs and new ones open almost daily. The therapeutic program industry is not supervised by an official governing body. A parent cannot tell which ones are excellent and which ones are questionable. If you believe that your child needs this type of intervention, I strongly urge every parent to work with an educational consultant. Call the Independent Educational Consultants Association (IECA) at 703-591-4850 for the names of Certified Educational Planners who visit these programs, get to know the therapists who work in them, and understand which programs are appropriate for the specific problems of your child.

Therapeutic wilderness programs are recommended for some students after other therapies and approaches have been unsuccessful. They employ techniques that are psychologically sound and insightful, but distinctly different from traditional psychiatric models. "Mother Nature," the outdoors, teaches children respect and consequences, while the therapists establish a trusting relationship with the children who are removed from the stimulation and distractions of their home environments. With a small group of fellow campers and field staff, in the high desert or forest, therapists help children evaluate their lives to date, gain insights about the impact of their behaviors, design new patterns for dealing with stress and temptations, and build self-esteem through mastery of wilderness survival skills. In group and individual counseling sessions, they begin the journey to emotional health. Parents are involved through regular telephone communication with the therapist and often by going into the wilderness with their child at the end of the program. The duration of the program can be three weeks to three months. Students usually return from the wilderness thanking their parents for "saving" them, and parents often report feeling profoundly rewarded.

In some instances, a therapeutic wilderness program is sufficient to enable a child to examine his or her choices and to experience a wake-up call. More often, it is the beginning of a longer healing process. Few students can sustain the dramatic improvement that occurs in programs by returning to the same school and conditions that contributed to the problems. Children can continue to gain emotional health by attending therapeutic schools. These schools rely on a combination of individual, group, and family therapy, highly structured days and evenings, positive peer culture, academics, and physical activity to continue to restore the young person to emotional health and responsible citizenship. Successful students emerge from these schools accountable for their own actions, and possessing more resources for dealing with temptation, frustration, sadness or any other of the emotional issues that beset them. The length of stay in any of the schools or programs depends upon the seriousness of the student's condition at the time of entry and his or her ability to make progress.

Unlike more conventional academic settings, therapeutic programs continue throughout the year and admit students on a rolling schedule as space permits. Students who refuse help may need a professional escort to take them to the program site.

With the specialized training of the staff, high levels of supervision, and lower faculty-student ratios, the costs are considerably higher at therapeutic institutions than conventional schools. The charge for a program that lasts for a few weeks can be $400 per day and a program that lasts several years can be $5,000 per month or more.

CONSIDERING AN INDEPENDENT SCHOOL

Should I consider applying for admission to an independent school for my child? Which is the best grade to enter?

A child needs the best possible education in the early, formative years. Children who have had the opportunity to acquire a love of learning and a good work ethic usually can make the best of any school. I have seen too many children who did not receive the attention necessary to maximize their potential in the early years. As a result, their performance in school declines annually. Some parents saved their money for an independent middle school, upper school, or college, only to discover that the child was not adequately prepared for an accelerated curriculum requiring a high level of motivation. On the other hand, many of the public elementary schools are excellent, and some of the public middle and high schools also provide excellent quality. I am extremely comfortable advising parents to enroll their child in a public school, as long as the child is in a social and academic environment that enables learning at a level consistent with his or her academic potential, is feeling good about himself or herself, and you are satisfied with the nonacademic culture.

You must weigh the relative merits of a neighborhood public school and an independent school based on your own values, priorities, financial resources, and the needs of your child. Please do not use your own educational experience as the only criterion. Both public and independent schools have changed in recent years.

There is an unfortunate misperception that enrollment in any one school is a ticket to a specific, possibly prestigious secondary school, college, or university. A high level of success in a fine school is a way to maximize future school options and does increase the opportunity for scholarships, but it is the child's achievement, not simply your investment, that makes the ultimate difference.

When a child enters an independent school, the family often gives up the advantages of a neighborhood school. In most cases include economic, racial, and cultural diversity, a sense of community, the child's close friendships with those who live nearby, even parents' relationships with neighbors.

Independent schools have important features that are not available in the public schools. The religious or values-oriented education of an independent school often has great appeal. Independent schools are characterized by less bureaucracy, less emphasis on testing, more control over financial resources, more opportunities for students to participate in sports and the arts in lower and middle schools. A selected enrollment and set of rules that require less disciplinary action can prevent classroom distractions. Teachers in independent schools have greater autonomy in the classroom, fewer administrative responsibilities, and, therefore, more time to develop personal relationships with their students. The ability of an independent school to control class size and identify and enroll the students who will learn from each other and flourish in its environment allows it to focus more attention on the individual student and deliver the kind of education that can enhance a child's abilities, interests, and confidence.

Regarding optimum time for enrollment, schools begin at many different grade levels (See the chart in chapter 1). Most schools increase the class size at certain grades. These grades with openings are sometimes called an enrollment window. I often hear concerns that acceptance in an independent school becomes more difficult at each advancing grade level. That is not always true because, in this city, often the largest number of applicants relative to the total number of spaces is at pre-kindergarten and kindergarten. In fact, there may be fewer applicants at the windows than at the beginning grade level. In general, there are relatively fewer places available at second, fifth, eighth, and eleventh grades because class size at those grades is rarely increased. Spaces that become available result from attrition. Unless a student has a strong academic record and extracurricular interests, acceptance is unlikely for the senior year.

Schools in the area end at varying times as well. (See the chart in chapter 1.) There are advantages to each of the age combinations. The school that is only a primary school and ends at second or third grade, or a junior school that invests all of its financial resources in that age group, creates places where children, at an early age, can experience leadership opportunities and a sense of belonging in a cozy environment that promotes confidence and a sense of well-being. The school that teaches ninth through twelfth graders can focus exclusively on age-appropriate opportunities for a limited age group. Schools that span the primary though high school years offer both students and faculty many excellent opportunities to grow within a consistent educational philosophy.

Over the years, schools have refined their ability to make admission decisions with increasing astuteness, but the fact remains that the needs of a child are more evident as he or she gets older. Making a decision for the educational future of a child who is less than a thousand days old is, at best, difficult, but this is necessary for children entering pre-kindergarten. There is no crystal ball in which you can foresee the future development of your child. Parents should be open every year to the possibility that a change of schools is advisable.

This is not to say that "the match" of student to school will likely be amiss and that you may have to go through the tedious admission process again. Nonetheless, you need to be vigilant and make sure that your child's school is the best available place for him or her at any given time.

We want our son to attend the school his brother attends. Should we worry about his acceptance?

In general, priority applicants are siblings, children of alumni, faculty, and, in some schools, members of that school's religious denomination. These students receive special consideration because all schools want to be responsive to the families who are already a part of the school community; however, schools with the most competitive admission may have twice as many priority applicants as the number of available places in a grade.

When applying to schools with highly competitive admission, parents should recognize that siblings cannot be guaranteed a place.

While Director of Admission, I was acutely aware of the school's dilemma. If we took a family new to the school, we may have denied a sibling. The new family is thrilled with the decision until they apply for another child who may not be admitted. Should schools be places that are loyal only to those families who are already in the school? How great is the responsibility to accept those without "connections" who go through an admission process expecting some degree of equality? These are tough questions for all schools with competitive admission, including colleges and universities.

If your child were denied admission, realize that it could simply be the lack of space. Class size must be controlled; even one more student for a teacher may reduce his or her ability to do the best for everyone.

If space is the only factor precluding acceptance, be patient and reapply at a later date.

It may be that not all children in your family would be well served in the same school. You should look at your child's learning profile. Use the admissions process to determine whether a school is appropriate for your child and, if not, which school would be more suitable. Look at each child as an individual and determine what is best for that child. Remember that you want your child to be where he or she will be more rewarded than frustrated.

A final note

When asked what I want children to gain from their education, I think of this quotation:

> The entire object of true education is to make people not merely to do the right things, but enjoy them; not merely [to be] industrious, but to love industry; not merely [to be] learned, but to love knowledge; not merely [to be] pure, but to love purity; not merely [to be] just, but to hunger and thirst after justice.
>
> —John Ruskin

This is a lofty ideal but a worthy one. My answers to questions are influenced by this ultimate goal that I hold for all children.